The Rise of the Community Builders

THE COLUMBIA HISTORY OF URBAN LIFE
KENNETH T. JACKSON, GENERAL EDITOR

THE
RISE
OF THE
COMMUNITY BUILDERS

*The American Real Estate Industry
and
Urban Land Planning*

MARC A. WEISS

NEW YORK
Columbia University Press
1987

Library of Congress Cataloging-in-Publication Data

Weiss, Marc Allan.
The rise of the community builders.

(The Columbia history of urban life)
Bibliography: p.
Includes index.
1. Land use, Urban—United States.   2. City
planning—United States.   3. Real estate development—
United States.   I. Title.   II. Series.
HD257.W46   1987   333.77'17'0973   87-5115
ISBN 0-231-06504-3

Book designed by Laiying Chong.

Columbia University Press
New York   Guildford, Surrey
Copyright © 1987 Columbia University Press
All rights reserved

Printed in the United States of America

The Columbia History of Urban Life

Kenneth T. Jackson, General Editor

CONTENTS

ACKNOWLEDGMENTS

The Rise of the Community Builders began as my Ph.D. dissertation at the University of California, Berkeley, and I once again thank my committee: Roger Montgomery, chairman; Barton Bernstein (of Stanford University), Martin Gellen, and Richard Walker. In my dissertation acknowledgments I thank many people, and I will not repeat all the names here, though my gratitude remains just as strong.

My greatest debt goes to Roger Montgomery, to whom this book is dedicated. Roger was the inspiration and the guiding light of the entire enterprise for the past nine years. He was both a trenchant intellectual critic and a constant source of encouragement and support. We have shared our lives in this project, and it is a special honor for me to have been a partner in such a great working relationship.

Michael Ebner believed in me, counseled me, and opened the doors for me in the history profession. Among many other kind acts of generosity, he arranged for Kenneth Jackson to read my manuscript for his History of Urban Life Series at Columbia University Press. I am grateful to Kenneth Jackson for giving my book a careful reading and for recommending it for publication with helpful criticism and enthusiastic praise.

Many other people have provided useful comments on my work as it has been steadily rewritten these past few years. Thanks to Eric Hobsbawm, Leo Grebler, David Goldfield, Seymour Mandelbaum, Elliott Sclar, Allan Heskin, Carl Abbott, Marilyn Weiss, Sam Bass Warner, Jr., Jon Teaford, Leland Burns, Lawrence Susskind, Raymond Watson, Alan Rabinowitz, Maury Seldin, Fred Case, James Graaskamp, Eric Monkkonen, Bernard Frieden, Robert Fogelson, Charles Orlebeke, Ann Markusen, David Dowall, Michael Teitz, Peter Hall, Melvin Webber, David Vogel, Alfred Chandler, Jr., Blaine Brownell, Barry Karl, Ellis Hawley, Mansel

Blackford, Melvin Holli, Carl Feiss, Coleman Woodbury, Peter Marcuse, John Reps, Mel Scott, Eugenie Birch, Donald Krueckeberg, Christopher Silver, Laurence Gerckens, Gordon Cherry, Anthony Sutcliffe, James Bennett, Douglas Mitchell, Allen Graubard, Doreen Massey, Howard Rosen, Mark Rose, Ann Durkin Keating, Jon Peterson, Christine Rosen, Judith Rosener, Spencer Olin, Jr., Joseph McGuire, John Mollenkopf, Michael Conzen, Kathleen Conzen, Henry Binford, Christine Boyer, John Forester, Pierre Clavel, William Goldsmith, Barry Checkoway, Albert Guttenberg, Louis Wetmore, Gill-Chin Lim, Dowell Myers, Bennett Harrison, Lynne Sagalyn, Matthew Edel, John Friedmann, Alan Kreditor, Richard Peiser, Lowdon Wingo, Jr., Peter Rowe, John Stilgoe, Stephan Thernstrom, Jose Gomez-Ibanez, Norman Krumholz, Frank So, James Greer, Joan Draper, Robert Bruegmann, J. Warren Salmon, Ashish Sen, George Hemmens, William Peterman, Dennis Keating, Marshall Feldman, Seymour Adler, Charles Downs, Robb Burlage, Joel Schwartz, Harold Platt, Marc Hilton, David Johnson, Daniel Schaffer, Hilary Silver, Charles Connerly, J. Paul Mitchell, Joe Feagin, Earl Lewis, Heywood Sanders, Richard Harris, Michael Heiman, Robert Beauregard, Susan Fainstein, Norman Fainstein, David Perry, Richard Florida, Clayborne Carson, Martin Schiesl, Michael Storper, Mark Gottdiener, Nancy Leigh-Preston, Zeynep Celik, Diane Favro, Martin Landau, Victor Jones, and Madeline Landau.

Two people who are now deceased helped me in conceptualizing this study: Harvey S. Perloff and William L. C. Wheaton. I wish they could both be here to read what they inspired.

To my graduate research assistants, John Metzger, Susan Vavra (who prepared the index), Nancy Strening, Chris Koziol, David Lehman, Tim McNulty, Arthur Alterson, and Janet Tarsitano, I am very grateful. I hope you all enjoyed studying history as much as I do.

For financial assistance I express my sincerest thanks to the following sources: the Homer Hoyt Advanced Studies Institute, for a research grant to study the history of urban land economics; the Herbert Hoover Presidential Library Association, for awarding me the Colonel Robert R. McCormick Research Fellowship; the Lincoln Institute of Land Policy, for a research grant to study financial institutions and negotiated development; the Nathalie P. Voorhees Center for Neighborhood and Community Improvement, for research support; the School of Urban Planning and Policy, University of Illinois at Chicago, for research support; and the Graduate School of Management, University of California, Irvine, for research support.

Of the many lectures and papers on urban history I gave at universities and academic conferences over the past several years, two were particularly important in shaping my argument: the Chicago Historical Society Urban History Seminar, and the Harvard University Graduate School of Design. I wish to thank Michael Ebner, Kathleen Conzen, Timothy Jacobson, and Russell Lewis in Chicago and Peter Rowe in Cambridge for giving me the opportunity.

Richard Pierce, former executive director of the Los Angeles Board of Realtors, provided me with the ancient and dusty files that I utilized in writing chapter 4, and also arranged my interview with Fred Marlow. Karen Switt, director of Library Information Services for the National Association of Realtors in Chicago, made available to me, with encouragement from Les Gaskins, the best workspace I have ever had, amidst the resources of the world's finest real estate library. Likewise, Jean Alcan and Beverly Martin provided me with materials from the library of the California Association of Realtors, Virginia Rees enabled me to study the city planning records of the Commonwealth Club of California, Jane McMaster provided me with a key document from the Ohio State University Library and Sally Wolf made available Gordon Whitnall's papers at the Los Angeles City Planning Department Library. To all the libraries I utilized and the many librarians who served me so well, especially to Arthur Waugh and Charles Shain at UC Berkeley, I say: THANKS!

Several people granted me interviews, including Fred Marlow, Huber Smutz, Senator Arthur Breed, Jr., Milton Breivogel, Harold Mayer, Dean McHenry, T. J. Kent, Jr., Corwin Mocine, Leo Grebler, Calvin Hamilton, Harold Jensen, Philip Klutznick, Albert Lepawsky, Robert Walker, Louis Wetmore, and Coleman Woodbury.

Janet Goranson typed the entire manuscript. I thank her for being a delightful, patient, and speedy perfectionist.

To my friendly and energetic editor at Columbia University Press, Kate Wittenberg, my manuscript editor, David Diefendorf, my designer, Lee Chong, my copywriter, David Bruce, and to all the other editorial, design, and marketing staff, I say thank you.

I also wish to acknowledge the hospitality of the hosts and hostesses of dwellings in which I wrote and rewrote parts of this book: Allan Heskin in Los Angeles; Gail Resnik in Santa Monica; the Canyon Ranch Inn in Sierraville, California; Roy Fried and Hilda Klimek in Elkhart Lake, Wisconsin; Charles Downs in New York City; and David and Annie Tucker and family in Iowa City.

My parents, Andrew and Ruth, my wife Marilyn, my son David, my former wife Ann, my sister Susan, my brother-in-law Terry, Don Baker, Holiday O'Dell, and all of my relatives and friends have granted me the gift of their love, which has made this project both possible and worthwhile.

My father, Rudolph Maximillian Froelich Getzel Spitzer, founder and president of the Realty Catalog Service in Chicago, died at the youthful age of 39 with many visions of how he planned to make urban areas better places to live. One contribution he probably never imagined he would make is that his son would write a book about the American real estate industry and urban land planning.

PROLOGUE

"In the proper relation between the subdivider and the regional planner, both are engaged in the work of building a metropolis unit by unit. Each subdivision becomes an added piece in the great mosaic that gradually assumes the physical shape determined by the design of the builders." [1]

"Subdivision of land is a step in community building and must so be considered, rather than as merely a process in the transfer of property. As such it must follow sound principles of community development rather than haphazard chance, unregulated individual design, or deliberate selfishness. Reconciling this aim with that of a proper return upon investment and establishment of adequate land values may be said to be the common field of the realtor and the planner." [2]

Hugh R. Pomeroy,
founding secretary, Los Angeles County Regional Planning Commission

"City planning is the production end of our business. Too long have we realtors given the major thought to the selling of real estate. It is time that we look well to the proper planning and the better building of the goods we sell. If we are to sell our goods with constantly increasing advantage to our clients and to ourselves, they must be planned well and built efficiently." [3]

Fred E. Reed,
California realtor and developer, chairman of the City Planning Committee,
and vice president, National Association of Real Estate Boards

CHAPTER ONE

BUILDING COMMUNITIES

Introduction

THE KEY TO UNDERSTANDING THIS BOOK is that it is about site planning and land development.[1] When we think of the image of a "builder," we imagine someone who puts together a physical structure. The image of a "community builder" concerns the land pattern in which the structures are placed and the relationship of the structures to one another. A community builder designs, engineers, finances, develops, and sells an urban environment using as the primary raw material rural, undeveloped land. In the parlance of the real estate industry, such activity is called the platting and improvement of subdivisions. As one developer stated in 1936, "Fundamentally the subdivider is the manufacturer in the field of real estate practice."[2] The history of the last century in American real estate is one of increasing growth in the average scale of development and the size of the land parcel, increasing sophistication in the scope and quality of the structural improvements to land and buildings, and increasing economic coordination and integration in the phases of the development process by the entrepreneurs.

The Rise of the Community Builders tells the story of what I call "the creation of the modern residential subdivision." That an urban land subdivision could be considered "residential" at the time the land was still being platted was a fairly novel concept in late nineteenth- and early twentieth-century America. Most land had previously been carved out into building lots and sold for whatever use the new owners intended. Subdividing land exclusively for residential purposes presupposed a level of planning and control that was certainly not the norm for American urbanization. Planning and developing for specifically residential districts or neighborhoods was first utilized by land subdividers in the case of high-income suburban communities. The technological and economic changes that made possible spatial separation of urban land uses were combined by the developer with substantial investment in landscaping and infrastructure improvements and legal use of deed restrictions to control and preserve a planned environment.

Creating residential subdivisions for builders and purchasers of expensive single-family houses represented the first phase of the modern transformation of urban land development by private real estate entrepreneurs. I call this phase "changes at the high end," which reached maturity during the 1920s. The second phase, "changes at the moderate end," completed the revolution in community building by the 1940s. In this phase, subdividers became full-fledged suburban housing developers, not only planning and improving large tracts of land, but building the houses on the lots and selling the completed package to the homebuyer. Often parks, schools, shopping centers, and other community facilities were also built. What made the Levittown story of the late 1940s so important was not just that the Levitts had found a way to mass produce affordable housing, but that the housing was an attractive investment for young families precisely because of the planning and construction of a complete community. Even where smaller subdividers only created modest-sized neighborhoods, what the average consumer was now purchasing or renting was a new dwelling in a new district of completed dwellings, rather than a vacant lot in an undeveloped area with an uncertain future. This phenomenon of "community building," particularly for the average modest-income resident, constituted a dramatic change from the speculative "lot-selling" practices of the preceding generation.[3]

That this change is of so recent vintage is attested to by Clarence Stein, the famous architect and planner who designed Radburn with Henry Wright, in comments about the crisis of American housing in 1930:

> The more I think of what has been happening in the field of housing in this country during the last decade the more strongly I feel that the essential lack has been our inability to see that the house itself is of minor importance. Its relation to the community is the thing that really counts. . . . It is not only the fact that a small house must depend on its grouping with other houses for its beauty, and for the preservation of light, air, and

the maximum of surrounding open space. What is probably more important is the economic angle. It is impossible to build homes according to
the American standard as individual units for those of limited incomes. If
they are to be soundly built and completely equipped with the essential
utilities they must be planned and constructed as part of a larger group.[4]

Subdividers who engaged in full-scale community development also
performed the function of being private planners for American cities and
towns. Working together with professional engineers, landscape architects, building architects, and other urban designers, residential real estate developers worked out "on the ground" many of the concepts and
forms that came to be accepted as good planning. The classification and
design of major and minor streets, the superblock and cul-de-sac, planting strips and rolling topography, arrangement of the house on the lot,
lot size and shape, set-back lines and lot coverage restrictions, planned
separation and relation of multiple uses, design and placement of parks
and recreational amenities, ornamentation, easements, underground utilities, and numerous other physical features were first introduced by private developers and later adopted as rules and principles by public planning agencies. I call this pattern "private innovation preceding public
action." One need only look at the Federal Housing Administration's
1940 publication, *Successful Subdivisions,* to see clearly and graphically how
the various innovations of a half-century of private development were
fully incorporated as public values to be standardized and emulated.[5]

The main method by which community builders implemented their
planning and design vision, other than through direct capital investment
and administrative coordination of the investment and improvement process, was through the vehicle of legally enforceable deed restrictions. These
restrictions, written into a private contract between the original seller and
buyer of the building lot, both mandated and prohibited certain types of
behavior on the part of the present and future property owner. Deed
restrictions, by virtue of being voluntary private contracts, often went
beyond the scope of public sector police power regulations, particularly
in the earlier years. These restrictions, which might even include barring
the owner from painting the house a certain color, constituted a very
significant abridgment of private property rights. That they were will-
ingly and in many cases eagerly accepted by purchasers opened the wedge
for the introduction and extension of public land-use controls. Deed re-

strictions, an innovation of community builders and their attorneys, served as both the physical and political model for zoning laws and subdivision regulations.[6]

Community builders did more than just serve as innovators for the land planning ideas that were spawned in the early 1900s and spread rapidly during the succeeding four decades. Many of the large subdivision developers played a direct role in actively supporting and shaping the emerging system of public land planning and land-use regulation. These community builders, most of whom developed stylish and expensive residential subdivisions and were leaders of the Home Builders and Subdividers Division and the City Planning Committee of the National Association of Real Estate Boards (NAREB), worked actively with city planners to establish public planning laws and agencies. J. C. Nichols, the developer of Kansas City's Country Club District, spoke for his colleagues among the community builders when he stated that the private planning of large residential subdividers could not succeed without "municipal assistance." What Nichols meant was that in addition to the public provision of infrastructure and services, private developers who scrupulously planned and regulated their own subdivisions needed the planning and regulation of the surrounding private and public land in order to maintain cost efficiencies and transportation accessibility and to ensure a stable and high-quality, long-term environment for their prospective property owners.[7]

The two most widely adopted land planning tools were zoning laws, which regulated the use, height, and bulk of structures on urban land, and subdivision regulations, which imposed minimum standards of lot size, street width and alignment, and other provisions for physical improvements in the subdividing of land for sale as urban building lots. Theodora Kimball Hubbard and Henry Vincent Hubbard, in their comprehensive and authoritative 1929 study of American city and regional planning, underscored the importance of zoning and subdivision controls as the key elements of public regulation to facilitate metropolitan residential development:

> The present field study proves that those charged with the responsibilities of planning all over the country are eager for facts and statements of experience. They look for future progress in their communities largely along

three lines: zoning, subdivision control, and major thoroughfare planning. They need to know the relation of these three most popular phases of planning to each other and to the remaining elements of comprehensive plans.[8]

Table 1.1, compiled in 1937, also demonstrates the commanding position of zoning laws and subdivision regulations as the two leading forms of public planning. These two, along with their necessary companion, the major street plan, were the most strongly advocated by community builders in their quest for "municipal assistance."

TABLE 1.1
City and County Land-Use Plans in the United States,
1937

Type of Plan	Number of Cities and Counties
Zoning Ordinance	1,360
Control of Plats (Subdivision Regulations)	517
Thoroughfare Plan (Major Streets)	229
Comprehensive Plan	217
Park and Parkway Plan	184

SOURCE: U.S. National Resources Committee, *Status of City and County Planning in the United States,* Circular 10, May 15, 1937, Washington, D.C. (Table compiled from Appendix B, p. 11, and Appendix E, p. 37.)

Community builders by no means represented the typical subdivider. In their support of public planning, as in most other aspects of their business operations, they were a distinct and fairly unrepresentative minority breed of real estate developers. The longer time-frame for development, larger scale of activity, greater degree and quality of design and improvements, and other features distinguished community builders from the average subdivider. Many subdividers were indifferent if not openly hostile to public planning regulations, although they often welcomed public investment. One group of subdividers, referred to variously as "curbstoners," "fly-by-nights," "land butchers," and "lot sellers," were a source of scandal and market instability that community builders hoped to eliminate as competitors through government regulation and private trade association agreements. An important goal of community builders was to stop the mania of land speculation that turned subdividing into stock-market-style gambling in vacant, unimproved lots heavily encumbered with private debt and public tax and special assessment obligations.[9] The battle between community builders and curbstoners and the many factions in between is a vital part of the story of the American real estate industry and urban land planning.

Community Builders and Subdivision Regulations

Community builders' desire for subdivision regulations encompassed three different forms of planning to address three sets of concerns: (1) planning as *coordination,* to ensure that new subdivisions would be accessible to highways, parks, and other public infrastructure and facilities, and would be properly aligned with existing and projected major and minor streets; (2) planning as *design and engineering,* to develop and enforce standards for streets, lots, drainage, and utilities in the laying out of new subdivisions that would enhance their marketability for residential construction (as opposed to pure speculation in vacant lots); (3) planning as *control,* to restrict competition in subdividing by regulating the procedures, increasing start-up costs and barriers to entry, and publicizing and penalizing fraudulent or misleading sales efforts, thereby reducing the overall supply of available lots and eliminating the curbstoners.

The first two forms of planning were responses to long-term changes in the structure of the real estate industry and real estate development, particularly residential development. The third issue arose directly in the context of the collapse of the early 1920s subdivision boom, when after 1926 a rapidly accelerating financial crisis in real estate induced some industry leaders to support government actions to help save their businesses. This cyclical crisis also provided the impetus for public intervention in the first two categories of subdivision planning.[10]

A key publication of the 1930s highlights this three-part planning relationship. *Subdivision Principles and Practices,* a collection of essays published by the California Real Estate Association, clearly details the community builders' approach to large-scale residential development. In an essay called "Selection of Property: Improvement and Development Program," Walter Leimert, one of California's leading subdivision developers, articulates the level of *design and engineering* standards for a successful high-income community builder development. Leimert, who employed the Olmsted Brothers as landscape architects on several of his California subdivisions, uses as his example of attractive, quality development the various residential subdivisions of Beverly Hills:

> Could Beverly Hills have been carried out by the methods of the old subdivider, who usually sold sixty to seventy per cent of his lots with a certain ease, during the period allotted for selling, which was generally too short, and then disposed of his thirty or forty per cent of "culls" at sacrifice prices? Of course not, for that sacrifice, which meant to him only the loss of dollars, was the sacrifice of the character and value he had promised the home seekers who first came at his promise of a good place to live.
>
> The present-day subdivider, through expert market study of his prospective buyers, intelligent restrictions, good quality of improvements, establishment of environment and general knowledge of the business in which he has engaged, finds that the last thirty or forty per cent of his lots can command very high prices. For he has protected those who already live there and his tract is becoming a stronger and stronger magnet to home seekers. This is the history of every development in the United States in which care, forethought and planning have been brought to development.[11]

Walter Leimert argues the case for excellence in design and engineering. Most of the local subdivision regulations administered by planning commissions during the 1920s and 1930s were concerned with minimum standards of street grading, drainage, lot size, availability of water, and installation of sewers and utilities. The purpose of these regulations was to avoid the burdensome future private costs to the lot and home purchasers, and public costs to the taxpayers, of adding or reconstructing essential subdivision improvements. The regulations were also intended to help avoid falling property values and disruption of real estate markets from excessive marketing of poorly subdivided and inadequately or improperly improved land. Rising costs and falling values had both become serious problems by the late 1920s, with widespread defaults on real estate loans and on property tax assessments, mostly related to subdivision lot purchases.

As the community builders became more economically integrated and sophisticated in their own methods of subdivision planning, their example helped set higher minimum development standards for the rest of the subdividers and for the lenders, insurers, and regulators. The FHA minimum subdivision standards of the 1930s were equivalent to advanced practice for the early 1920s.

A second essay in the California anthology, by the real estate commissioner, describes the subdivision *control* procedures under the California Real Estate Act. The commissioner, realtor J. Mortimer Clark, was a former president of the Long Beach Realty Board and vice-president of the California Real Estate Association. Under California law, the real estate commissioner's office was required to investigate all subdividers offering lots for sale in the state, to issue a public report on each subdivision, and to stop the sale of lots if any fraudulent practices were discovered. Planning as *control* was combined with planning as the requiring of minimum *design and engineering* standards by local planning agencies to achieve the clear purpose of restricting the ability of curbstoners to participate in the marketing of urban subdivisions. In particular, these two forms of regulation joined forces to try and prevent curbstoners from flooding the market with an oversupply of cheap subdivision lots, and destabilizing investor or consumer confidence in real estate through speculative overpromising and scandalous practices. Subdivision *control* was supported by community builders as well as by many larger realtors, lenders, insurers, and other elements of the real estate industry. Commissioner Clark explains the rationale for community builder support:

> Remembering some of the bitter subdivision tragedies of the past, and their bad effect on the entire real estate structure, it is easy to realize the vital necessity for these provisions of the law. They are designed not only to protect the public from ignorant and fraudulent practice, but to protect the legitimate subdivider as well from unfair competition. As a matter of fact, they were written into the law at the urgent request of the subdividers themselves.[12]

A third essay in the California real estate collection discusses planning as *coordination*. This essay is written by Charles D. Clark, subdivision engineer of the Los Angeles County Regional Planning Commission.[13] The *coordination* function of subdivision regulations was the most closely associated with the rise of the master plan in public land-use planning. It was also the least controversial of the three. Whereas the majority of subdividers bitterly opposed subdivision *control* and often deeply resented the intrusive regulation of the *design and engineering* of their subdivisions, most subdividers welcomed planning agency *coordination* as an important service that could only enhance the sales value of their land.

An example of this viewpoint is displayed in the 1926 demand by San Bernardino realtors and subdividers for local subdivision planning and regulation:

> Members of the San Bernardino Realty Board launched a campaign to present before the public the question of the forming of a city planning commission with a view to bringing enough pressure to bear on the City Council that a permanent planning commission will be instituted, according to I. W. Gilbert, secretary of the board. "This is the big objective of the Realty Board for the coming year," Mr. Gilbert declared. . . . "We will adopt any means necessary to present our plans to the public so that they will understand what we are trying to do and fall in behind us." . . . "It is because the city is growing so rapidly that a planning commission must be forced. Unless it is, we will find ourselves in the same position as a large number of other cities in this state and the rest of the country, which now are having to spend millions upon millions of dollars for street reconstruction." [14]

While the first two forms of subdivision planning were related to cyclical crises and the aftermath of boomtime abuses, *coordination* planning was much more the offspring of structural changes in real estate development practice. As residential developers began to scatter urban subdivisions farther away in all directions from the center of the city, and as the automobile and other technological innovations were increasingly utilized to reshape urban spatial patterns, large subdividers became interested in coordinating their individual developments with surrounding private land-uses and with public extension of streets, parks, and other forms of infrastructure and services. In 1909 the first state subdivision planning law was passed in Wisconsin. This law authorized Wisconsin cities to regulate the width and alignment of all subdivision streets that were proposed for public dedication. Two years later the state of Washington passed a bold act requiring subdividers submitting plats for map filing in or near major cities to dedicate small public parks in their subdivisions. California's first *coordination*-based subdivision planning laws were approved in 1913 and 1915. The primary purpose of the California laws was the regulation of street width and alignment.[15]

During the "City Beautiful" period of downtown reconstruction, planners and subdividers realized that millions of dollars in public street openings and widenings could have been saved if only the original subdividers had dedicated the appropriate street size and arrangement when they first developed their acreage into urban lots. Both subdividers and planners strongly desired to pursue such far-sighted cooperation in the future and avoid the costly mistakes and uncertainty. However, public-private partnership of this nature could not be undertaken on a piecemeal basis. In order for the subdivider to know what to dedicate, the planner had first to devise a master street plan as the basis for any individual subdivision regulations. As Charles Clark put it: "The 'backbone' of the subdivision ordinance is the master plan of major and secondary highways."[16]

American regional planning traces its origins to the 1920s as metropolitan highway planning and subdivision regulation. The very idea of comprehensive planning was a direct outgrowth of the uncoordinated subdivision mania and subsequent private economic collapse and public fiscal crisis of the late 1920s. Residential subdivisions with well-planned public thoroughfares that avoided costly special tax assessments on property owners were in the best position to thrive or at least survive, and city and regional planning could help assure the developer's survival.

Community Builders and Zoning

Community builders wanted zoning to help stabilize the pattern of land usage in residential subdivisions and surrounding areas. The executive director of the National Association of Real Estate Boards stated in 1947: "We helped think up the idea of city zoning ordinances thirty years ago. Their purpose was to protect good residence neighborhoods from trade uses that would destroy values."[17] For community builders and realtors who specialized in developing and selling lots and houses to a relatively high-income market, *protection* was indeed the primary motivation for zoning. Through the use of private deed restrictions, residential subdividers had already market-tested the value of land-use regulations and found them to be most desirable.

Community builders needed public zoning to supplement private restrictions and especially to regulate areas not covered by deed restrictions. They believed that their interests would be adequately represented in the public planning process, enabling them to continue to exercise a great deal of private control over development and sales competition. The idea of *protection* in zoning, however, was not intended to be universally applied. It was to be extended mainly to "good residence neighborhoods," as the NAREB statement clearly indicated.

Since good residence neighborhoods were the principal kind that most community builders were in the business of creating, they naturally were strong and early advocates for the zoning concept. "Good" in this case meant the quality of landscape design and improvements, and it also generally meant designed primarily for higher-income purchasers. Private restrictions, for example, normally included such provisions as minimum required costs for home construction, and exclusion of all non-Caucasians from occupancy, except as domestic servants.[18]

In chapter 4 I describe the Los Angeles "Use of Property" survey and the Realty Board's campaign against the "overzoning" of certain use categories. During the 1920s and 1930s most of the privately owned land area in large central cities was not zoned for *protection*, even where neighborhoods were already built up with many single-family houses. Middle-income residential areas were generally zoned for multiple dwellings, and all major streets were zoned for commercial use. Low-income residential areas were usually zoned for either industrial or unrestricted use. As Barbara Flint noted, "The St. Louis City Planning Commission felt that where property was developed with homes of low value, even though they were single-family homes, multiple-family houses and other uses did not impair the value of these areas."[19]

In all different cases and classes of property use, zoning was normally devoted to stimulating more or less compatible forms of high-value development. Where residential areas were planned for or built up with expensive single-family houses, *protection* to facilitate or preserve this particular form of high property values was considered to be a worthwhile objective; in middle-income residential areas, *promotion* of higher-density, higher-value multifamily apartment buildings, hotels, stores, offices, and other residential and commercial uses was combined with the necessary *protection* of these uses from industrial "nuisance" encroachment; in low-income residential areas, *promotion* of industrial uses was the primary objective, with absolutely no *protection* of the local working-class population. Indeed, some of the more sophisticated zoning laws, such as Berkeley's, actually created exclusive industrial use districts to protect factory owners from complaints and lawsuits by low-income residential neighbors.[20]

Community builders frequently came into conflict with the majority of realty agents over zoning, with the community builders generally on the side of imposing stricter and more uniform public regulations. Most small realty operators wanted to promote the highest speculative values and fastest turnover for each individual property they owned or represented as agents, irrespective of neighborhood-wide or market-wide impacts. With the collapse of the 1920s urban real estate boom and the creation of the Federal Housing Administration (FHA) mortgage insurance program in the 1930s, the three-class model of zoning began to change. Beginning in 1935, *protection* for single-family residences was finally extended to middle-income, though still not low-income, residential neighborhoods.[21] For the period of the 1920s and early 1930s, however, community builders relied on tightly drawn and vigilantly enforced deed restrictions, ownership of large land parcels with protected borders such as rivers or parklands, incorporation of suburban government enclaves, and the establishment of county and regional planning agencies as their main lines of defense against the threat of curbstoner zoning.

California as a National Innovator

California was selected as the focus of chapters 4 and 5 because private and public forces within the state exercised national leadership by innovative example in three overlapping spheres: (1) in the growth, organization, and regulation of the real estate industry; (2) in the creation of land-use regulations and planning agencies; (3) in the extensive involvement and strong support of California realtors for state, county, and city planning efforts.

In real estate regulation, California led the nation. The first state real estate brokerage and sales licensing act in the U.S. was signed into law in California in 1917. During the 1920s, the California Legislature expanded the scope and enforcement powers of the Real Estate License Law into new regulatory arenas. California had the largest number of licensed brokers and salesmen of any state in the 1920s, and it also contained the largest number of realty boards and board members (realtors). The title insurance and trust companies and real estate lending institutions, particularly the savings and loan associations, grew to national prominence during this period. Most importantly, the large-scale residential subdividers, the community builders, were more prevalent among California's realtors than in any other state. California's community builders played a notable leadership role within the National Association of Real Estate Boards, and particularly within NAREB's Home Builders and Subdividers Division.[22]

With the creation of zoning regulations during this period, California was among the top five states in the 1920s in the number of local ordinances, and clearly dominated in the western half of the United States. The City of Los Angeles passed the country's first zoning law in 1908, successfully fought the national legal battle to establish the police power validity of citywide land-use zoning (1908–1915), and later established the nationwide legal precedent for the zoning of districts exclusively for single-family residential use (1921–1925). Both of these new forms of public planning intervention spread rapidly to other California cities, suburbs, and towns, making Los Angeles a state pace-setter as well as a national model.

Los Angeles County also led the nation in pioneering metropolitan regional subdivision regulation, part of southern California's contribution to national trends in the development of the modern residential suburb. In December of 1922 the Board of Supervisors created the Los Angeles County Regional Planning Commission, with the power to plan for and regulate the use of land in all unincorporated areas of the huge county. The Commission, the first of its kind in the U.S., was also charged with coordinating its county land-use planning activities with the city planning commissions of Los Angeles, Pasadena, Long Beach, and the county's other incorporated cities.

Los Angeles' key innovation of county planning, established in order to aid in subdivision development through plat control, zoning, and highway and infrastructure planning, was emulated in 1927 by Santa Barbara County. Ten counties in other states had also established Los Angeles-style county or regional planning commissions by 1927. After the California Legislature passed the 1929 Planning Act, which legally mandated the adoption of county subdivision regulations and the creation of land-use planning agencies, 34 California counties had planning commissions in operation by the mid-1930s.[23]

During the dramatic year of 1927, according to the chairman of NAREB's City Planning Committee, "The first state to take advantage of the Hoover Act was California."[24] The 1927 California Planning Act, adopted with considerable realtor support while the U.S. Department of Commerce's 1928 *A Standard City Planning Enabling Act* was still in draft form, had a significant impact on the nationwide fortunes of urban planning initiatives. The purpose of the 1927 law, superseded by the 1929 Planning and Map Filing Acts, was to meet the needs of primarily residential developers whose activities were extending further and further beyond the built-up portions of the established cities.

California was also widely regarded in the 1920s as the state in which realtors as an organized force were most strongly involved in promoting and shaping urban land-use planning legislation and implementation. Chapters 4 and 5 document realtors' participation in public decision-making on zoning and subdivision regulations. Sponsorship by the California Real Estate Association of an annual statewide California Conference on City Planning from 1926 to 1932 was considered by many community builders, planners, realtors, and civic leaders throughout the United States to be especially noteworthy, as Hubbard and Hubbard described:

> The outstanding example of state-wide real estate interest in comprehensive planning appears in California, where recent leadership has made the California Real Estate Association one of the most potent state influences on planning progress. A series of annual city planning meetings sponsored by the association, beginning in 1926, has attracted statewide and national interest and promoted the formation of many city planning commissions throughout California. It is interesting to note that by 1928 forty California realtors were serving on such commissions, seven being commission chairmen.[25]

Design of the Book

This book is primarily a study of the interactions between two groups of people: community builders and urban planners. In each case I have chosen to analyze both individual and organizational behavior. For urban planners I have studied specific people in their various roles as private consultants and public administrators, and collective behavior through two principal associations, the National Conference on City Planning (NCCP) and the American City Planning Institute (ACPI).[26]

Community builders likewise are researched and analyzed both as entrepreneur-developers and heads of real estate firms, and as actors in their principal trade association, the National Association of Real Estate Boards (NAREB) and its many affiliated state associations and local boards. From 1914 to 1923, the City Planning Committee of NAREB was the main organizational voice of America's community builders. From 1923 to the early 1940s, the Home Builders and Subdividers Division of NAREB was the key meeting ground for community builders. In the 1940s, two spinoffs of NAREB, the National Association of Home Builders (NAHB) and the Community Builders' Council of the Urban Land Institute (ULI) supplanted the realtors' association as the primary spokesmen for community builders. Thus for the time frame of my book, 1890 to 1940, NAREB is the focal point.[27]

Accordingly, chapter 2 emphasizes two analytical tasks. First, I explain the organization of real estate brokers into the trade association of NAREB. Most major subdivision developers also headed brokerage firms. Secondly, I explain the many institutional and structural changes in the real estate industry and urban real estate development that led to the rise of community builders as a business institution and to community building as the creation of modern residential subdivisions.

In chapter 3 I introduce urban planners and explain why community builders and urban planners worked together to produce both a new system of private land planning and a new system of public planning. I tell the story of the organizational cooperation beginning in 1914 and of the more extensive partnership in the mid-1920s that led to the important 1927 NAREB-ACPI *Joint Statement on Subdivision Control*, one of the key planning and development documents of the decade.

Chapters 4 and 5 are case studies of the Los Angeles Realty Board and zoning, and the California Real Estate Association and subdivision regulations. These case studies reveal that the community builders were not entirely satisfied with the apparatus of urban land planning agencies that they had helped create during the 1910s, 1920s, and early 1930s. While they continued to support planning in general, they often were opposed to particular proposals, decisions, and laws. They also encountered a great deal of conflict not just with planners and public officials, but with colleagues and competitors from within the ranks of the real estate industry. As a consequence of this dissatisfaction, community builders began searching for alternative and additional vehicles of land-use control, including stricter and more extensive private restrictions, establishment of newly incorporated suburban government jurisdictions and of metropolitan-wide regional planning agencies, and support for real estate business regulation in place of planning commission authority.

Chapter 6 documents the successful completion of this search for a better source of control through the powerful national intervention in the mid-1930s of the Federal Housing Administration (FHA). FHA, in close alliance with the large community builders and the major real estate lending institutions, imposed standardized land planning requirements on private subdividers and state and local governments. By 1940 FHA's influential Land Planning Division was fully implementing a set of public-private planning goals that had been the basic suburban housing development agenda of community builders and urban planners for three decades. The creation of the modern residential subdivision, best symbolized in the 1950s by the Levittowns and Park Forests, was essentially accomplished by the late 1930s.[28]

stoner"—the real estate broker with his office in his hat. He has no regular place of business, but is always on the street looking for prospective customers. He hangs around the depot and watches for the stranger, or on the sidewalk in front of some well-advertised firm. His only asset is a slick tongue and he catches many a "sucker" and sells him a worthless piece of land. He always has a "bargain" that may look good to you on the surface, but generally has a flaw in the title or some other defect that you do not discover until too late. The California State Realty Federation has introduced a bill in the present Legislature to put this class of men out of business.[1]

The California State Realty Federation (CSRF), founded in 1905, was one of the oldest and largest state associations of local realty board members. At the time the ad appeared, the CSRF was at the peak of its pre-World War I strength, with 26 local boards and approximately one thousand members.[2] Two years later, in the face of a depression in residential real estate brought on by the War, the State Federation nearly dissolved, as did many of the smaller local boards. The struggle of the "First Class" firms continued unabated, however. A real estate sales licensing bill passed each biannual session of the California Legislature beginning in 1913, and was signed by the governor in 1917 to inaugurate the first state Real Estate License Law in the U.S. In that year, the CSRF changed its name to the California Real Estate Association (CREA), which in the 1920s became a powerful voice for state regulation of the real estate industry.[3]

This chapter examines the structural transformation of American urban development that spawned the "First Class" real estate firm as a central node of a much broader network of entrepreneurial institutions in real estate finance and insurance, land subdividing and development, construction, and property management. As brokers, the "First Class," joined in the 1920s by elements of the "Second Class," organized into local real estate boards and state associations and a national association as mechanisms designed to reduce competition within their highly competitive industry and to rationalize and standardize economic relationships more favorable to the larger realty dealers. The goals of the "Realtors," as the board and association members called themselves, included: (1) expanding the share of the total dollar volume of real estate transactions handled on a commission and fee basis by the brokerage industry; (2) stabilizing the wide "boom-bust" sales activity and price cycles that often undermined investor and consumer confidence in real estate purchase; and (3) improving the pattern of urban land-use and quality of development to increase the attractiveness, security, and growth potential of real estate investment.

Goal #3 constituted the core program of what was often referred to as "scientific city planning." Certain members of the real estate boards and associations, particularly the brokerage firms that specialized in direct large-scale land subdividing for residential development, were frequently strong supporters and even leaders in the movement to establish local planning commissions to guide public improvements and regulate private land-use. This group of real estate executives I call "community builders." The fight for urban planning was an integral part of their local, state, and national battle with the "curbstoners," and was also a source of conflict among their fellow realtors.

The community builders began as land subdividers and evolved into homebuilders between 1890 and 1940, particularly during the 1930s with the encouragement and assistance of the Federal Housing Administration. While some large subdividers and many operative builders were not members of real estate boards, the Home Builders and Subdividers Division of the National Association of Real Estate Boards (NAREB) was the main organizational framework within which most of the community builders operated during the 1920s and 1930s. On the vital public issues of land planning and regulation for development of the urban periphery, the leading residential subdividers inside NAREB were more active and influential lobbyists than any other organized group from the entire real estate industry. They also played an important role both as allies and adversaries of professional city planners. In the pages that follow, I will describe and analyze the changing pattern of economic and political relationships between the community builders and the curbstoners.

The Competitive Environment

Real estate brokerage is essentially a sales-oriented service in which a broker acts as agent for a principal in arranging the selling, purchasing, or leasing of real property, including facilitating the completion of a sometimes complicated set of related legal and financial transactions. The bulk of standard brokerage income has generally derived from commissions as a percent of the sales price paid by the selling owner when the agent sells a property on the owner's behalf. Income also derives from arranging rental leases, managing property for an owner, appraising property, selling property insurance, arranging and servicing property loans, and a whole range of other activities, but sales commissions have always been the bread-and-butter of the average brokerage business. The broker gets his or her name by being the agent who represents the property owner (or seeker, but mostly owners); this differentiates her or him from sales personnel ("salesmen"), who are employed by brokers, generally on a commission basis, to help the broker sell property. Realty clients pay their commissions directly to brokers, not to salesmen; sales personnel are paid by the broker.[4]

While some form of brokerage has probably always existed, real estate brokerage in eighteenth- and nineteenth-century America was not so nearly widespread an occupation as it subsequently became. Most people one hundred or more years ago bought and sold or leased real estate for speculation, investment, production, or consumption, directly on their "own account." The wealthy often employed middlemen or agents in various phases of land transactions, but most other property owners acted as their own trading representatives. A large number of new realty agents first emerged most prominently in connection with the expansion of interstate railroads and later with the growth of intra- and interurban transit companies. These railway corporations platted, subdivided, and promoted the sale of vast tracts of rural and urban land to international and interregional migrants. Real estate agents employed by these transportation concerns helped promote the initial land sales, although the subsequent resale market frequently reverted back to direct "own account" transactions between owners and purchasers (assuming there was a genuine resale market rather than a speculative collapse).[5]

The largest and most stable of the more modern version of urban realty brokers grew up with the advance of urban technology in the latter third of the nineteenth century. These real estate leaders were closely allied with the major transport companies, utilities, and other large landholders and residential subdivider/developers, as well as with the newly formed giant corporations that were changing the face of the fastest-growing cities with the advent of the downtown headquarters "skyscraper."[6]

With the increasing pace of urbanization and the tremendous mobility and constant turnover of the urban population, the volume of metropolitan real estate sales transactions both for vacant lots and for existing buildings grew rapidly, providing vast opportunities for realty agents to earn commissions by seeking out prospective purchasers among the anonymous city populace.[7] This new source of income and employment in realty sales mushroomed in the 1880s and early 90s, but there were several serious problems with its potential long-run growth and success.[8]

The first set of problems applied to the buyers and sellers who dealt with the agents. The industry had total ease of entry. It required no capital to enter—anyone could call him or herself a real estate "agent."[9] Since all but the most sophisticated and professional buyers and sellers entered the market only very infrequently in any single geographic area, they were often quite unfamiliar with the salesmen, sales techniques, laws, prices, customs, and even the physical property over which they were bargaining. Thus they might be easy prey to unscrupulous real estate operators, who could engage in substantial misrepresentation and even outright fraud and then simply "fly by night," free of the business constraints that reputation imposed in a more closed community setting. Since buyers and sellers were legitimately uncertain as to which realty agents and proposed deals to trust, the real estate market periodically suffered from halting fluctuations that in times of falling prices could escalate to panic levels of disinvestment and "no confidence."[10]

The second set of problems belonged to the brokers. Given that there were so many other sales agents in business, how could a broker wholeheartedly pursue the sale of a property when the commission could so easily be lost to a competing agent working to sell the same property, or when the owner might play off a number of agents against one another and then sell the property "independently" and refuse to pay any commission? How could a broker charge a reasonable fee when he or she was so vulnerable to being undercut by a "curbstoner"? Given the general level of mistrust, how could an honest broker engage in fair practices without being out-competed by less scrupulous rivals, and how could such a reputable dealer distinguish both the firm and the industry as being sources of reliable and trustworthy service? Was there a way for brokers to share market information without sacrificing deals? Could realty agents work together to enhance the quality of real estate development in the community, as a more long-range strategy for expanding sales opportunities and increasing property values?[11]

That the ultracompetitive situation caused serious problems for the larger brokers can easily be gleaned from this admonition published in the *San Francisco Real Estate Board Bulletin* in 1918, urging its members to "COOPERATE WITH YOUR FELLOW BROKERS AND BOOST."

> If the client of another office makes a purchase and asks for your opinion, don't tell him he has been robbed, that you could have sold him the same piece or a better one for less money. Don't boost one part of town by knocking another. Real Estate is a commodity the sale of which depends largely on confidence in values, future prospects and the broker's expert advice. How can we build up a Real Estate Market, if, for every broker who through hard work and sincere optimism effects a sale, there arise a dozen knocking, disloyal malcontents who impugn the buyer's sanity, the broker's honesty, the value or prospective value of the property?[12]

For some of the more prosperous and ambitious realty brokerage firms in a number of the fastest-growing cities (particularly in the midwest and far west), the answer to the various sets of competitive problems lay in the formation of an industry trade association. Such an association would act as an informal cartel to standardize transaction procedures, reduce competition both within the association and especially from without, encourage cooperation among members, enhance the public image of brokerage and of real estate investment, and act as a lobby to win needed institutional changes from other private industry sectors and from different levels of government. The primary vehicles for achieving these aims were the local real estate boards, the state associations of local board members, and the National Association of Real Estate Boards (NAREB), founded by 19 local boards and one state association (California) in 1908.[13]

The initial agenda of NAREB was articulated by its executive secretary during its first year of operation:

1. Organize in some way that will give a rating of men who handle real estate, "something similar to Dunn's or Bradstreet's, but a moral rating not a financial rating."
2. Have some sort of sign to be displayed on every member's office wall showing membership in the National Association of Real Estate Boards.

3. Secure uniform state laws as to deeds, mortgages, and real estate contracts.
4. Establish exclusive agency. "Exclusive agency would revolutionize our whole business." Local exchanges told him this was hard to do. Members said that owners wouldn't agree to it. Nevertheless, urged Halsey, "if we can say to owners you must sell through some one man or you cannot sell through any of the members of this board, we can make it stick."[14]

The first big debate in NAREB was over the issue of whether a broker was an entrepreneur in the sense of being a dealer and speculator in real estate, or whether brokers were professional fiduciaries, akin to lawyers who represent a client's interest subject to strict rules to avoid conflicts of interest. NAREB essentially opted for the latter approach, which constituted the beginnings of the "professionalization" of realty brokerage. Probably the key step was taken in 1915 when the national conference in Los Angeles agreed that

> An agent has no right to sell his own property to his client, or himself buy a property from a client who is paying him a commission for his services as agent, unless he has his client's full knowledge and consent. Nor is it permissible for a broker in the employ and pay of one of the parties to make a deal to take compensation from the other party to the transaction without the knowledge and consent of each.[15]

Once the local real estate boards firmly decided upon the notion of providing a service as a fiduciary agent rather than competitive self-dealing or double-dealing, the way was then clear to push for the major structural changes that have made the modern brokerage profession possible, namely "exclusive" agency made legally binding by written contracts, the multiple listing system, and standard fixed commissions with clear and enforceable guidelines among realty agents for splitting commissions. The exclusive agency provision and the standard commissions introduced the elements of monopoly the brokers felt they needed in order to ensure adequate remuneration for their efforts; the multiple listing system and the cooperative commission arrangements organized the real estate market such that the elements of monopoly also expanded rather than contracted the range of service and market coverage that a client could receive from any one particular agent. Brokers could now share market information and even sales efforts without undercutting each other or risking loss of compensation.[16]

The principal means that the local boards used to pursue the above-outlined institutional rationalization was by exercising a form of collective market differentiation and market power. Members of local boards were advertised by the board and advertised themselves individually as being part of a select, elite group. After 1916, all members of NAREB, and *only* members of NAREB, were legally entitled to use the new brand name of "Realtor." To deal with a "Realtor," a client was generally asked to agree to exclusive agency, written contracts, and standard commissions and fees, and in exchange would receive the advantages of multiple listing of the property through a wide network of active and reputable agents.[17]

The image of a "Realtor" was further reinforced by NAREB's promulgation of a Realtor's Code of Ethics, beginning in 1913. The Code of Ethics created internal rules for enforcing relations between realtors in order to put substantial teeth behind the new cooperative arrangements. A realtor who failed to obey the rules could be fined, censured, or even expelled from the board, in which case he could no longer call himself a "Realtor" and would be denied access to the economically advantageous Multiple Listing Service. The Code also contained standards of fair practice for dealing with clients and with the general public, such that a client or citizen could file a complaint to the local board, whose Grievance and Arbitration Committee would presumably investigate and take punitive or corrective action where appropriate. Realtors' willingness to act as monitors of honest business behavior served to enhance their reputation vis-à-vis their numerous agent-competitors, to help exorcise what they saw as a "curbstone" mentality from their increasingly professionalized approach. Since most of the realtors, as local board members, were in fact a select group of the more prosperous and well-established metropolitan firms, the Code of Ethics and the "Realtor" name became self-fulfilling prophesies both of structural change in the industry and of the concomitant rise in economic and cultural respectability.[18]

Being a select group, however, had both positive and negative aspects. The positive side was that the realtors managed to successfully differentiate their own image from that of the run-of-the-mill ("Second Class") agent and particularly from the "curbstoner." The negative side was that there were still hundreds of thousands of these other dealers in the U.S. busily seeking after and brokering realty transactions, inflicting a great deal of competitive impact on the real estate industry's image, on its cost and price structure, on supply and demand, and on physical urban development patterns and practices.

The privately administered Code of Ethics could only be used to discipline a small portion of the total number of full- and part-time realty dealers. Even the worst sanction that could be applied under the Code was expulsion from NAREB, which still allowed the presumably guilty broker to continue to engage in disapproved business methods. To solve this dilemma, NAREB members turned to state governments for assistance. They demanded that all real estate brokers and sales agents be licensed and regulated by state authority.[19]

Beginning in 1913, when the California Real Estate License Bill passed the legislature but was vetoed by Governor Hiram Johnson, realtors waged a vigorous campaign for state licensing. By 1919 California, Michigan, and Oregon had license laws on the books. A decade later 27 states were enforcing regulatory real estate licensing procedures covering approximately 115,000 brokers and 150,000 salesmen.[20]

The various state license laws all required registration for a modest fee, complete with personal references and sometimes with an entrance examination and/or the posting of a performance bond. The fees covered the administrative costs of the real estate commissions or licensing boards that were newly established in most states to enforce the license laws. These state agencies were generally empowered to investigate citizen complaints and to suspend, deny, and revoke licenses. In some cases and states, licensing boards could require certain forms of public disclosure of financial information in connection with real estate transactions, could issue cease-and-desist orders to block sales, and order that refunds be paid to aggrieved purchasers and clients. Many states also required prospective licensees to fulfill certain educational requirements and to pass written examinations. A few states even utilized a portion of the license fees to fund college-level real estate education and research.[21]

The professed goal of many of the "First Class" realty dealers was to use licensing both to regulate industry behavior and to eliminate and exclude the bulk of existing and potential agents from the real estate profession. The leading realtor-advocates of licensing wished to make the registration process expensive to the applicant, to require stringent educational and other qualifications for acceptance into the field, and to make enforcement against abuse swift, strict, and certain. In no state were any of these conditions ever realized. However, it is probably fair to say that licensing did act as a very mild deterrent to entry into the business, as well as helping to curb some of the worst abuses. The state secretary of the California Real Estate Association in 1928 expressed both the modest reality and his fervent hope:

> The ratio of brokers to population is steadily falling under the present laws. . . . The writer foresees the day when a real estate broker's license will be on par with a seat on the stock exchange, or Wall Street. The prices may never reach from $50,000 to $300,000 a seat, but surely in their evolution, the real estate men will inevitably see that to handle other people's money, they should put up financial security with the State. This, to the writer's mind, is inevitable, if the business is to ultimately approach the standing of banking or medicine, and is run on a scientific basis.
> A hit-or-miss policy in modern business life is destined to be crushed out under the law of the survival of the fittest, the educated and the financially responsible.[22]

The hoped-for transformation was never so dramatic as the largest of the "First Class" brokers envisioned, probably because the average realtor still operated on a scale that by overall U.S. industrial or commercial standards was considered a very small enterprise. Nevertheless, the advent of licensing represented another important manifestation of the major structural shift that was occurring, and NAREB rose to prominence partly as a result of its leading role in the licensing crusade. In nearly every state, the local real estate boards and state associations were a key lobbying force behind state legislative and executive actions.[23]

Licensing was seen quite explicitly by many government officials and NAREB supporters as a method of imposing the Code of Ethics on the multitudes of non-"Realtor" brokers and salesmen. Many of the state agencies established to enforce license laws were directly controlled and administered by real estate board leaders from their respective states; in some cases the license laws expressly mandated such control. The connection between state licensing and NAREB was so close that in 1924 NAREB, a distinctly nongovernmental body, organized the National Association of Real Estate License Law Officials. This body met annually as part of NAREB's own national conference to exchange ideas between realtors and public officials about extension and enforcement of state license laws.[24]

One need only look at some relevant numbers to understand the inordinate influence of the realtors on state real estate regulation in relation to the overwhelming majority of those being regulated. In California, for example, the California Real Estate Association had 70 members in early 1920. Total local board membership statewide, including the flagship Los Angeles Realty Board, was approximately 400. And yet in 1920, the California Real Estate Department issued licenses for 30,000 brokers and saleswomen and men, many of whom "were bitterly opposed to the Act and sought every opportunity to discredit it."[25] Most issues of the department's *California Real Estate Directory-Bulletin* contained proceedings from the CREA annual convention or other statements by leading realtors. All licensed brokers in the state received copies of CREA publications. The state real estate commissioner, a well-known realtor, openly promoted local real estate board and CREA membership among the state's licensees. By 1927 the number of licensees in California reached 68,000, and CREA membership had climbed to a prosperous 5,000. Perhaps it is reasonable to say of California's license law that "with its passage organization of the State real estate business became possible by the Realtors."[26]

Another illustration of the close relationship between NAREB's leadership and state regulation of the real estate business came in the 1930s when the Nebraska legislature wrote the entire text of the Code of Ethics into the state license law. Later on a number of other states followed suit.[27]

The fact that real estate board members were generally larger in business size than the typical real estate broker was confirmed by two major national surveys conducted in the mid-1930s. The first was a 1933 survey of NAREB members. This survey, compiled for the U.S. National Recovery Administration (NRA), covered all 10,641 active NAREB members, representing a dramatic Depression-induced decline of nearly 16,000 from the peak membership year of 1926.[28] The second survey, of 36,137 real estate agencies and brokerage offices, was undertaken in 1936 by the U.S. Bureau of the Census. The latter survey took place under somewhat improved economic circumstances for the real estate industry. It established that California was the leading state in the number of real estate offices, and New York state was first in total real estate employment, and in brokerage income.[29]

The Census Bureau analysis stated that "many proprietors reported no paid employees whatsoever, and many others represent one-man establishments except for the services of a single clerical employee."[30] The average number of clerical and sales employees per establishment in the Census study, including proprietors and executives, was 1.3. Among NAREB members, however, the average number of office executive, clerical, and sales workers per business was 3.4.[31]

An additional finding of the NAREB survey was that for the larger brokers that engaged in property management, the 2,400 who engaged in office and business property management employed an average of 5.5 workers directly related to this function, and the 1,900 NAREB members engaging in apartment building management employed an average of 6.3 workers. These figures cannot be compared to the Census survey, however, because the latter study did not report data on direct employment in property management.[32]

NAREB Influence in Washington, D.C.

NAREB's rise to prominence as a national organization and its strong role in federal policymaking began in 1917 with the advent of U.S. entry into World War I. Headed during the war years by Los Angeles realtor Colonel William May Garland, NAREB actively assisted the federal government in appraising and acquiring property and facilitating new construction. Many leading realtors were instrumental in creating the Real Estate Division of the U.S. Housing Corporation (USHC). This Division established a special federal mortgage loan program to stimulate private construction of moderate-cost housing for war workers, supplementing the government housing construction program of the USHC directed by city planner F. L. Olmsted, Jr.[33]

With the accession of Herbert Hoover as secretary of commerce in 1921, NAREB became an important and highly favored trade association working closely with the Commerce Department's newly created

Division of Building and Housing, as well as with other federal agencies. By the early 1930s NAREB was a major presence at the U.S. President's Conference on Home Building and Home Ownership in 1931 and a key national lobbying force behind the creation of the Federal Home Loan Bank System, the Federal Housing Administration, and a number of additional federal policies and programs.[34]

The most visible symbol of the realtor's national power came in 1933, when the National Recovery Administration (NRA) was promulgating restrictive federal codes of "Fair Competition" for every substantial industry in the country. In September of 1933, NAREB submitted to the NRA proposed codes for the "Real Estate Business," separated into five distinct components: (1) "Real Estate and Insurance Brokerage Business"; (2) "Real Estate and Building Management Business"; (3) "Real Estate Mortgage Business"; (4) "Land Development and Home Building Business"; and (5) "Real Estate Appraising Business."[35] In its cover letter accompanying the proposed codes, NAREB's president and its Code Committee chairman stated:

> Real Estate has frequently been estimated to comprise at least one half of our national wealth. In spite of its importance, however, real-estate methods are generally unstandardized. The National Association of Real Estate Boards is the only articulate nation-wide body representing real estate in all of its branches. The Association believes that a great opportunity exists at this time to standardize and coordinate the work it is doing and the work that is being done by several other national associations covering important but restricted fields, such as the National Association of Building Owners and Managers, Mortgage Bankers Association of America, the National Association of Apartment House Owners, and others.
>
> Because of lack of coordination, there has not been sufficient planning with respect to the production of improvements and their adjustment to current needs. As a consequence we have periods of feast and famine. Lack of coordination has also produced costs that are frequently excessive and that are an obstacle to home ownership. The present crisis offers an opportunity for the major interests and activities in the real-estate field to work together for more intelligent development of sites, better planning and construction, sounder financing methods, and more productive management.[36]

The first of the NAREB codes officially approved by the NRA was for the "Real Estate Brokerage Industry," in April of 1934. This code re-

quired *all* "Members of the Industry" to register with the Code Authority and to pay a registration fee to finance the administration of the Code
Authority, which was the NRA-designated national code enforcement
body for the particular industry. The Real Estate Brokerage Code specified that the national Code Authority would consist of 11 voting members, 8 of whom must be appointed by NAREB. It further stated that
local code control boards would be created to aid in enforcing the new
industrial law. The Code mandated that these local code boards would
be established by local real estate boards, or, where no realty board existed, by NAREB. The section of the Code on Trade Practice Rules
enumerated "methods of unfair competition" that would be considered
illegal violations of the NRA Code if practiced by any registered Member
of the Industry (any unregistered broker would automatically be in vio-
lation), subject to fines and imprisonment. Not surprisingly, the 18 Trade
Practice Rules were quite similar to the Realtor's Code of Ethics.[37]

Linkages and Institutional Transformation

The fact that NAREB drafted the proposed five NRA codes for "real
estate in all of its branches" was a sign of the increasing institutional
interconnectedness that had been spawned in the real estate industry during the preceding three decades. The largest of the brokers now stood
near the center of a broad network of economic actors shaping the development process.[38] (See table 2.1.)

Having first organized a trade association and licensing laws to secure
strong market power within real estate brokerage, the large brokers enhanced this power through their central position as an integrating force
in the increasingly complex institutional process of urban land development. Many of the larger brokers and builders became "developers," providing the service of managing and linking together the various stages of
transforming parcels of unimproved land, from the initial subdividing
process through the construction of improvements to the selling and
renting of the completed structures. These stages became increasingly
integrated in each decade from the 1900s to the 1930s; however, even
when the stages were disconnected by transfer of ownership, large real
estate brokers were often involved in each different stage of ownership

TABLE 2.1
The American Real Estate Industry, 1890–1940

Brokers and Sales Agents
Renting and Leasing Agents
Building and Property Managers
Appraisers
Operative Builders
Contractors and Subcontractors
Equipment, Materials, and Appliance Manufacturers and Suppliers
Subdividers and Land Developers
Transportation and Utility Companies
Architects and Civil Engineers and Landscape Architects
Lawyers and Accountants
Fire and Property Insurance Companies
Title Insurance and Trust Companies
Commercial Banks
Life Insurance Companies
Mutual Savings Banks
Building and Loan Associations (Savings and Loans)
Mortgage Companies (Mortgage Bankers)

transaction. The new production-oriented broker-developers went one step further, actually coordinating multiple activities and involvement of financial institutions and insurance companies, contractors and subcontractors, architects and engineers, and other key actors in the development process. The overall institutional changes in land development practices that led to greater control by substantial private firms and public agencies also enhanced the central position of the biggest real estate broker-developers, the leaders of NAREB's Home Builders and Subdividers Division—the community builders.[39]

Finance

The single most important institutional change in urban property development after 1900 was in the area of real estate finance. Up to the late nineteenth century the vast bulk of real estate transactions were financed either directly from personal savings or through small loans informally arranged through relatives, friends, or very small local lenders.

By the early twentieth century this situation was dramatically shifting. Both the proportion of real estate transactions financed through mortgage debt and the proportion of mortgage debt held by financial institutions were rapidly rising. Property acquisitions often carried multiple mortgages on them. Commercial banks, mutual savings banks, life insurance companies, and savings and loan associations all significantly expanded their mortgage lending. The average length and the loan-to-value ratio of first mortgages began increasing, and self-amortizing repayment schedules grew in usage. In the 1920s, mortgage bonds appeared as a major new source of financing, and mortgage guarantee insurance and secondary mortgage markets also grew in importance.[40]

In 1923, the U.S. Census reported that the number of mortgaged homes (as opposed to debt-free) nationwide had increased by 43 percent between 1890 and 1920, with a steady upward trend in the intervening years. The actual number of existing home mortgages grew by 350 percent during these 30 years, with the amount of debt increasing six-fold to six billion dollars.[41] The Census survey was taken in a real estate depression year, 1920, and before the unprecedented expansion of mortgage lending that dwarfed all previous statistical peaks, with the total residential mortgage debt more than tripling between 1920 and 1930.[42] This Census study, prepared by economist Richard T. Ely, also revealed that mortgage financing, which in 1890 was confined mainly to upper-income purchasers, had by 1920 extended to smaller, lower-priced, middle-income housing, symbolizing another key change in institutional real estate development patterns.[43] The revolutionary rise in higher loan-to-value debt financing for residential realty, often ascribed to the post-World War II era, clearly began in the early decades of this century.

Between 1850 and 1900 a national urban network of all of the main types of modern financial institutions took shape. After 1900, substantial growth in institutional mortgage debtholding occurred, foreshadowing the floodtide of real estate lending during the 1920s boom. For example, the institutional share of residential mortgage debt increased from 49.5 percent in 1896 to 66 percent by 1912.[44]

Savings and loan associations, originally called "Building and Loan," first experienced dramatic growth in the 1880s. After the depression of 1893, they settled down to a more modest growth rate.[45] By the 1920s, however, "S&Ls" had emerged as the top mortgage lender among all competing financial institutions, particularly in 1–4 family residential dwellings.[46] To illustrate the scale of institutional growth, in 1893 the total number of properties mortgaged by S&Ls in the previous 31 years was just over 300,000. Yet in just 10 years, between 1920 and 1930, savings and loans mortgaged 4.35 million properties, totaling more than 15 billion dollars in loans.[47] Acknowledgment of their growing role in real estate finance reached national headlines in 1932 when President Hoover and Congress created the Federal Home Loan Bank System.[48]

Prior to the 1920s, mutual savings banks were the largest residential mortgage lenders, and their lending activities also steadily increased in the post-1900 period.[49] The main reason for their declining relative share of total institutional lending was their concentration primarily in just one region of the country, the northeast. Within that region, however, they exercised considerable influence on real estate market activity.[50]

State-chartered commercial banks were among the oldest of institutional mortgage lenders, dating back well into the nineteenth century. The rise of commercial banks as major mortgage lenders did not begin until the early twentieth century, when the Federal Reserve Act of 1913 and a key amendment passed in 1916 paved the way for federally chartered commercial bank involvement. National bank real estate lending was further expanded with the passage of the McFadden Act in 1927, and again through the creation of the Federal Housing Administration (FHA) in the 1930s.[51]

Life insurance companies in 1900 were the third largest institutional residential mortgage lenders after mutual savings banks and savings and loans.[52] As a percentage of their own total assets, however, life insurance companies have traditionally been very heavily involved in mortgage investment, more than any other financial intermediary except savings and loan associations. Dating from the 1860s, anywhere from one-quarter to one-half of the total U.S. life insurance company portfolio has consisted of real estate mortgage loans, with another major portfolio segment invested in direct real estate ownership.[53] Life insurance holdings of mortgages grew enormously during the 1920s. The larger companies played a particularly important role in handling the big commercial and industrial mortgages, and in creating and standardizing the national mortgage market for lending on residential property.[54]

Mortgage companies, also known as mortgage bankers, were yet another key financial innovation to grow in institutional status during the early twentieth century. In a sense these companies were engaged in mortgage brokerage, as they basically acted as intermediaries between prospective borrowers and prospective lenders. They would originate loans, both first mortgages and especially second or junior mortgages, and then sell them to financial institutions or investors, often continuing to manage the loan and receiving a fee for this service.[55] This institutional arrangement was a vital forerunner of the secondary mortgage market that reached national fruition with the establishment of the Federal National Mortgage Association (FNMA) during the 1930s.[56] Perhaps a related development to mortgage banking in the 1920s was the growth of mortgage bond houses, who sold securities to investors backed by real estate mortgages. The main difference was that mortgage bankers sold individual mortgages mostly to financial institutions, whereas the bond brokers sold mortgage-backed securities primarily to individuals.[57]

Realtors were vitally interested and in many cases intimately involved in promoting the expansion of financial institutions into real estate lending. Since realty brokers' primary source of income came from earning commissions from the sale of real property for clients, the brokers were anxious to pursue any means of widening the market for their product. Availability of financing became increasingly important with the changing pattern of realty transactions beginning in the 1880s. The organization by NAREB of a separate Mortgage and Finance Division in 1923 was a recognition of this crucial connection.[58]

Many of the larger real estate brokers were actively engaged in financial operations both as agents of other institutions and as lenders for their own institutions. The most common form of involvement was as an agent. Reputable brokers would steer prospective borrowers to financial institutions with which they had ongoing relationships and receive a percentage fee from the value of every mortgage loan they successfully "brokered." In some cases, they were officially authorized to initiate certain types of mortgage loans for these institutions. Many of the major life insurance companies maintained "correspondent" relationships with realtors in various cities.[59]

In addition, the bigger realty brokers generally had their own "Mortgage and Loan" departments to make, sell, and service loans. Some realtors would spin off separate mortgage companies to expand their business in the area of financing, usually as a supplement but occasionally as an alternative to brokerage. Such an orientation explains the very close connection between NAREB and the Mortgage Bankers Association of America (MBAA), which was founded in 1914. The Mortgage and Finance Division of NAREB wrote the proposed NRA code for the "Real Estate Mortgage Business" in conjunction with the MBAA.[60]

Moreover, beginning in the early twentieth century major real estate brokers often directly controlled, or were very closely associated with directing, local financial institutions. As Leo Grebler has pointed out, "realtors, for example, have sometimes controlled savings and loan associations or country banks to such an extent as to make them adjuncts to their operations."[61] Economist Herbert Simpson, writing about the role of financing in the tremendous wave of suburban land speculation during the 1920s, underscores this growing link between realty brokers and financial institutions:

> A particularly ominous development was the expansion of the banking system itself for the specific purpose of financing real estate promotion and development. Real estate interests dominated the policies of many banks, and thousands of new banks were organized and chartered for the specific purpose of providing the credit facilities for proposed real estate promotions. The greater proportion of these were state banks and trust companies, many of them located in the outlying sections of the larger cities or in suburban regions not fully occupied by older and more established banking institutions.[62]

Another indication of the substantial difference between the average small realty broker and the larger realtor was in the area of real estate finance. The U.S. Census of Business reported for 1936 that of the 36,137 real estate agencies surveyed, the average income from "placing of loans and mortgages" was just 5.8 percent of average total income.[63] For the 10,641 realtors surveyed by NAREB in 1933, income from negotiating, renewing, and servicing mortgages was significantly higher than the Census figures both in average dollar amounts and as a percentage of total income. Thus the realtors were much more involved in financing and earned more from doing so. About one-fourth of the NAREB members surveyed were heavily engaged in mortgage brokering, and 190 of the

NAREB members maintained simultaneous membership in the Mortgage Bankers Association of America.[64]

Insurance

The selling of property insurance (fire and casualty) overlapped significantly with the growth of the modern realty brokerage industry. The majority of brokers, both large and small, generally sold some form of property insurance on a commission basis.[65] In this case their paying client was an insurance company. During the latter decades of the nineteenth century, with the explosion of high-density city-building, fire insurance sales entered a period of rapid expansion. Many of the large realtors maintained strong ties to the big fire insurance companies and their local agents. The Los Angeles Realty Board, for example, created in 1903 a local association of fire insurance agents, using the Realty Board's office and staff.[66]

According to the 1933 NAREB survey of its members, realtors engaged in a larger number of business transactions selling property insurance policies than they did in selling real estate. The Census of Real Estate Agencies and Brokerage Offices found that 60 percent of all realty offices were actively engaged in selling property insurance in 1936. As a consequence of this strong link, NAREB maintained good relations with the National Association of Insurance Agents, an organization founded in 1898 to represent fire and casualty insurance firms.[67]

A closely related link in the transformation of the property development industry was the rise of title insurance and trust companies. Real estate lawyers led the effort to organize private title abstract companies in the late nineteenth century in order to rationalize and coordinate the burgeoning and expensive title search process. Once good abstracting services were established, the financial intervention of title insurance soon followed. The creation of title insurance played a critical role in facilitating and standardizing real estate transactions: transfer of title at once became safer for the purchaser and easier for buyers, sellers, and brokers. Adding the trustee function, the holding of deeds in trust for property owners, further improved the reliability and efficient organization of realty transactions.[68]

In most large metropolitan areas title insurance and trust companies held oligopoly or even monopoly status, and exercised a great deal of economic and political power in the real estate field. Prominent real estate brokerage firms often were closely connected to the title companies. The American Title Association, organized during the national "Panic" of 1907, worked together with NAREB leaders on many issues of mutual concern. The California Land Title Association and the California Real Estate Association went a step further, sharing their magazine, *California Real Estate*.[69]

Property Management

Big real estate brokerage firms generally handled sales, leasing, and management for large-scale landowners and property developers. In some cases the major downtown realtors developed and owned their own office buildings with one floor as headquarters and the rest of the space for lease. This entrepreneurial role was in addition to their acting as agents for other central business district property owners. Many of NAREB's leaders were closely intertwined with the members of the National Association of Building Owners and Managers (NABOM), founded in 1908. NABOM, whose monthly magazine was called *Skyscraper Management*, was a strong lobby for the urban land-use interests of large downtown corporations and office building developers and investors. Particularly when real estate boards were located in sizable central cities, there usually was a contingent of realtors who worked together with the local building owners and managers organization on issues of common concern.[70]

Real estate board members also acted as brokers for major land-extensive owner-developers on the outskirts of the spreading metropolitan areas. These included most significantly the electric urban transit companies, but also involved other large private utilities owners, newspaper publishers, manufacturing and mining corporations, railroad companies, and major agricultural interests. Periodically there existed much common ground between the realtors and these more powerful economic institutions regarding the adoption of public and private policies to stimulate urbanization and urban property development.[71]

Builders

Builders, like real estate agents, were very numerous, and most of them operated on a very small scale with few if any regular employees. The majority of general contractors and special trade subcontractors were actually building trades journeymen who moved back and forth between hiring construction crews and working on them. The bulk of building construction work performed was done under contract. Even in the area of housebuilding, contract construction executed by small local contractors and subcontractors was the norm. Owner-built homes were more common than housing built on speculation for direct sale.[72]

Estimates of the total number of contractors and subcontractors active during any one year in the latter 1920s ranged from 140,000 to 200,000. Disparities in scale of operations between big and small were quite substantial. The U.S. Census reported for 1929 that the top twenty percent of contractors and subcontractors averaged more than $200,000 worth of annual business, whereas the remaining 80 percent averaged less than $9,000.[73] Of firms in all branches of building and nonbuilding construction, residential building, particularly housebuilding, ranked at the lowest end of the average scale of operations. The U.S. Bureau of Labor Statistics calculated in 1938 that even in the largest cities, the typical housebuilder constructed less than four houses a year, with most building only one or two per year. Very few firms built more than 10 houses annually.[74]

Building contractors and subcontractors engaging in large-scale construction generally did so under contract, with payment by the purchaser of the construction services. The profit on construction work was assured regardless of the ultimate economic fate of the building once completed. Often large commercial office buildings, hotels, apartment buildings, and other facilities were built on speculation for sale or lease, but the speculators were real estate promoters, financiers, and investors, not building contractors. Operative or operating builders, also known as speculative or merchant builders, were very much the minority breed within the construction industry. These were builders who constructed buildings for their own account, as owners rather than under contract, in order to sell the completed building or lease space in it for a profit. Among the high volume builders in 1929 (the top 20 percent), the U.S. Census determined that only 2.5 percent were "operative builders."[75] These were the cream of their trade, occasionally venturing to erect office or apartment buildings, but generally concentrating on speculative homebuilding. Many smaller individuals and firms in the construction trades periodically built one or several dwelling units on speculation for sale, but few engaged in operative building on a sustained year-round basis. With the exception of construction equipment and materials manufacturers and distributors, the "construction industry," meaning contractors, sold services, not products.

Who sold the products? Real estate dealers did so, either as brokers for an owner-client, or directly for their own account. In the process of production that led to new building construction, a broker might sell a piece of land to an investor, who would then contract with a builder to erect a structure, and then engage a realty broker to either sell the completed building, or lease the building space and manage the property. Alternatively, a broker would sell land to a user-purchaser who would then contract with a builder to construct a facility for the purchaser's direct consumption. The broker might also help arrange mortgage financing for the purchaser, for an additional fee. In another common scenario, a speculative builder would buy land from a broker acting as agent for a subdivider or lot owner. The builder would then construct one or several houses on the land, and then hire a broker on commission to sell the house or houses. Larger merchant builders who constructed groups of houses on a more sustained basis often made special arrangements with brokers for selling their properties at a flat fee or commission rate somewhat less than the standard rate for an individual sale. Excepting such large-scale homebuilding operations, the typical relationship between operative builders and real estate brokers and salesmen was as follows:

> A builder may employ licensed real estate salesmen on a weekly salary basis or on a fee basis at less than 5 percent, but broker members of real estate boards have fixed the fee at 5 percent of the value. Nevertheless, in the transactions connected with one final sale a real estate broker may obtain even more than this share of the value. For instance, he may negotiate the sale of the land, for which he receives a 5-percent fee, and later, when the houses are built, he may negotiate their sale, for which he receives another 5-percent fee. Moreover, he may act as mortgage broker in obtain-

ing the financing and receive three-fourths of 1 percent on the amount of the mortgage. Thus the real-estate business obtains a fairly large share of the total housing price.[76]

The untypical, but more important relationship, was that the larger merchant builders were primarily real estate dealers, and only secondarily general building contractors. In some cases, building materials manufacturers also engaged in merchant housebuilding in order to test, model, publicize, and market their materials. Most of the time, however, the large operative builders were first and foremost real estate firms. The 1930 census reported that "Many real estate firms act" as "operative or speculative builders."[77] They made their profits off the sale or lease of land and buildings, and not off the construction of buildings per se. Construction services as general contractors were performed "at cost" to themselves, simply as an adjunct to the principal business of real estate promotion. The U.S. Census study aptly characterized this duality:

> As a general rule, he was not in the construction business to make a profit, and the contract value which he put upon his buildings was approximately what actually cost him to build them. He had, as it were, two edges to his sword, and the one which cut profits out of the sale or actual operation of his buildings was the sharper of the two.[78]

Land Subdividers

With the increasing spread of urbanization and suburbanization made possible by transportation and utility improvements and the expansion of urban employment opportunities, many real estate entrepreneurs entered the subdivision business beginning in the 1870s and 1880s. Subdividers would purchase multiple acreage of undeveloped agricultural land at the fringe of the growing city, and "subdivide" the land into allotments or building lots for individual purchase. These lots were sold either directly to prospective owner-residents, or to speculators interested in profitable resale, or to operative builders.[79]

Subdivision quality varied enormously. Many subdivisions consisted of no more than a few stakes in the ground, an ungraded road, an unrecorded plat, and a defective title. Others were elaborately landscaped with full streets and utilities already installed. Mostly unimproved subdivisions (though with clear title) were the typical variety up to and including the 1920s. Public improvements came after sales, through special tax assessments on the new lot owners. The more ambitious, larger-scale, and less speculative-minded subdividers distinguished themselves as being genuine land "developers" by contracting for extensive engineering and landscaping improvements. Despite this form of development, however, they usually erected few if any buildings on the subdivided land prior to commencing lot sales.[80]

Real estate brokerage firms were involved with subdividers in two different ways. First, brokers and salesmen sold subdivision lots, on either a commission fee or salary basis, for subdividers. Second, many brokers were themselves subdividers, buying tracts of land and selling subdivided lots for their own account, or subdividing and selling land by contract with the landowners. Lot purchasers, if they were either speculative builders or nonspeculative consumers, usually made their own arrangements for erecting dwellings or other structures on their lots. Occasionally the brokers or the broker-subdividers directly assisted the purchasers in arranging for financing contract construction on the lot. This assistance would be provided for an additional fee. The primary business of the subdivider was selling the lots, and not contracting for building construction either before or after land sales.[81]

Subdivision sales to the middle classes became more widespread in the early twentieth century, and particularly in the 1920s, when subdividers essentially entered the financing business by selling lots on land contract with 10 to 20 percent down and the rest due in monthly installment payments.[82] Realtor-subdivider William E. Harmon of New York is generally credited as being a pioneer of land contract installment selling. Harmon's ideas for mass production and sales of residential subdivision lots also included increased land planning to rationalize the development costs and enhance the marketability of large-scale subdivisions. His favorite design feature was the dedication of subdivision acreage for parks and recreation areas, which he claimed always boosted sales prices and profits, despite the added costs.[83]

During the 1920s and 1930s, some of the larger subdividers began evolving into merchant builders, putting up homes directly for sale with the lots, rather than on contract after lots were sold. The initial impetus for this change was the competition for lot sales due to the tremendous oversupply of subdivision lots in most urban areas by the mid-1920s. A few of the large-scale subdividers had earlier moved into the homebuilding field, especially in the Midwest, and these real estate dealers discovered that combination lot-house sales were more stable, profitable, and marketable than pure lot sales. Once the speculative subdivision resale boom had collapsed by the late 1920s, other subdividers with sufficient capital or credit began to follow suit.[84]

The transformation from broker to land subdivider to homebuilder as an economically integrated community builder was already evident by the latter half of the 1920s. The following testimony, given before the U.S. Temporary National Economic Committee in 1939, clearly delineates the structural transition from subdivider to subdivider-homebuilder:

MR. DAWSON: My name is Allen H. Dawson, and I live in Glenview, Ill.

MR. O'CONNELL: And your business—

MR. DAWSON: And I am a partner in the firm of Smith and Dawson. We are developers and builders of homes.

MR. O'CONNELL: You are builders and developers of real estate properties?

MR. DAWSON: Yes.

MR. O'CONNELL: How long have you been in this business?

MR. DAWSON: Why, we originally went into the business about 1926 and we were more then in the selling of the vacant land up until about 5 or 6 years ago; we didn't do an awful lot in the construction end of it, and when it became so difficult we couldn't sell the land we started building homes.

MR. O'CONNELL: Prior to 1928 had you had practical experience in the construction business?

MR. DAWSON: No; I didn't have any experience before that time.

MR. O'CONNELL: Since you have been in business I take it that you have developed a number of subdivisions, so to speak?

MR. DAWSON: Yes; we have developed approximately 1,500 acres of land and we sell—we formerly sold anywhere from 2 to 5 acres of ground and now we sell about an acre of land with each house, and we find that that is plenty of land for the average home owner to buy.

MR. O'CONNELL: Speaking at the present time, do you only sell improved lots, that is improved by construction of homes, or do you also sell subdivided land unimproved?

MR. DAWSON: We sell both and if we weren't able to sell the land and make a profit on the land in addition to what we are making on each house sale, why I don't think we could stay in business. It takes that additional profit of the additional land sales to make it work out for us.

MR. O'CONNELL: Have you any particular development under way at the present time?

MR. DAWSON: Yes; we have one development located north of Chicago; it is about 22 miles from the center of Chicago and that comprises about 300 acres of land. We started that approximately 3 years ago; the first year or so we didn't do an awful lot with it until we were able to get F.H.A. loans, and we were able to do that and have now between 140 and 150 homes there.

MR. O'CONNELL: When you say you started about 3 years ago you mean you bought the land about that time?

MR. DAWSON: We bought the land and cut it up in acre tracts and subdivided it in that form.[85]

Within the field of land subdividing, many of the larger subdividers also ran brokerage firms and belonged to NAREB. In addition, major realtors who were not themselves subdividers usually acted as selling agents for many large-scale landowners and subdivider-developers. At the other end of the spectrum, many of the smaller subdividers were precisely the type of "curbstoners" that real estate board members strongly disdained. Subdivision sales practices often produced the worst and most widespread examples of public fraud and abuse within the entire real estate business.[86]

The majority of real estate board members were general brokers who sold subdivision lots as agents but did not engage in direct subdividing. The majority of subdividers, many of whom were not licensed brokers or salesmen, did not belong to real estate boards. But the largest of the subdivider-brokers were realtors. Frequently these subdividers were leaders of the local boards because their firms tended to be better capitalized and have higher incomes than their fellow realtors. For the same reason, many of the big subdividers were leaders in the state associations and in NAREB.[87]

The 1933 NAREB survey revealed that 60 percent of the members engaged in a "general brokerage business," whereas the remaining 40 percent specialized in particular aspects of the business, from mortgage brokering to appraising, or maintaining exclusive listings of only industrial or commercial property. Of the specialists, 12 percent were subdividers and 10 percent were homebuilders, with considerable overlap between the two categories. This group was a subset of a broader group of major commercial, residential, and industrial property developers, that are today simply called "big developers." Their leadership as broker-developers in NAREB was a very important force from 1908 onward.[88]

In 1923 NAREB created several special divisions starting with a Brokers Division, which represented the majority of local board membership. The other seven membership divisions were: Appraisal, Cooperative Apartment, Farm Lands, Home Builders and Subdividers, Industrial Property, Mortgage and Finance, and Property Management. The second largest of all the divisions was the Home Builders and Subdividers Division.[89]

NAREB's Home Builders and Subdividers Division was the principal, indeed the only, organized voice for the homebuilding industry in the U.S. That this voice should come from real estate firms is striking testimony to the transformation within real estate development and residential building patterns that was then taking place. When the National Recovery Administration in 1935 published a list of 68 trade associations representing "The Construction Industry," NAREB was the only representative listed for homebuilding.[90] Seven years later, NAREB's 105 large-scale residential developers spun off their Home Builders and Subdividers Division and created a new independent organization, the National Association of Home Builders (NAHB). Most of the nation's 10,000 home builders at that time operated on a very small scale, building only a few scattered houses per year. By contrast, the big realtor-subdividers were more than home builders: they were community builders.[91]

Community Builders

In his classic book, *Production of New Housing,* Leo Grebler states that

research on the operative builder must take account of the great variety of types of entrepreneurs and activities covered by this term. They range from the fly-by-night operator, who takes an occasional fling at housing production, to the large-scale "community builder" who develops integrated communities with specially designed street patterns and commercial and other facilities.[92]

The community builders were subdividers who changed the nature of American land development during the early decades of the twentieth century. They did this initially by taking very large tracts of land and slowly improving them, section by section, for lot sales and home construction. Strict long-term deed restrictions were imposed on all lot and home purchasers, establishing uniform building lines, front and side yards, standards for lot coverage and building size, minimum housing standards and construction costs, non-Caucasian racial exclusion, and other features. Extensive landscaping and tree planting were emphasized to accentuate the natural topography and beauty. Public thoroughfares included curved streets, cul-de-sacs, and wide boulevards and parkways. Often special areas were set aside for retail and office buildings, apartments, parks and recreation facilities, churches, and schools. Private utilities and public improvements were coordinated as much as possible with present and future plans for subdivision development and expansion.[93]

Prior to the 1940s, the market for most "community builder" subdivisions was high-income. In the post-World War II era, many of the features of community building were extended to developments for middle-income homebuyers. The phrases "community builder" and "community building" were current among real estate board members during the 1910s and 1920s, either in connection with discussions of city planning or in directly referring to large-scale private subdividing and residential land development. A particular slant on this definition pertained to the establishment of whole new residential suburbs, which might or might not also contain commercial or industrial districts. In 1927 several city planning enthusiasts in Los Angeles began publishing a magazine called *The Community Builder,* which was strongly supported by the California Real Estate Association (CREA).[94]

In 1944 the Urban Land Institute (ULI), a small NAREB spin-off organization, established an elite 27-member Community Builders' Council, and three years later ULI published the first edition of *The Community Builders Handbook.*[95] The Chairman of ULI's Community Builders' Council in 1944 was a man who 20 years earlier was a leader of NAREB's Home Builders and Subdividers Division, and 40 years earlier, as a Harvard-educated "young turk" in the real estate profession, had taken the lead in establishing both the image and the principles of the modern community builder. Jesse Clyde Nichols, real estate broker and developer of the spacious Country Club District of Kansas City, Missouri, first achieved national prominence by delivering a landmark speech to the 1912 NAREB convention in Louisville, Kentucky. Calling his address "Real Estate Subdivisions: The Best Manner of Handling Them," Nichols described in detail his six years of innovative experience in developing what was then more than 1,000 acres of exclusive residential property. He challenged the prevailing assumptions of the subdivision trade regarding such shibboleths as cost minimization and sales philosophy. His was a much grander, more long term, and, he asserted, ultimately more profitable vision:

> The best manner of subdividing land should not necessarily mean the quickest sale. The destiny and growth of your town is largely affected by the foresight of the man who subdivides the land upon which you live. The most efficient manner of platting land should be the plan which gives the greatest value and security to every purchaser, adds the greatest amount of value and beauty to the city as a whole, yet produces a big profit to the man who plats the land. To follow this method, one must have supreme imaginative confidence in his city and its future.[96]

Not all of the big subdivision developments produced by community builders were as beautifully designed as the Country Club District, nor were they all aimed at large-lot upper-income residential homebuyers.[97] The unifying feature of the community builders was the very substantial scale of development, the control of large parcels of land by a single developer, the use of deed restrictions and other legal instruments to reinforce that control, the ability to win cooperation from private utilities and public agencies and to utilize this cooperation to best development advantage, the degree of long-term planning, and the level of integration of the brokerage function with financing, insuring, and building operations.

A preeminent example of a community builder operating at as big a scale as J. C. Nichols but less "high-grade" in marketing and development strategies was Harry H. Culver. Culver was a Los Angeles realtor who bought a 200-acre barley field for a down payment of $3,000 in 1912 and turned it into Culver City, a fast-growing Los Angeles suburb by the early 1920s, best known as the headquarters of the MGM motion picture studios. Culver City was fairly conventionally platted and built up with smaller lots and much more modest dwellings than neighboring developments such as Beverly Hills. Culver's ambitious development philosophy certainly qualified him as a charter member of NAREB's Home Builders and Subdividers Division. In addition to heading his own real estate brokerage and development firm, Harry H. Culver & Company, "a $2,000,000 corporation" (in 1926), Culver was president of the substantial Pacific Building and Loan Association (a Los Angeles S&L), vice-president of the still larger Pacific-Southwest Trust and Savings Bank, and director of the Lincoln Mortgage Company. He was also president of four separate neighborhood associations in Culver City, each designed to control enforcement and extension of deed restrictions and establishment of special street and other public improvement benefit assessment districts for the major Culver subdivisions. His concerns about good transportation access in and through Culver City led him to serve on both of the major highway and traffic commissions for Los Angeles. Finally, Harry Culver held the realtors' "Triple Crown": president of the CREA in 1926, president of the Los Angeles Realty Board in 1927, and president of NAREB in 1929.[98]

By the late 1920s many community builders began to see that they could enhance the marketability of their subdivision property if they erected houses on at least a portion of the available lots. One major subdivider who pioneered in the homebuilding field was Irving B. Hiett, a realtor who had built 7,500 homes in Toledo, Ohio, by the time he became president of NAREB in 1922.[99] Subdivider-homebuilders played a very significant leadership role in NAREB from its founding, despite the fact that they were a numerical minority in an organization consisting predominantly of nonsubdivider brokerage firms.

Indeed, from the time that the Home Builders and Subdividers Division was established in 1923, 8 out of the next 11 NAREB presidents were subdividers of community builder status. When the subdivision bubble burst in 1926 and the crisis of slow lot sales and falling lot prices precipitated the structural transformation of subdividing into homebuilding, the Home Builders and Subdividers Division provided national leadership in the area of housing and land planning policy, lobbying and providing guidance to the federal, state, and local governments. Officers of the Division headed NAREB as presidents for 7 consecutive years, from 1928 through 1934. The last of these presidents, Hugh Potter, developer of River Oaks in Houston, Texas, was a founder of the ULI Community Builders' Council a decade later.[100]

Conflicts Within NAREB Between Brokers and Community Builders

A significant conflict existed within the ranks of the realtors, between those brokers who engaged in a general brokerage business or specialized in other aspects of real estate, and those brokers who specialized in large-scale subdividing and homebuilding. Real estate board membership was separated into three categories: active members, who could vote and hold office and who essentially ran the board; associate members, who were primarily salesmen or other employees of the active member firms; and affiliated members, who were prominent bankers, lawyers, and other nonbrokers with a close interest in the real estate field.[101]

Active real estate board members were required to be principals or owners of local firms at least partly engaged in a currently active realty brokerage business (defined as selling, renting, or managing real estate for others) or mortgage brokerage business (defined as loaning money on real estate for others). Brokerage firms that specialized in large-scale subdividing and homebuilding were a distinct minority within local real estate boards, though they also were among the biggest, most prestigious, and highest income of the member firms, comparable to the largest of the firms that specialized in downtown property management. Sometimes the same firms specialized in both types of development and management.

Not all large subdividers were real estate brokers, and hence did not belong to local boards or NAREB except as affiliated members. In fact, for a time in the 1920s there was a separate trade association for community builders, the National Conference of Subdividers, headed by J. C. Nichols. Nichols was also a broker and a long-time leader of the Kansas City Real Estate Board and a very influential executive officer and director of NAREB, but some of the other leading subdividers did not have this dual distinction. Even though most of them were active brokers, the differentiation in business emphasis meant that the Home Builders and Subdividers Division of NAREB constituted a kind of "special interest group" somewhat distinct from the mainstream majority ranks of the realtor-brokers, and this distinction was very important where urban planning was concerned.[102]

On the general brokers side, the typical realtor was an enthusiastic booster of urban planning and land-use regulation, mostly beginning around 1914 and particularly during the early 1920s. Zoning restrictions and civic improvements were the areas of greatest interest to most brokers, some of whom were strictly focused on commercial or industrial property or on the central business district, and most of whom dealt primarily with selling, renting, and managing many scattered individual buildings and vacant lots in certain built-up neighborhoods. Their chief concern was with maintaining and increasing the immediate market value of their own listed products that they sold on commission, the liquidity and marketability of their listed properties. Except in the cases where brokers specialized in long-term leasing and management of commercial or industrial properties, or in brokering mortgages, the general real estate brokerage business attitude was extremely short-term in time horizon. Brokerage income depended primarily on commissions and fees, and it increased only through faster turnover and higher sales prices.

Realtors regarded zoning and city planning as one of the most important ways to "protect and serve the commodity in which Realtors deal."[103] They believed that the main value of planning was its ability to boost property values and liquidity by stimulating the demand for real estate as an attractive and safe investment. "Speculation" rather than development or purchase for use was considered acceptable and even popular with many brokers, so long as it promoted more frequent sales at rising prices. Zoning and city planning were not seen as being opposed to "speculation" per se, but simply another vital public tool for stimulating current and future demand.

Homebuilders and subdividers, unlike brokers, were concerned not just with selling the commodity but also with producing it. Thus they had a much greater orientation toward issues concerning the *supply* of factors in real estate production, and not just in the factors affecting the market demand for the sales product. Large-scale subdivider-developers viewed urban land-use planning as a means of rationalizing the cost of land and building development and of protecting their own considerable direct investment over the necessary period of years required to realize their full return. Certainly they desired a salable product and therefore wanted also to protect the purchaser's investment in order to expand market demand. Yet they had an equally clear-cut interest in private and public methods of supplying a greater amount of needed and good-quality improvements at a more efficient, lower cost per unit of sales product. This explains the strong focus on rationalizing the development process itself, a debate in which community builders and financial institutions led and the brokerage industry followed. Planners shared the orientation of the large-scale subdividers toward issues of improving the quality of the actual development product and rationalizing the coordinated public-private investment process in land development to produce better housing at less total cost. This shared orientation explains why urban planners generally maintained much better personal, professional, and political relations with community builders than with realtors in general.

The outlook of the large subdivider as a producer of a huge and indivisible commodity was well expressed by Edward H. Bouton, realtor and developer of two of the most famous community builder subdivisions, Roland Park in Baltimore and Forest Hills Gardens in New York. In a speech to the National Conference on City Planning in 1916, Bouton outlined the community builder's need for zoning, subdivision regulations, and comprehensive public planning of urban expansion:

I refer to the necessity that usually exists in a high-class development of controlling a large area of land in order that a general plan and proper restrictions may be extended over the whole region.

We, land developers, are manufacturers; our raw material is the acre tract, the finished product is the building lot. We differ from other manufacturers in this, that an ordinary manufacturer, who buys a year's supply of raw material in advance, is considered provident. In order to protect a neighborhood we deliberately provide raw material for ten years or more in advance and we have to carry that burden. To my mind, this necessity for carrying large investments in land far in advance of their needs is the fundamental financial difficulty that confronts those engaged in the better type of development. . . . If our municipalities could be given power to district the city, so that protection could be afforded the various neighborhoods in advance of their actual development, the advantages resulting from the judicious exercise of such a power would extend over the whole city.[104]

Large subdividers differed from realtor-brokers in the length of their time commitment to a single real estate production process and also in the breadth of land coverage of that process. Realtor-brokers listed and sold many individual properties, usually concentrated only in certain neighboring parts of the metropolis, but nonetheless spatially and financially disconnected from one another. This explains their willingness to manipulate zoning on a very property-individualized basis, frequently attempting to rezone or "spot zone" specific parcels on single blocks or even single lots. Planners often decried this seemingly contradictory attitude, particularly of smaller brokers and developers, of on the one hand supporting zoning restrictions in general and on the other hand being willing to undermine zoning's effectiveness in order to manipulate present and future values for any particular property.

Community builders, by virtue of developing vast contiguous parcels of land, were much more likely to assume the broader and more generalized land-use perspective advocated by planners. The public manipulations these subdividers engaged in, of course, also took place on a much grander scale, yet even that aspect of their business behavior served to enhance their strong interest in promoting and controlling public planning as a vital adjunct to their own private production process. Since the big subdividers actually engaged in extensive land planning and employed numerous landscape architects, civil engineers, architects, and lawyers in the process, they shared more of a genuine common interest with the planning professionals in the principles and methods of cost-saving and quality-enhancing land development practices. Sometimes the subdividers were really kindred land-planning professionals, in the sense that they developed the land for a commission or fee on behalf of a major landowner, rather than owning the land themselves. This was true of realtors such as Edward Bouton and Duncan McDuffie. The longer-term perspective and concern with stabilization of future property values and future liquidity was shared by mortgage lenders; and property insurance companies shared the perspective on the future quality and stability of development. Brokers, who lived or died on current sales commissions, were structurally more divided in their interests and loyalties with regard to land-use planning and regulation. The key differences were: (1) length of payback period; and (2) degree of concern with the costs of production, and stability and quality of the product.

Conclusion

This chapter has outlined the structural transformation of the real estate industry, which established the institutional context for the emergence in this century of a new sector of large residential subdivision developers. With the advent of FHA mortgage insurance and the FHA Land Planning Division in the mid-1930s, many land subdividers also became large-scale developers of suburban single-family housing. By surveying the real estate industry "in all of its branches," this chapter points clearly to the central role of the community builders from the Home Builders and Subdividers Division of NAREB, who provided powerful leadership in both public and private sector debates on the principles and applications of urban land planning and land-use regulation techniques.

commercial businesses depended on strengthening the downtown's accessibility and "image." Typically the city's biggest corporations with office headquarters in the central business district, plus the main daily newspaper publishers and the principal department store and hotel owners, constituted the key business support for "City Beautiful" plans. Realtors who routinely sold, leased, and managed substantial amounts of downtown property for their major clients were also involved, but since their clients were often much wealthier and more politically potent, the local real estate boards usually followed the planning crusade rather than leading it.[2]

Once public regulation of private land-use became the top issue in planning, however, real estate boards leaped from the shadows to the forefront. With the single exception of New York City's zoning resolution, which was designed primarily to remedy the real estate conflict in Manhattan, zoning in all other municipalities was much more strongly stimulated by a desire to regulate residential expansion than to facilitate central business district restoration. The further from the downtown one got, the more important the realtor's role became. In Chicago, for example, the Real Estate Board played a minor part in initiating and promoting the famous 1909 Burnham Plan, which was sponsored by the corporate Commercial Club. The 1923 Zoning Ordinance, on the other hand, was passed almost entirely as a result of the realtors' strenuous lobbying efforts. The Chicago Real Estate Board wrote the bill and shepherded it through the political terrain, such that Everett Hughes in his classic sociological study maintained that the Board was "the real father" of Chicago zoning. Similar relationships between realty boards and local land-use regulation were repeated in most U.S. cities during this period.[3]

Beginning in 1914, the attention of city planning began to shift dramatically away from the downtown and onto the peripheral growth of metropolitan areas. Debate over proposed public improvements moved from civic centers to major streets and highways. Moreover, an additional vital element was added to the universe of planning discourse: regulation, coordination, and planning of *private* land-use through zoning laws and public review of subdivision plats. As metropolitan decentralization and suburbanization raised the curtain on a new scene in American urban history, community builders began moving to the center of the stage. Thomas Ingersoll, executive secretary of the National Association of Real Estate Boards (NAREB), explained the new involvement of subdividers in planning to the National Conference on City Planning in 1917:

> Four or five years ago it was difficult to get the interest of real estate men in city planning, and I think the reason for this was that the idea they had was city re-planning, which has been thoroughly explained by your very capable and interesting secretary, my good friend Flavel Shurtleff, who told us that the real meaning of city planning is to develop the new sections of our city along the right lines.[4]

The City Planning Committee of NAREB formed in 1914 was composed entirely of brokers whose primary interest was in land development, residential subdividing, and homebuilding. Just as the big downtown realtors were naturally interested in the issue of "re-planning," the community builders were understandably very enthusiastic about developing "the new sections" of the city along "the right lines." As they saw things, they were the people who were actually carrying out this important task. What they hoped planning experts and the planning movement could provide them with was (1) public recognition of their contribution to community building; (2) scientific advice as to how to develop better subdivisions and communities; (3) government legal and financial assistance to help them plan and develop their subdivisions more cost-effectively and protect and enhance their considerable financial investment. In short, they hoped that planning and planners could both widen the market for subdivided land and make their long-term market prospects more secure and predictable.[5]

A 1914 article on the "Science of City Planning" in the official magazine of the California Real Estate Association (CREA) explained the brokers' interest, the subdividers' interest, and the special focus on planning for *new* development:

> There is no class of people in the business world who should take a more active interest in the science of city planning than the real estate fraternity. Every precept, every theory of that science contains a lesson for the man who sells or buys real estate. And its value is still more great to those who promote projects connected with subdivision of property or the opening of new towns.
> City-planning is meant to make a city or town a more pleasant, convenient, healthy and attractive place in which to live. Once the ideas to this

end are carried out, there is no difficulty in making them plain to the prospective buyer of property. The merits of a scientific town stand out all over it. It is so apparently superior to the old-fashioned community laid out more or less at random and left to itself to grow, that even the man of the least practical ideas can see for himself the great advantages of living and owning property in the scientifically planned community.

The theory of city-planning has taken a firm hold upon the ideas of the real estate promoters of our own State. Some of the communities being planned and developed at the present time are models of the new science.[6]

Once the ideas of city planning began to spread in the public's imagination, the large subdividers started to present themselves as the true guardians of a community's down-to-earth planning efforts through their role as private land developers. The chairman of CREA's Subdividers and Homebuilders Division, a leading southern California subdivider who sat on the Pasadena City Planning Commission and later chaired the advisory committee on subdivision controls for the California State Senate, summarized this perspective quite succinctly: "The subdivider is the practical city planner. The actual working out of a city plan lies largely in the hands of the subdivider. He is creating the city of the future on the outskirts of the city of today."[7]

Among the majority of the larger subdividers, the bandwagon for city planning did not proceed apace until well into the 1920s. During the pre-World War I period, however, a relatively small band of community builders took up the cause of private and public land-use regulation and planning as a serious issue. Beginning in 1914, a group of community builders from NAREB's City Planning Committee exchanged ideas with the landscape architects, civil engineers, architects, and lawyers who predominated in the National Conference on City Planning (NCCP), founded in 1909. Together, these community builders and the NCCP activists worked to promote planning legislation among other entrepreneurs in the real estate industry, to the general public, and within state and local governments.[8]

Many realtor-subdividers were familiar with the leading planning consultants, particularly the landscape architects such as Frederick Law Olmsted, Jr., and John Nolen. These and other consultants had traveled the continent preparing "City Beautiful" plans for a wide range of cities and towns, and had also worked as designers or advisors to a number of the larger real estate developers. In turn, the planning consultants were well aware of what they considered to be the best in modern community design by "progressive" subdividers, such as the ones named by John Nolen in his landmark 1916 article, "Real Estate and City Planning":

> Not only has the developer of the Country Club District of Kansas City practiced his own preaching, but the advantages of good planning have been recognized and applied particularly in the last two or three years by subdividers in all parts of the country: on the east coast, in Roland Park out of Baltimore, and in Forest Hills Gardens, the Russell Sage Foundation development on Long Island, N.Y.; in the south, by the Stephens Company, of Charlotte, N.C., and in the steel city of Fairfield, Ala., one of the developments of the Jemison Company, of Birmingham; in Ohio, by the E. H. Close Company of Toledo, the Kissell Companies, of Springfield, the King Thompson Company, of Columbus, and in the Ottawa Heights development, of Cleveland; in Indiana, by the Wildwood Builders, of Ft. Wayne; on the west coast, in St. Francis Wood, developed by the Mason-McDuffie Company, of San Francisco, and at Atascadero, a new made-to-order city in Southern California. And this is only a partial list.[9]

Not surprisingly, the real estate broker-developers of Nolen's most admired subdivisions were among the planning consultants' closest allies in the drive for public acceptance of land-use regulations. Four of these community builders were included in the 52 founding charter members of the American City Planning Institute (later the American Institute of Planners) in 1917: (1) J. C. Nichols, developer of the Country Club District; (2) Edward H. Bouton, developer of Roland Park and Forest Hills Gardens; (3) Robert Jemison, Jr., the deep south's largest developer, who became president of NAREB in 1926; and (4) Lee J. Ninde, head of Wildwood Builders, who as president of the Indiana State Association of Real Estate Exchanges in 1916 launched a new organization called the Indiana State Campaign for City Planning to lobby for planning legislation at the state and local levels.[10]

Other community builders active in promoting land-use planning during the pre-1920 years were as follows: three of NAREB's first presidents, Alexander Taylor of Cleveland (1910), Samuel Thorpe of Minneapolis (1911), and Henry Haas of Pittsburgh (1916); Paul Harsch, vice-president of the E. H. Close Company of Toledo, developer of Ottawa Hills, "a perfect example of City Planning" according to a 1916 advertisement; King Thompson of Columbus; Harry Kissell, an Ohio community builder who served as NAREB president in 1931; Fred Smith, a leading Minneapolis subdivider and homebuilder; and Duncan McDuffie, developer of California's first restricted subdivision, St. Francis Wood (1912), and other large subdivisions in the San Francisco Bay Area. McDuffie was the founding vice-president in 1914 of the California Conference on City Planning, a statewide lobbying group for planning legislation, and he also initiated and headed the first city planning commission in Berkeley, California, beginning in 1914.[11]

Edward Bouton, by virtue of his connection with the Russell Sage Foundation, actively participated in the National Conference on City Planning (NCCP) from its first year, 1909. Broader cooperation between community builders and city planners at the national level began in earnest during 1912 and 1913, when larger numbers of subdividers and realtors started attending national planning conferences. In 1913 J. C. Nichols joined the General Committee of the NCCP, and the following year the conference initiated a major national study of "The Best Methods of Land Subdivision," directed by John Nolen and Ernest P. Goodrich. NAREB's newly formed City Planning Committee, headed by Lee Ninde and including Edward Bouton, Paul Harsch, Robert Jemison, Jr., Duncan McDuffie, J. C. Nichols, and King Thompson, worked closely with the planners in encouraging this research agenda. Presentation and discussion of the study was the major topic at the 1915 National Conference on City Planning in Detroit. This also was the first year that several realtors were featured as speakers at the annual planning conference.[12]

The focus on land subdivision and the scheduling of prominent realtors as speakers continued for the 1916 and 1917 NCCP conferences. By 1916 no less than 10 realtors, including NAREB President Henry Haas, sat on the NCCP General Committee. The following year J. C. Nichols headed the Committee on General Arrangements for the 1917 NCCP conference, held in his hometown of Kansas City. When the ACPI was formed at that conference, both Nichols and Ninde were elected to its first Board of Governors. Private subdividing and residential construction slowed to a standstill after America's entry into World War I in April of 1917, but national public cooperation between planners and community builders reached new heights through the medium of the land development and homebuilding for war workers orchestrated by the U.S. Housing Corporation and the Emergency Fleet Corporation. NAREB and ACPI leaders worked together on these efforts more closely than any previous joint activity, and the legacy of this cooperation continued on in the 1920s under the auspices of Herbert Hoover and the U.S. Department of Commerce.[13]

During 1917 and 1918 J. C. Nichols headed NAREB's War Service Board, and leading realtors including NAREB President William May Garland, Irving Hiett, Samuel Thorpe, Alexander Taylor, and Henry Haas worked for war agencies on real estate appraising, acquisition, and development. ACPI member and future NAREB President Robert Jemison, Jr., directed housing and land development for the Housing Division of the Emergency Fleet Corporation. When the United States Housing Corporation (USHC) was created in June 1918, several NAREB leaders served as officers and directors of the corporation, and ran its Real Estate Division, which provided subsidized financing for private residential developers building "priority" war worker housing.[14]

Frederick Law Olmsted, Jr., directed the United States Housing Corporation's Town Planning Division. Olmsted's well-known landscape architecture firm had previously planned private subdivisions for E. H. Bouton, Duncan McDuffie, and several other community builders in NAREB. The USHC's Town Planning Division built a number of public residential subdivisions for war workers, as well as assisting in the private efforts. John Nolen, George Ford, Ernest Goodrich, Henry Hubbard, Charles Cheney, Stephen Child, and Arthur Shurtleff were among the many urban planners who worked on USHC projects. In his 1919 presidential address to the National Conference on City Planning, F. L. Olmsted, Jr., argued strongly for greater cooperation between private subdividers and local government through the establishment of city zoning and subdivision regulations and planning. Olmsted concluded from his development experience with the USHC that large subdividers needed public assistance in planning for the provision of infrastructure and services while land was still being platted, prior to sales and development:

It has been fully established that a well located school and playground, or even a site for the same, definitely fixed and known to be embraced in the program for school authorities, adds to the value of all the remaining land in the territory to be served by the school more than the value of the land withdrawn for the purpose, just as a local park of suitable size, location and character, and of which the proper public maintenance is reasonably assured, adds more to the value of the remaining land in the residential area which it serves than the value of the land withdrawn to create it.

Enlightened realtors who are engaged in the legitimate business of producing and selling what the ultimate consumer wants, for the best price that a satisfactory article will bring, know these things, and act accordingly when circumstances are favorable. The speculative subdivider who seeks his profit in selling to suckers, themselves largely speculators on a small scale, like Wall Street lambs, or who relies for his profit more on abstract skill in salesmanship than on the inherent value of what he offers, generally does not.

But even the thoroughly legitimate and thoroughly enlightened realtor whose subdivision is considerably less than will support a school and playground, or a local park, cannot afford to contribute land for the whole thing largely for the benefit of other subdivisions. He can perhaps afford to do somewhat more than his share but not much more.[15]

Timing of the New Cooperation

The reasons for the emergence of subdivision planning as a field of common interest between NAREB and NCCP beginning in 1914 were three-fold: (1) technological changes, particularly in transportation, utility, and construction improvements; (2) market competition and institutional changes in the scale and private control of urban land development; (3) the inadequacy of the existing public legal and governmental framework to respond to these changes.

The transformation of American urban development utilizing the combination of automobiles and commuter trains was only in its infancy at that time. The previous wave of residential decentralization, already proceeding for several decades prior to 1914, was based on electric transit as the primary mode of urban transportation. The need for subdivisions to closely surround traction lines dictated a continuously compact form of urban development. Many property owners believed that urban middle-income residential subdivisions would eventually be engulfed by high-density congestion and possible transition to commercial or industrial land uses. Those far-sighted developers and planners who rejected the pattern of past development experience in favor of a new model were just beginning to work together to search for new legal, financial, and institutional forms to adapt to what they saw as changing times.[16]

Edward Bassett's remarks during the subdivision discussion at the 1915 National Conference on City Planning illustrate the novelty of this search for new answers:

> In the law office with which I am connected we make a good many first mortgages to small builders in the Borough of Queens, and during the last six months I have heard from at least ten builders who usually construct houses on lots of about 20 to 30 feet in width and 100 feet in depth. Now they want wider lots in order to leave a space for automobiles between the houses. They tell me that if this is not done it hurts in the selling of the house. These houses sell for $3800 to $4500. You cannot make a building lot much under 100 feet in depth and still provide a living place for a small household with the conveniences that seem to be coming in the future, reckoning as one of these conveniences, the low priced automobile, which seems to be taking the place of the summer vacation for many families of moderate means.[17]

Redesign of building lots was only one aspect of the many changes in land subdividing contemplated at the dawning of the modern suburban era. A much more important issue was the redesign of street patterns in the newer areas, as well as replanning and rebuilding of streets in older areas. Streets and the increased need for coordination of the public and private roles in their platting, development, and maintenance started becoming a concern of the community builders in the 1910 decade, though it did not become a general public issue until the mid-1920s.

Key to all discussion of changes in private subdividing and public planning were two concepts: (1) spatial separation, and (2) permanency of land and building use. Technological innovations were making it increasingly possible to lower urban densities and spread the various working and living spaces over a wide metropolitan area. This separation could only be sustained, however, if there were some means of stabilizing land uses such that urban physical investment would have a longer and more predictable life. "Building for permanency" would allow differential classification and development of varying lot sizes, street sizes, infrastructures, utility load capacities, building sizes, and building types. Further, construction could proceed without the costly intrusion of constant public and private reconstruction that was then so common a feature of urban growth.

Real estate subdividers were already working on private means of stabilizing development through the use of deed restrictions, and planners were assisting them in these efforts. Both developers and planners were becoming increasingly interested in public restrictions through zoning and subdivision controls, and public planning, to supplement their private efforts. Discussions of the possibility for public "districting," or zoning, were a vital element of the NAREB-NCCP-ACPI cooperation.[18]

A second important reason for the timing of the growing interest by real estate entrepreneurs in "the best methods of land subdivision" was the general weakening of the urban real estate market beginning in 1914, simultaneous with a heightened competition for the sale of "the best deals" in suburban residence property. The coming of the Great War in Europe significantly slowed foreign immigration to U.S. cities, increased U.S. agricultural exports and farm prosperity which considerably slowed U.S. rural-to-urban migration, and drove up interest rates and shifted debt and equity capital from urban real estate development to foreign loans and related industrial and commercial investments. The net effect of all this was to cause a major urban real estate recession. Demand for subdivision lots and construction of new residential dwellings fell off substantially after 1913.[19]

At the same time, the growth of aesthetic consciousness from the "City Beautiful" campaigns, the increasing availability of private automobiles for upper- and middle-income purchasers, the public acceptance of deed restrictions in property ownership, the expansion of urban transit lines, and other factors combined to stimulate a nonspeculative market for suburban residential building lots in relatively new and well-planned subdivisions. Developers who could offer a complete package of futuristic improvements, attractive surroundings, and deed-restricted exclusivity could beat out their competition and sell higher-priced lots and homes much faster, thus saving on the burden of excessive carrying charges and avoiding the curse of low profits. The time was right for existing community builders, would-be large-scale residential subdividers, operative homebuilders, and real estate brokers who previously sold or desired to sell higher-grade suburban residence property to focus their collective attention on "scientific city planning."

The official magazine of the California Real Estate Association, reporting on the real estate recession that hit that state beginning in 1914, noted the one remaining bright spot in a generally declining market. First the bad news:

> In common with other sections of the country, following the readjustment of business conditions made necessary by the war, the demand for property diminished. This condition was more noticeable here, probably than in other localities owing to the briskness of trade previously.

Then the good news:

> Residence lots have formed a large part of the business of the real estate men. . . . Country property in small tracts, usually one acre, have been the salvation of the dealers in both selling and exchanges.[20]

This induced the Los Angeles Realty Board and the Los Angeles Chamber of Commerce to initiate a massive promotional campaign of noon-hour downtown lectures for office workers, with the goal of

> educating the city lot owner to the possibilities of a home surrounded by a small piece of ground. The talks are illustrated with slides and are designed to inform the office man, the clerk, the mechanic and urban dweller generally how he may reduce the cost of living and even add to the family income by working two hours a day in growing things on a fifty-foot lot.[21]

King Thompson, who sold lots and homes to a relatively high-income clientele, was a Columbus, Ohio, community builder and NAREB leader. In 1915 Thompson told the NCCP that good planning, including curved streets, was the key to gaining a competitive sales edge in what was clearly a buyer's market for subdivision lots:

> During the past six months the sale of lots in ordinary straight street subdivisions has been very slow, and I believe the measure of success which has come to us would have been impossible if we had not had the inspiration of the Columbus city plan and if we had not in accordance with

that plan laid out a subdivision which will afford the people of Columbus not only better access to the city, but more beautiful drives and more park space. We have planned out streets and thoroughfares to anticipate the needs of future generations and we have added as much beautification as possible, always being careful not to interfere with the main purpose of streets, that of conveying traffic.

I believe that with facts and figures I can demonstrate to any hard-headed subdivider that beautification pays in dollars and cents. I believe that I can go further and say that if local conditions are met, a plan of beautification and a scientific study of streets and thoroughfares are indispensable to success. I think I would not as soon attempt to build a house without the services of an architect as I would lay out a subdivision without the help of a landscape architect.[22]

Defining an Agenda for Public Action

In 1916 J. C. Nichols delivered a major address to the National Conference on City Planning that rivaled in importance his well-known NAREB speech four years earlier. The 1916 talk, "Financial Effect of Good Planning in Land Subdivision," outlined the broad contours of the urban land planning agenda that would accompany and help foster the emerging transformation in the institutional processes of urban land development. His speech clearly underscored the crucial interconnection between the changing nature of residential development and the creation of land-use regulations and planning agencies in American cities. It also described the basis of cooperation between community builders and city planners from the developer's viewpoint, a similar task to that performed by John Nolen in his very important article, "Real Estate and City Planning," which presented the planner's perspective on the same issues.[23]

J. C. Nichols began his address with a complaint and a lament. The complaint was that "Eighty to ninety percent of our city property is covered with residence districts, and yet ninety percent of the discussion in city planning conventions I have attended is directed to traction problems and downtown development."[24] His own participation and that of other community builders helped to considerably change the latter percentage.

The lament was that in order for community builders to successfully develop a large subdivision, the amount of land they needed to control and the length of time it took to sell all the parcels imposed huge financing problems on the subdivider, despite the profitability of individual lot sales. Nichols pointed out that the true community builder must take a long-term approach to development of a very big tract of land, and yet time is his enemy in being able to financially afford to hold onto the land. By rejecting the method of selling cheap unrestricted speculative lots for quick turnover, the developer exposed himself to the financial risk of not being able to sell high-quality restricted lots rapidly enough to stay afloat for the long haul.

Nichols then listed the various ways that good planning, including deed restrictions, attracted greater amounts of longer-term and higher loan-to-value mortgage lending from banks and insurance companies, saved money in land development costs (particularly on street layout), and generally brought much higher and more enduring property values and sales prices. "But this private planning must have municipal aid," he insisted. "Now, how in the world can the private developer, without municipal assistance, expect his property to succeed, if he is to work with unregulated development all around him?"[25]

The solution for Nichols was quite clear: public regulation of all private development. Subdivision controls would establish different classes of property development in different locations (as part of a master plan) and then ensure that a new high-grade subdivision in an undeveloped area would eventually be ringed by like-minded neighbors, what Nichols called "the cumulative effect." "The constant effort of the operator is to try to get surroundings that are entirely congenial to what he has placed upon his property, and to do that successfully we absolutely must have municipal control of the surroundings on the adjoining lot."[26]

In addition to the control of new subdividing, Nichols called for continuing municipal regulation of building use, size, land coverage, and setback, or what was called districting or zoning. Zoning would classify each type of development and make future development stable and predictable at any given building site. He extolled the ability of private deed restrictions to create monopoly value and hence extra profits for the developer, and asserted that public restrictions could achieve similar results:

Now, if in developing our subdivisions, we can limit the quantity of certain classes of property, if we can create the feeling that we have a monopoly of that class of property around a little plaza or square, if we give the prospective buyer notice that if he doesn't buy that property today somebody else will buy all that is left of it tomorrow, we are assisting in the sale of that property, and the man that has it won't give it up except at an advanced price, and we can raise the prices of the adjoining property.[27]

Finally, Nichols argued that the developer needed municipal assistance in aligning his subdivision with future plans for extension of major streets and highways, as well as the placement or extension of public parks and recreation land, schools, utilities, and the entire range of municipal improvements and services. In the next two decades this notion of coordination-based regulation between public and private development was to become the central logic of land-use planning for urban expansion: (1) the comprehensive land-use plan, (2) the capital improvements budget, (3) the Official Map of public land reservations for future uses, and (4) the staff planning agency to work with the subdivider to correlate public and private development plans and establish rules for accepting dedications of prospective streets, parks, and other land from private subdividers for public development and maintenance. Nichols also stated that community builders needed the same type of coordination-based cooperation from other key private concerns including financial institutions, street railway companies, and churches.

The essential thrust of Nichols' comments was a community builder's manifesto on the need for local government planning. He advocated a public-private partnership in the preparation and execution of private urban land development at a level of resource commitment and regulatory intervention much greater than had been applied by American local government since colonial times. If "progressive" meant to stand for drastic change, then John Nolen's description of Nichols and his colleagues on NAREB's City Planning Committee was certainly appropriate. Nichols concluded his address with a plea for the assistance of city planners in implementing this new approach:

> I believe that the work the subdivision men have done in this country has been, in a certain degree, the foster mother of the city planning movement. The fact that we have struggled along for many years with practically no cooperation and are beginning to make it win, has given the city planners courage to look at the city as a whole, in the same way we have looked at our own subdivision.

Now, with this cooperation that we have given you, we want you city planners to again realize that a great part of your work of city planning turns on how to help us make our land increase in value rapidly enough for us to afford to do the best things in city planning, and make them permanent, and mark up our prices to enable us to meet our carrying charges.[28]

The needs described by J. C. Nichols and the policy tools which formed the basis of the planning response—Master Plan, Official Map, zoning map and laws, set-back requirements, subdivision map filing regulations and planning agency review, capital budget—defined the direction taken by both the community builders and the planners in modern U.S. city planning's first big decade, the 1920s. At first the focus was on establishing zoning laws. In 1921, Secretary of Commerce Herbert Hoover appointed an Advisory Committee on Zoning, which published *A Standard State Zoning Enabling Act* in 1924, and later in 1928, as the renamed Advisory Committee on City Planning and Zoning, published *A Standard City Planning Enabling Act*. Together these two documents outlined the basic principles for state and local governments to follow in implementing the comprehensive urban land-use planning agenda. Many state legislatures adopted one or both of the model enabling acts almost verbatim. NAREB President (1922) and community builder Irving B. Hiett served on both Advisory Committees, along with nine men closely associated with the newly emerging city planning profession: attorneys Edward Bassett and Alfred Bettman, landscape architect F. L. Olmsted, Jr., civil engineers Charles Ball, Morris Knowles, and Nelson P. Lewis, housing specialists John Ihlder and Lawrence Veiller, and good government publicist J. Horace McFarland (Knowles and Ihlder both represented the Chamber of Commerce of the United States).[29]

In 1931 President Hoover's Conference on Home Building and Home Ownership expanded the public urban land planning agenda by detailing the means by which the federal government, in association with financial institutions, building products manufacturers, utilities, and trade associations from various branches of the real estate and construction industries, could help speed the transition from subdividing to homebuilding as a large-scale, standardized, modernized, and economically integrated sector of production. Community builders were prominent participants in the Conference, and "community building" as a goal was very highly valued in the conference recommendations.[30]

Three years later, Thomas Adams, who had directed the New York Regional Plan, codified and summarized the best planning knowledge to date in *The Design of Residential Areas*. In the mid-1930s the federally owned greenbelt towns furthered the state-of-the-art in public community building that had previously been explored by the U.S. Housing Corporation. The private Radburn, New Jersey, experiment of the late 1920s, "a town for the motor age," as well as various development efforts by innovative subdividers, also broke new ground in establishing better planning standards. The last and in many ways the most effective step in tying the entire planning package together came through the federal rationalization of housing development and financing initiated by the FHA in the mid-1930s. FHA's Land Planning Division played a crucial role in institutionalizing as part of the housing tract development process the very forms of "municipal assistance" and regulatory intervention that J. C. Nichols had called for in his 1916 NCCP speech. The FHA's Land Planning Division was originally headed by Seward Mott, who became executive director of the Urban Land Institute (ULI) in 1944, the same year that ULI organized the Community Builders' Council with J. C. Nichols as chairman. One of Seward Mott's first major actions at ULI was to coedit and publish *The Community Builders Handbook*.[31]

Deed Restrictions—Private Innovation Preceding Public Planning

When J. C. Nichols called the subdivision work of the early community builders "the foster mother of the city planning movement," his statement may have been considered far too self-congratulatory by professional planning consultants, but it was essentially correct. Indeed, planning consultant and former NCCP President George Ford corroborated this line of reasoning in a 1925 speech to NAREB's Home Builders and Subdividers Division when he opined that "It is the Realtor subdivider who is really planning our cities today, who is the actual city planner in practice."[32]

Neither Nichols nor Ford meant to claim that subdividers *per se* were "city planners" simply because they platted undeveloped land into salable lots. Rather, their point was that the most innovative of the large subdividers were working out "on the ground" the newest and most advanced principles and techniques of urban land planning. More specifically, they acted as pioneers in developing the physical design standards and establishing and improving the first widely used mechanism for asserting long-term control of large parcels of urban land owned by many small private owners: deed restrictions.[33]

The initial step in the long march toward achieving "public control of private real estate," as the planners called it, was attaining a measure of private control. Deed restrictions legitimized the idea that private owners should surrender some of their individual property rights for the common good, including their own. By 1914, it was becoming clear that the rising land values of deed-restricted property demonstrated that it was quite beneficial for individual private owners to participate in collective land-use control, and that many prospective land purchasers, builders, and occupants understood and appreciated its advantages. As J. C. Nichols noted in his 1912 NAREB talk: "In the early time (1906–1908) I was afraid to suggest building restrictions; now I cannot sell a lot without them."[34]

Deed restrictions did more than legitimate the concept of land-use control, however. They also were the principal vehicle by which subdividers and technicians tested and refined the methods of modern land-use planning. In this important activity the community builders led the economic charge, but received a great deal of guidance and assistance from leading landscape architects, civil engineers, architects, and other professionals. The finest designers frequently were the planners of the best deed-restricted private subdivisions. For example, F. L. Olmsted (Sr.) and Calvert Vaux laid out Riverside, Illinois, the Chicago residential suburb that set the early and long-held standard for excellence of planning and for the creative use of deed restrictions. Riverside, platted in 1869, served as the inspiration and example for Roland Park in the 1890s, landscaped by F. L. Olmsted, Sr. and Jr., and for the 1911 design of Forest Hills Gardens by F. L. Olmsted, Jr., and Grosvenor Atterbury. Forest Hills, owned by the Russell Sage Foundation, was developed by realtor and community builder E. H. Bouton, developer-president of the

Roland Park Company. In the planning of the Country Club District, modeled to a certain extent on Roland Park, J. C. Nichols utilized the services of noted landscape architect S. Herbert Hare.

Duncan McDuffie employed landscape architects F. L. Olmsted, Jr., and John Olmsted, and California beaux arts architects John Galen Howard and Louis Mullgardt, to design elements of St. Francis Wood in 1912. John Nolen designed both Kingsport, Tennessee, and Mariemont, Ohio, just after the end of World War I. F. L. Olmsted, Jr., and Charles Cheney designed Palos Verdes Estates in 1923. Clarence Stein and Henry Wright planned Radburn for developer Alexander Bing in the late 1920s. The list goes on.[35] The key point is that all of these land development plans and many other similar efforts were implemented by private developers using deed restrictions as their only effective means of retaining control in executing the plan once the lots were subdivided and sold to individual private owners. John Nolen emphasized their importance as a planning tool in 1916:

> The principle of restriction in the subdivision and use of land is well understood in the United States and very frequently applied. In fact, it is so well understood and so highly valued that it is most often applied in a thoroughgoing way by the real estate operator himself in his own interest. The restrictions placed upon a purchaser in the conveyance of a plot of land often include a long list of the kinds of business which are classified as nuisances, and which may not be established or maintained upon the property; regulation as to stables and garages; fences and walls; set back of buildings from streets and from lot lines; minimum cost of buildings; easements and rights of way for public utilities; and in some cases, even the approval of plans and specifications of buildings including their nature, shape, kind, height, material, color scheme and location; also the grading plans of the plot to be built upon. These restrictions, or, as some operators happily term them, "safeguards," are often placed for a period of twenty-five years or more with the right of renewal subject to the assent of the owners.[36]

Community builders worked together with planners to privately establish the framework for most major aspects of what later became public planning—building restrictions; classification and separation of land uses; integrated planning and design of streets, blocks, and lots, such as the "superblock"; planning and design of open space between buildings and within and between subdivisions; uniform set-backs; advance reservation and dedication of subdivision land for public use—the list is long and covers a wide range of applications of zoning and subdivision regulations and urban design and engineering. Even on the commercial side, the basic concept of the modern suburban shopping center was first developed by J. C. Nichols and widely introduced as a new innovation in residential subdivision planning by community builders.[37] The paramount importance of private development deed restrictions as the model and precursor of public land-use regulation is highlighted by New York City Assessor Lawson Purdy in explaining why the 1916 New York zoning law was understood and supported by real estate developers, brokers, lenders, insurers, and appraisers:

> I sat in the room where the hearing was going on, and my associates asked me to attempt to reply. There were many men engaged in the real estate business there. They were all familiar with that with which you are so familiar here, the practice of real estate developers of putting restrictive covenants in the deeds which they gave to purchasers, not to decrease the value of the thing they had to sell, but to protect the buyer and to enhance the value of the thing they had to sell. And I attempted briefly to answer the objections that these regulations would reduce the value of real estate by saying that for two years the Commission that had been appointed, after very careful consideration, which was composed of men familiar with real estate conditions in the city of New York, some of them professional developers of real estate and others of them representing great lending institutions (and by the way, all of the lending institutions of New York City substantially approved the regulations that were adopted by the Board of Estimate); I said such a commission has done that for the city of New York which every private developer attempts to do by restrictive covenants which he himself puts in the deed he gives to prospective buyers; it has attempted to impose regulations on the city of New York which will enhance the value of the land of the city and conserve the value of the buildings. And I believe they have done that with success.[38]

Members of the real estate business community understood that private restrictions were no panacea and could not substitute for public regulation. J. C. Nichols made this point quite forcefully in his 1916 speech to the National Conference on City Planning. Seven problematic issues rendered private restrictions inadequate: (1) They were difficult to establish once land was subdivided and sold to diverse owners. Thus they could only be easily applied to new subdivisions, and not in already built-up areas. (2) They were often difficult to enforce through the civil courts. Property owners could not depend on their future effectiveness with any certainty. (3) They generally were only considered to be legally enforceable for a limited period of years, at which point the restrictions would completely expire and the area would be officially unprotected. (4) They were very inflexible. Once written into the original deeds, they were extremely difficult to change, even where new and unforeseen conditions clearly warranted certain modifications. (5) They only applied to whatever size parcel of land could be controlled by a single owner or subdivider. All land surrounding a restricted subdivision could remain unrestricted, subjecting the subdivision's border areas to the threat of encirclement by "undesirable" uses. (6) Even where deed restrictions were applied to a number of tracts, each subdivider used a different standard, leaving a complete lack of uniformity between each private effort. (7) In addition to the lack of coordination between privately restricted and unrestricted land uses, restricted subdivisions were not at all coordinated with public land uses and future public land-use plans.[39]

Leading subdividers and realtors advocated public planning to overcome the deficiencies of private restrictions and to supplement their strengths. Without the visible precedent of private planning efforts by community builders and their advisers and allies within the city planning profession, the establishment of public land-use regulations would no doubt have taken longer to accomplish and the newly created public planning agencies would have been far less knowledgeable in their initial attempts to set reasonable standards for urban land development.

The Community Builders and the Standard Planning Act

Just as the initial cooperation between NAREB's City Planning Committee and the National Conference on City Planning beginning in 1914 had helped set the planning agenda for the early 1920s, a renewed and more extensive cooperative effort commenced ten years later that produced one of the most important planning documents of the decade: *A Standard City Planning Enabling Act* (1928). The immediate stimulus for such realtor-planner dialogue was the subdivision crisis of the mid-1920s.

The massive urban population increase in the 1920s in many metropolitan areas combined with a period of relative prosperity and rising real incomes stimulated a subdivision boom in the early 1920s that quickly took on the character of a speculative frenzy. By 1923 there were already many warning signs that the house of cards of "shoestring" purchases and leveraged credit would soon come crashing down, and the level of complaints and horror stories of investors being swindled began to accelerate sharply. In some cities lot prices and sales activity were already leveling off or declining. By 1926 activity had peaked nearly everywhere and the long and steep descent into bankruptcy, foreclosure, default, and "frozen assets" was commencing. The capstone event was the collapse of the notorious and highly publicized Florida land boom, in which enough land (some of it underwater) had been subdivided to house the entire U.S. population. Florida's boom began faltering in the fall of 1925 and by the fall of 1926 was in full-scale decline, sending shock waves through the nation's financial and real estate markets.[40]

The Home Builders and Subdividers Division of NAREB took organized action for the first time at the June 1925 NAREB convention in Detroit when it voted to establish a Committee on Subdivision Control in Metropolitan Areas. Irenaeus Shuler, the chairman of NAREB's Home Builders and Subdividers Division and of the new Committee on Subdivision Control, had invited the professional city planners of the American City Planning Institute (ACPI) to come to Detroit and discuss subdivision control with the realtors. As a result of these discussions, the ACPI set up its own Committee on Subdivision Control to work together with NAREB in hopes of defining a consensus position. Shuler strongly criticized the inadequacy of existing planning efforts in addressing the problems of large residential subdividers. He said that "city planning as practiced in America has had to do mainly with the built-up areas. In all of our cities most of the efforts along this line have been devoted to correction of mistakes of the past."[41]

Irenaeus Shuler had earlier conducted a study for NAREB on regional subdivision control in 24 U.S. cities, concluding that the planning of future street extensions was now required for the entire metropolitan area, and that new subdivisions should be regulated according to a "master plan" to assure uniformity of street width, grade, and alignment and to provide for proper drainage, water and sewer systems, and other utilities. Arguing that poor street systems in urban areas "have retarded city growth and have necessarily kept down land values," the study concluded that "the advent of the automobile has brought a new emphasis on the need of regional rather than merely city planning."[42]

The spirit in which even the largest and most prosperous realtor-subdividers took action, however, was highly defensive. Shuler told his more than one thousand colleagues assembled in the Detroit convention hall that the "successful subdivider" had actually pioneered the methods of private control through deed restrictions, large-scale land planning and construction of improvements, arranging purchaser financing, and home-building—in short, the complete development of communities. "If these things were always done with reasonable thought and care, values would be created and maintained and there would be much less need for public or civic control of the subdivision of land."[43] However, he continued, "private control has its limitations," and any standards promulgated through the 20,000 members of NAREB "can only extend to the voluntary adoption of its individual members" at best, and not at all to the "many other men . . . engaged in the subdivision of land who take no part in the affairs of this or similar organizations."[44] Shuler warned his fellow realtors that the level of subdivision crisis was heading to a point that some public action would eventually be necessary: "I realize the viewpoint of the subdivider who objects to control over the subdivision of land, on the ground that it may become burdensome, and the operation of such control might be placed in the hands of political agents. Public demand, however, will bring about this condition sooner or later, unless the subdivider himself devises means of reasonable control. We all realize there are some subdividers who will not exercise proper private control."[45]

N. P. Dodge, the chairman of the Committee on Legislation, reinforced Shuler's comments with a report which endorsed some form of public subdivision regulation, but only if planning boards "are composed of experienced Realtors in good standing, or at least a majority of the board is made up of such men." Otherwise there is a "danger of over-regulation" if planning commissions are "composed of inexperienced men and women" who might have "unreasonable and extreme views."[46]

Dodge urged that control of subdivisions be exercised countywide, "for nearly all new platting is outside the city limits." He listed three main purposes of plat control: (1) that the subdivider be required to connect up with existing or proposed streets, (2) that the streets be improved to permanent grade before lots are sold, or a bond posted to guarantee that streets will be improved within a reasonable time, and (3) that a minimum lot size be required, to prohibit the selling of "lots of such small dimensions as to constitute a fraud by misleading the buyer concerning the cheapness of the lot." In these three recommendations we see the three key motivations of the real estate industry for subdivision regulation: (1) *coordination*, (2) *design and engineering*, and (3) *control*.[47]

The NAREB committee and the ACPI committee deliberated for the next two years, with the realtors coming to a tentative agreement on principles at their June 1926 convention in Tulsa, and a final position was hammered out and approved by the NAREB Board of Directors at a business meeting, appropriately located in Miami, Florida, in January 1927. (See exhibit 3.1 at the end of this chapter.) The planners evidently were somewhat unhappy with the document, as it took them another four months and one additional meeting with NAREB leaders before the ACPI approved the report in May 1927. The statement of principles was identical from both committees, though the ACPI changed some of the text of the preamble, the most interesting change being that the realtors stated that planning should not be so "idealistic" as to "destroy real property values," whereas the planners stated that planning should not be so "idealistic" as to "destroy all real property values." The one issue on which there seemed to be genuine controversy was the question of whether subdividers should be required to dedicate a certain portion of their land to parks and open space without public compensation. At least some planners were in favor of this, but the realtors wanted voluntary dedication of small parks and public acquisition of larger park lands as determined by a master plan for the broad urban area.[48]

The NAREB-ACPI joint statement in 1927 was so influential that it formed the basis of the U.S. Department of Commerce's *A Standard City Planning Enabling Act.* In this document the Commerce Department recommended to state governments that they pass enabling legislation, using the Standard Act as a model, to facilitate local and metropolitan land-use planning and regulation in all 48 states. A key section of the suggested planning enabling act dealt with subdivision control. The

Standard Act formed the basis of most state and local subdivision control and planning legislation for the next several decades.[49]

The work of NAREB's Homebuilders and Subdividers Division in initiating the joint statement with ACPI, and in encouraging the spread of what many realtors called "the Hoover Act," is often forgotten in the current canons of American city planning history. Perhaps a measure of the importance of this initiative can be gleaned from Edward Bassett's comment in the following story.

When the National Conference on City Planning held its annual convention in St. Petersburg, Florida, in the spring of 1926, one of the key issues on the agenda was a progress report of the joint ACPI-NAREB discussions on subdivision regulations. The NCCP delegates were welcomed by the president of the Florida State Association of Real Estate Boards, who, not surprisingly, given the real estate crisis brewing down there, announced that his State Association was "considering the promotion of legislation to regulate and control subdivisions." Edward M. Bassett, a member of the U.S. Department of Commerce Advisory Committee on City Planning and Zoning, and a leader of the city planning profession, stated enthusiastically after hearing the subdivision committee progress report: "I prophesy that some of us in this room today will look back upon this St. Petersburg Conference as being almost the first groping after lawful methods to bring about comprehensive planning."[50]

Conclusion

In this chapter I have demonstrated the fundamental basis for cooperation between the community builders and the urban planners in achieving certain goals of mutual importance to both groups. For the community builders, these goals were shaped by the changing institutional nature of the real estate industry, as I have explained in chapter 2, and by cyclical economic crises. The planners' goals were formulated according to cultural conceptions of good city form, design, and living standards. In the following two chapters, I will describe the conflict that emerged between developers and planners within the context of this cooperative framework.

EXHIBIT 3.1
NAREB-ACPI JOINT STATEMENT ON SUBDIVISION
CONTROL, 1927
RECOMMENDATIONS

We therefore recommend the following:

First: That State Planning Enabling Acts should be enacted, delegating to cities and other political subdivisions the authority to prepare general plans and to approve subdivisions.

Second: That under the authority of such an Enabling Act a master plan should be prepared for the area of control, showing the location of main thoroughfares, recommendations for open spaces and designating land areas for specific uses.

Third: That the control of the platting of subdivisions should be authorized under the act and this control exercised by the local planning commission.

Fourth: That the planning commission should be an appointive, non-political board, serving without compensation, and the members should hold no other municipal office, excepting that certain legislative or representative officials should be ex-officio members of the commission.

Fifth: That the master plan and the control exercised should extend out beyond the municipal limits into the nonmunicipal territory which will sooner or later be developed as a portion of the city. This control to be developed in accordance with a Regional Plan in cooperation with the adjoining territorial governments.

Sixth: That the planning commission be authorized to adopt regulations providing for the location, continuity and width of streets, to safeguard travel, prevent congestion and provide proper drainage. Such regulations to include, where and when practicable, the minimum size and area of building lots and the extent to which street improvements, such as water and sewer provisions should be made before approval of plats. In some states bonds are required from the land owner, guaranteeing the installation of these improvements. This seems to be practicable.

Seventh: The general requirements for principal public parks and recreational spaces and sites of public buildings should be included as a part of the master plan. Where a land owner has submitted a plat of his land and the authorities have designated in it such a principal public park, recreational space or public building site as part of the master plan, the municipality should take prompt steps to acquire such land, or failing so to do, should act upon the plat, so that the owner can make use of his property. The subdividers should be encouraged to provide small private recreational parks.

State Enabling Acts, as recommended in the foregoing, should be broad in their authority. The extent to which this authority shall be accepted and exercised by each municipality will remain for local determination. It is also the work of the local real estate boards, chambers of commerce, and other civic organizations to advance and support local ordinances, putting into effect the purposes to be accomplished under the authority of State Enabling Acts. The city officials in whom is vested the power to appoint members of the planning commission, if supported by public opinion and by civic organizations, will see that a capable planning commission is provided to carry on this important work.

Signed: for the National Association of Real Estate Boards:
Irenaeus Shuler, Omaha
(Chairman, Committee on Subdivision Control in Metropolitan Areas)
J. C. Nichols, Kansas City
J. J. Hurst, Baltimore
R. G. Lambrecht, Detroit
Guy S. Greene, Detroit
Robert Jemison, Jr., Birmingham (President, 1926)
Nathan Upham, Duluth (Advisory Board of Past Presidents)
Arthur M. Suor, Buffalo

Signed: for the American City Planning Institute:
Morris Knowles
(Chairman, Committee on Subdivision Control)

Jacob L. Crane	Lawrence Veiller
T. Glenn Phillips	Robert Whitten
Irving C. Root	Frank B. Williams

SOURCE: "Subdivision Control," *Annals of Real Estate Practice, Volume III, Home Building and Subdividing* (Chicago: National Association of Real Estate Boards, 1927), pp. 332–34; "Subdivision Control," *Planning Problems of Town, City, and Region* (Philadelphia: William F. Fell, 1927), pp. 200–1.

CHAPTER FOUR

THE LOS ANGELES REALTY BOARD AND ZONING

Introduction

FROM ITS INITIAL GROWTH spurt during the boom of 1887, Los Angeles has done everything in a big way. The leaders of the Los Angeles Realty Board, ardent supporters of the city's extensive public works projects and nationwide promotional campaigns, were full participants in this sense of bigness. Perhaps also because much of the land around Los Angeles was still in single ownership as huge Spanish ranches, land subdividing and residential development were undertaken by community builders on a very large scale. These developers fully understood the need for planned infrastructure to support their realty projects, and they were quite willing to utilize government for such purposes.

In the dream of creating a prosperous homeowners' paradise, the southern California community builders' positive view of government action translated into a major push for strict land-use regulations. The Los Angeles Realty Board played an important role in establishing America's first citywide use-zoning law in 1908, and leaders of the Board fought in the 1920s to strengthen and extend the powers of zoning. The community builders who governed the Realty Board even hired their own professional city planning consultant in 1920 to write a new zoning law for the Los Angeles City Council.

The community builders lost as many battles as they won in their zoning crusade. To begin with, the Realty Board was divided over the issue, with many members wanting to use zoning to *promote* property speculation and higher density commercial or residential development, not to *protect* sprawling partially developed areas for future development as neighborhoods of single-family houses. Secondly, the vast army of small-scale realty dealers, builders, and property owners who fervently believed in the Los Angeles promise of perpetual real estate "boom" were bitterly opposed to strict land-use controls. Thirdly, many members of the Los Angeles City Council were responsive to the speculative fever and manipulated the zoning categories accordingly.

Responding to both internal and external opposition, the community builders on the Realty Board engaged in three strategies: (1) They searched for political power to strengthen their cause both with city officials and with other property owners. Through the Federal Housing Administration and its mortgage insurance program, the community builders found a sympathetic agency that was willing and able to force long-desired changes in land planning and regulation onto the local public and private sectors. (2) They established tough, enforceable deed restrictions as a fairly reliable method of controlling large, newly subdivided residential and commercial developments. (3) They helped create separate suburban jurisdictions and resisted their annexation to Los Angeles. To the community builders, these smaller municipalities were generally more dependable and cooperative in their implementation of land-use regulations. In addition, the Realty Board helped create the Los Angeles County Regional Planning Commission, to facilitate suburban growth and circumvent the need for involvement by the City of Los Angeles in land-use regulation, infrastructure and service provision, and property taxation. These strategies were all formulated in response to the early controversies over city zoning in Los Angeles. This chapter provides an overview of the conflict and the compromises.

Pioneers of American Land-Use Zoning

Los Angeles business and civic leaders acquired a justly deserved reputation in the early twentieth century as aggressive boosters of an arid, semitropical area that possessed no natural advantages save two: a lovely climate and attractive landscape. The efforts to make up these deficiencies in infrastructure—water supply, harbor, railways and transit, energy—are well known. Equally as noteworthy are the massive advertising campaigns to market Los Angeles as a haven of the "good life" in order to sell real estate to tourists and homeseekers. Because the beauty of the surroundings and the luxuriance of the lifestyle were such an important part of the sales pitch, which was carefully targeted to the middle and upper classes of the rural and urban American east and middle west, public action to preserve physical image was a key element of the growth and sales strategy of the real estate sector.[1] From its inception in 1903, the Los Angeles Realty Board expended considerable energy on public and private action to clean up vacant lots (of which there were still many left over from the collapsed boom of 1887), protect tourists from street hawkers, limit the height of buildings (a 1906 charter amendment created a 150-foot maximum), and promote "public art" including civic centers, parks, and boulevards as recommended by Charles Mulford Robinson in his 1909 report to the Municipal Art Commission.[2]

One of the most important initiatives to maintain and market Los Angeles' physical beauty was the creation of zoning laws. Los Angeles led the nation in regulating private land-use under the municipal police power by establishing the first major use-zoning law of any American city, a full eight years before the famous New York City ordinance. On September 14, 1908, the Los Angeles City Council passed the "Residence District Ordinance," mapping out three large areas of the city within which:

> It shall be unlawful for any person, firm or corporation to erect, establish, maintain or carry on . . . any stone crusher, rolling mill, machine shop, planing mill, carpet beating establishment, public laundry or washhouse, fire works factory, soap factory or any other works or factory where power other than animal power is used to operate, or in the operation of same, or any hay barn, wood yard or lumber yard.[3]

On the same date the City Council passed a companion "Industrial District Ordinance" defining the areas in which the above prohibited activities would be permitted, subject to certain fire regulations.[4] The "Residence District Ordinance" not only prohibited new businesses from operating in the residential districts, but it also applied retroactively. An existing business could be forced to vacate its current location, without compensation, under the terms of the 1908 law.

Los Angeles created America's first use-zoning law during a period when the Realty Board and the local real estate industry were suffering from the aftereffects of the national "Panic" of 1907 and the subsequent collapse of the city's recent real estate boom. The long drought of Los Angeles realty sales after the frenzied 1888 real estate debacle had finally turned into steady, sustained sales growth beginning in 1901, culminating in a speculative boom during 1906. The post-Panic slide turned 1908 into an uneasy year for the realty business, the worst year in the Los Angeles Realty Board's brief history. Since subdividing and selling suburban-style residence property was still a lucrative area of business for the larger realtors, and because there already was a substantial political constituency of prosperous homeowners among the city's growing population, land-use regulation was quickly identified as an important vehicle for strengthening Los Angeles' most appealing selling point.[5]

The case for public planning was articulated by Dana Bartlett in his 1907 book *The Better City:* "Climate has a cash value. . . . As the Greater City comes nearer to its realization, the leaders in social thought are more and more determined that it shall be a city of homes, and therefore a city without slums."[6] Accordingly, civic and business leaders promoted Charles Mulford Robinson's plan for "The City Beautiful," and the landmark "Residence District Ordinance." The rationale for this 1908 zoning innovation was explained by Los Angeles City Prosecutor Ray Nimmo in a 1913 article entitled "Accomplishing the Segregation of Industries":

> There is a well-defined movement in many of the European cities toward industrial segregation, but, until recently, no American city has attempted to execute this plan of civic improvement. This has been a subject of municipal legislation generally considered impossible to treat of, and it was left to the city of Los Angeles first to undertake a plan for the separation of its homes from its works and factories. In this city by the western sea, situated as it is, in the heart of the Southern California Riviera, there have gradually developed extensive and beautiful residence districts traversed by miles of smoothly paved streets and embellished with a wealth of trees and flowers. *The business enterprise of real estate operators,* combined with the civic pride and home life of the people of Los Angeles, have given the city a deserved reputation for its ideal residence conditions.
>
> Accordingly, the preservation of these conditions has been considered a matter of paramount necessity. (emphasis added)[7]

Industrial segregation under the 1908 law also provoked opposition from some groups. The *Los Angeles Times,* for example, editorialized in 1909 against the new zoning law, fearing that it would be an obstacle to the city's industrial growth. The editorial particularly objected to the retroactive provision in the ordinance. The *Times* did not advocate that zoning be eliminated, however, only that it be modified. The editorial supported the basic principle that industries should be barred from operating in "exclusively residential districts."[8] Since the owners and publishers of the *Times* were among the largest real estate developers in southern California and members of the Los Angeles Realty Board, it appears that the conflict over whether the future of the city was to be "the Riviera of the nation" or "the Detroit of the West" included a consensus among business and civic leaders that zoning would be an important part of that future.[9]

Legal authority for Los Angeles public regulation of private land-use in 1908 came from two sources, both deriving from the local government's police power authority to control "nuisances" in the interest of "the immediate preservation of the public peace, health, and safety."[10] The first source was the legal precedent of previously upheld regulation and prohibition of certain industrial activities publicly considered to be injurious to nearby citizens. In fact, the idea of establishing "residence districts" in Los Angeles was the direct outgrowth of earlier "industrial districts" that had been created during the preceding two decades to limit and control certain fire hazards.[11] In accord with this tradition, the industrial portion of the 1908 zoning law was officially labeled "An ordinance creating the Office of Fire Marshal and prescribing his powers and duties."[12] Los Angeles already had laws on the books restricting the location of oil-well drilling, the manufacture and storage of inflammable and explosive substances, carpet beating, gas works, and beef slaughterhouses and tanneries.[13]

The second source of legal precedent was also derived from "nuisance" law, but contained a very different social purpose—racial and ethnic segregation. W. L. Pollard, well-known city planning attorney for the Los Angeles Realty Board and the California Real Estate Association, stated the issue clearly: "It may sound foreign to our general ideas of the background of zoning, yet racial hatred played no small part in bringing to the front some of the early districting ordinances which were sustained by the United States Supreme Court, thus giving us our first important zoning decisions."[14] In California during the 1880s, San Francisco, Modesto, and several other cities passed laws restricting the location of hand laundries. The reason for these restrictions was that hand laundries in these cities were primarily owned and operated by Chinese immigrants. Thus laundry regulation was a clear-cut proxy for Chinese exclusion from certain "Caucasian" neighborhoods.[15]

Numerous California court decisions upheld the legal validity of these anti-Chinese zoning laws. The broad scope of the legal permission granted in the Hang Kie, Yick Wo, and similar court decisions also helped facilitate local police power regulation of other "social nuisances," in addition to hand laundries and washhouses, such as bars, liquor stores, and dance halls. Restrictions of this type were applied by Los Angeles prior to 1908.[16] Recognition of the purpose of zoning as stabilizing and enhancing the value of real estate had already been legally acknowledged by the California Supreme Court in the 1886 Yick Wo decision, when the Court ruled that a laundry could be legally prohibited from locating in a particular area because it "depreciates the value of property."[17]

Los Angeles' zoning laws created seven Industrial Districts, primarily along the Los Angeles River and the various freight railroad lines that coursed through the city's eastern, central, and southern areas.[18] Most of the remaining built-up portions of the city were placed in the Residence Districts, with "residence exceptions" spotted throughout these districts. These numerous "exceptions," an early form of zoning variance, included undertaking districts, cow districts, cemetery districts, motion picture districts, billboard districts, and poultry slaughterhouse districts, to name but a few. Anything that was legally excluded from the residence districts could be included by the City Council through the creation of an "exception." By 1915 there were nearly 100 "residence exceptions," ranging from a large section of the central business district to a single city lot.[19]

After 1908 the Los Angeles City Council continued to pass districting legislation of four basic types: (1) to create "exceptions," (2) to change the boundaries of existing districts, (3) to add new legal requirements and restrictions to the 1908 laws, (4) to create new districts covering areas of the city left untouched by previous legislation. The latter task posed a continuous problem for the City Council because the corporate boundaries of Los Angeles were rapidly expanding during these years through frequent annexations. Most of the territory being added to the city was very sparsely developed, and normally was placed in a Residence District, with some "exceptions." One of these areas, the little town of Colegrove which was annexed to the city in 1910, became the center of a bitter zoning controversy ten years later under its new name, the Wilshire District.[20]

In describing the passage of the Residence District Ordinance in 1908, Ray Nimmo stated:

> A few years before it was considered that the Constitutions of the state and the nation had raised insuperable barriers to any project embracing the prohibition of industrial expansion, but the zealous eye of the Los Angeles home-builder watched the approach of business activities with alarm, and necessity became the mother of legal invention.[21]

California's courts wholeheartedly approved of this new legal invention, upholding the Los Angeles zoning laws in three separate decisions between 1911 and 1913, involving city prohibition of the location of a Chinese-owned hand laundry, a lumber yard, and a brick yard. The case of the brick yard was the most controversial, as it invoked the retroactive feature of the zoning law. The owner, Mr. Hadachek, was forced by the city to abandon his current location in a Residence District and move to an Industrial District, at his own expense. The fact that he had owned the land and building and had been operating the brick yard prior to 1908 was not considered sufficient to merit an "exception." Both the California and U.S. Supreme Courts affirmed the Los Angeles zoning laws in the Hadachek litigation.[22] These decisions cleared away the constitutional obstacles to the adoption of zoning laws in cities throughout California and the nation.[23] In the preparation of New York's 1916 zoning law, the 1908 Los Angeles law and the 1915 U.S. Supreme Court Hadachek decision were cited by New York zoning supporters as key legal precedents.[24]

In California the Los Angeles zoning model spread rapidly once the legality was clearly upheld by the California Supreme Court in its 1913 Hadachek decision.[25] Particularly after the real estate market became depressed beginning in 1914, many California realty boards and city councils turned to Los Angeles-style districting laws as a method of stimulating residential sales and development. Between 1913 and 1917, Redondo Beach, Oakland, Pasadena, San Mateo, Burlingame, Turlock, Piedmont, and Sacramento were among the cities and towns adopting some form of districting ordinance.[26] Despite the Hadachek decision, or perhaps because of the controversy surrounding it, many of these laws were not retroactive. After 1917, the influence of New York's law and more fine-grained zoning ordinances in Berkeley, Alameda, Palo Alto, and other cities helped create a new California fashion in land-use regulation that rendered the 1908 Los Angeles ordinance somewhat obsolete.[27] In the pre-1917 period, however, Los Angeles zoning was the state and national model. For example, Oakland's 1914 law was definitely based on Los Angeles' "industrial" and "residence" districts. The zoning legislation was introduced by Mayor Frank Mott, past president of the Oakland Real Estate Board and the California State Realty Federation. At an Oakland City Council debate in 1914, Mayor Mott explained

> the protective nature of the proposed industrial zone ordinance, which is aimed at the inclusion of all industries within definite areas for the protection of people who desire their homes to be located far from the annoyances of shops and factories. He said that there are at least 10,000 acres of land in the city available for industrial purposes, and that it is desirable to keep manufacturing plants segregated from homes. The ordinance was prepared by (Deputy City Attorney) Earle and is taken with few modifications from the Los Angeles ordinance, which has been sustained by the Supreme Court.[28]

The Battle for a New Zoning Law

The passage of Los Angeles zoning laws in 1908 clearly reflected a strong push by the Los Angeles Realty Board to reassure prospective lenders and purchasers that the city would continue to be a spacious residential paradise of fine homes and quiet, clean surroundings. The success of this growth strategy was reflected in the statistics on Los Angeles' economy, which revealed a growing population both much wealthier than the national average and much more concentrated in professional, service, and other white collar occupations than most large cities.[29] Also in contrast to some fast-growing urban areas, the housing stock consisted mostly of detached homes, although, despite the homeownership sales pitch, many of these houses were occupied by tenants.[30]

The 1908 zoning ordinance was applied on a highly selective basis. In some cases property owners could petition the City Council to protect a certain area from an "undesirable" use that was threatening to move in; in the Hadachek case, they even forced an existing business to move out. But the blanket nature of the law over such vast territory meant that the City Council was constantly creating "exceptions" for a whole variety of land uses that could not be kept too far away from the residential portions of the city, such as specially created "public garage districts" needed to accommodate Los Angeles' growing automobile culture. Given that one of the city's biggest industries was real estate sales and development, including related sectors such as finance, insurance, and manufacturing of building materials, the City Council was just as likely to allow exceptions to "encroach" as it was to take action to "protect." In addition, the original districting ordinance did not distinguish between detached homes, apartment houses, hotels, movie theaters, commercial offices, or retail stores, which were legally permitted to exist side by side in the residence districts. Judged by the standards of deed-restricted subdivisions, which were already establishing the latest trends in modern suburban living, the residence district ordinance was very weak and ineffective.[31]

During the period when Los Angeles' pioneering districting law was making its way through the higher courts, establishing legal history and gaining national recognition, the real estate market in Los Angeles went through another cycle of growth and stagnation. Real estate sales and construction activity rose from 1910 through 1913, fed by burgeoning immigration of "native white homeseekers."[32] But the realty market started declining when the population influx and capital availability both dried up with the beginnings of World War I. The national depression of 1914 and 1915 hurt Los Angeles considerably. Many workers left the area in search of industrial employment elsewhere. The Los Angeles tourist industry was notably hard hit from 1914 to 1919, and the huge real estate and construction sector stagnated. Population growth, while slowed from its dizzying pace, continued, however, and the strongest element of real estate market demand was in large lots and luxury homes on the outer fringe of the city. This pattern of growth reinforced the viewpoint of the

Los Angeles Realty Board's leaders, who wanted to establish stronger public land-use regulations to protect these subdivisions from unwelcome neighbors.[33]

During the worst years of Los Angeles' real estate depression the Realty Board membership dwindled considerably. The remaining members congratulated each other on simply being able to stay financially solvent.[34] In the summer of 1916 the Los Angeles Realty Board formed a committee of their most distinguished leaders to "call the attention of the Banks to the injury they were doing the real estate business" by refusing to make loans and by "advising their clients not to make loans on real estate or to purchase same at the prevailing prices."[35] During 1917 and 1918, the years in which the United States government entered the War, residential and commercial construction slowed to a standstill as the rising costs and shrinking availability of building materials and labor and lack of real estate financing converged to form a nearly impassable bottleneck. Residential rents started rising in this period due to growing population and employment, combined with the wartime embargo on residential construction. The value of unimproved urban property, however, fell sharply. Indeed, with little possibility for building, the market for vacant lots was nearly frozen.[36]

The situation began to change with the end of the War. Tourism resumed in 1919, and demand for housing picked up considerably. Lack of financing and rapid inflation of building materials prices created a situation where demand considerably outran existing supply. Tourists went back east after winter excursions to Los Angeles complaining of a severe housing shortage. The Realty Board blamed the financial institutions for holding back the supply of mortgage funds, stating that "there is an unsatisfactory and illiberal condition existing in this city between sources of supply and those who would like to develop and improve their property." They pleaded with bankers to provide more mortgage loans at lower interest, "to encourage home-builders generally."[37]

As the year went on, building activity did improve for year-round residences, although the housing situation for tourists as the 1920 winter season approached was still very tight. Tourist accommodations were in such short supply that the Hotel Keepers' Association wanted the Los Angeles booster agencies to tone down their advertising in the east and midwest in order to avoid a repeat of 1919, when the hotel room crisis gave Los Angeles tourism a bad reputation. The Los Angeles Realty Board strongly opposed such timidity on the part of the Hotel Keepers, and enlisted the major newspapers, the Apartment House Association, and other organizations in a publicity campaign to dispel any rumors that short-term or long-term housing was unavailable in Los Angeles. According to the Realty Board, the tourist influx was of critical importance to the business of selling property in Los Angeles: "From the real estate man's point of view there must be an increasing number of homeseekers and tourists to purchase and occupy the new homes that are built and will continue to be built during the summer."[38] Realty agents would be waiting at the train stations with convincing sales arguments for the potential purchaser.

Building permits were on the upswing after 1919 but most of the new housing was being built for the upper-income population. Apartments and low-cost bungalows were still at a premium, and thus for workers the housing shortage of 1919 and 1920 was still a serious problem, and rents were rising rapidly. Pressure began to build for the Los Angeles City Council to pass a rent control ordinance. The Realty Board, denying the existence of any "rent-gouging," was unalterably opposed to rent controls. As an alternative, the Realty Board, with the Chamber of Commerce and the *Los Angeles Times,* launched a campaign to "Own Your Own Home," urging bankers "to loan more freely in order to encourage the wage-laborers to build and own their own homes and to encourage home-builders generally."[39] The Realty Board also formed, together with the Los Angeles Chamber of Commerce and the Merchants and Manufacturers Association, a Fair Rent Committee to investigate charges of "alleged exorbitant rents" and to get favorable publicity about the housing situation in the city.[40]

The "Own Your Own Home" message against rent control was largely rhetorical. But the "Own Your Own Home" campaign to attract many more prosperous tourists and year-round residents was a matter of economic survival for a real estate industry that had been through five or six years of relatively hard times.[41] For some of the large downtown brokers and the residential community builders in the Los Angeles Realty Board, a vital aspect of this economic growth strategy was the passage of a new zoning ordinance.[42]

Many Realty Board members desired to replace the 1908 residential district ordinance with a new comprehensive zoning law for four principal reasons. First, they wanted to preserve Los Angeles' image as an expanding enclave of luxury homes and estates. Land on the western side of the city had been partially developed with expensive detached homes, and some key Realty Board leaders, particularly the big residential subdividers, hoped to protect the existing areas and maintain the wider west side as the sphere of middle- to upper-income residential growth. Due to extensive land speculation during the previous 30 to 40 years, however, much of this land had already been subdivided and was not subject to any enforceable, long-running deed restrictions. As the building slump began to abate in 1919, certain well-known realtors and community builders from the Los Angeles Realty Board mobilized to halt what they saw as an imminent invasion of the west side by apartments, stores, warehouses, and small factories.[43] The residential district ordinance was not considered to be adequate protection; a new zoning law was required that would zone the entire area for exclusive single-family residential use. On the other hand, a number of west side brokers in the Realty Board, eager to earn commissions and sell frozen properties after the long sales downturn, opposed any zoning initiative that would constrict their ability to unload listed properties, regardless of the intended use.[44]

The second reason, intimately related to the first, was that the most powerful Realty Board members wanted to maintain the downtown commercial district as the primary office and retail center of Los Angeles. The Realty Board was dominated by the largest of the downtown commercial realtors, and they greatly feared the potential impacts of commercial decentralization on central city land values. Their fears were well grounded: the share of Los Angeles' retail trade conducted in the central business district declined from 75 to 25 percent during the 1920s.[45] In 1919, when the downtown was still preeminent, the major commercial realtors hoped to use a new zoning ordinance to stem the tide of outlying commercial growth at the downtown's expense. They hoped that by zoning the entire west side exclusively for single-family residential use, except for a modest amount of neighborhood commercial uses at some of the main traffic intersections, the wealthy residents would be forced to continue shopping downtown and professionals would continue to occupy office space in the city's center.

The third reason was that Los Angeles had fallen behind as the nation's pacesetter with regard to city zoning. Advances made by New York, Berkeley, St. Louis, Portland, and other cities, plus the passage of the zoning enabling act by the California Legislature in 1917, and the city's U.S. Supreme Court victory in the Hadachek case[46] convinced the Realty Board leaders that future zoning laws in Los Angeles should strictly separate residential, commercial, and industrial land uses in a much more systematic fashion than the 1908 ordinance. Realty Board members feared that Los Angeles would suffer in its promotional campaigns to attract real estate investors and consumers in the absence of the most up-to-date zoning regulations. In order to compete successfully with its local and national rivals, Los Angeles had to enhance its reputation as America's best planned and best regulated city.[47]

Fourth, having suffered through several depression years and watching Los Angeles largely excluded from the war-induced industrial growth, some real estate and business interests were concerned to expand Los Angeles' manufacturing base and year-round employment opportunities, decreasing the heavy dependence on tourism. Development of the harbor, highways, hydroelectric power, labor immigration, and other key factors had made industrial growth possible in Los Angeles, particularly in clothing, building materials, food processing, consumer durables, oil refining, and several other sectors.[48] Many manufacturing corporations who were considering the establishment of branch plants in Los Angeles were reportedly concerned about the existing zoning system. They felt that the piecemeal nature of the districting ordinances combined with the retroactive feature subjected potential industrial companies to uncertainty as to their ability to remain at a given location free from harrassment and residential encroachment. From 1908 through 1919 the attention in Los Angeles zoning had been on keeping undesirable nuisances away from housing. The Chamber of Commerce now sought to reassure outside capital that through passage of a new law industrially zoned land would be better serviced and protected.[49] Some members of the Realty Board concurred with this approach. Others, especially large residential brokers and subdividers devoted to promoting Los Angeles as America's "Riviera," feared that industrial growth strategies might hurt the market for high-income housing and related commercial developments.

The issue that precipitated the Realty Board's campaign to pass a new zoning law was the threatened invasion of the west side's Wilshire and

West Lake residential neighborhoods by a clothing factory and a warehouse in the spring of 1919. Under the Residence District Ordinance the City Council generally required that a property owner desiring a "residence exception" on a particular site must first gather petition signatures from 20 percent of the neighboring property owners in support of the proposed change. Since so much of the land on the west side was vacant and owned by speculators, small investors, lenders, or realty agents, all of whom were seriously hurt by the decline in property values which had become severe in 1917 and 1918, many of these property owners were glad to sign a petition that could stimulate sales interest and new construction of any sort. Intensive uses, if they could drive up the rents and sales prices of nearby land parcels, were particularly welcome.[50] The property owners requesting building permits for the clothing factory and the warehouse were able to get the required signatures and present their petitions to the City Council.

Realty Board leaders, many of whose brokerage firms specialized in handling downtown commercial properties and elegant west side residential subdivisions, mobilized to oppose the petitions.[51] This particular coalition of prominent Los Angeles realtors not only demanded that the City Council vote to deny the two petitions for residence "exceptions," but that a new zoning law be immediately passed that would restrict virtually the entire west side of the city for exclusive single-family residential use. On May 29, 1919, the Realty Board's Governing Committee took its first major step in fighting the battle for west side zoning by appointing a special committee "to urge the adoption of suitable ordinances to protect residential sections of the City from the erection of warehouses, factories, etc., and to protest in the name of this organization against any movement to create industrial districts, or otherwise to commercialize those parts of the city now devoted exclusively to homes."[52]

In June 1919, the Realty Board went public with its opposition to the petitions and managed to forestall City Council action.[53] The Realty Board also joined a Chamber of Commerce committee to prepare a new zoning law.[54] The Chamber was particularly concerned that adequate areas be zoned for industry. In early 1920 the Los Angeles City Club hosted a conference in which representatives of the Chamber of Commerce, Realty Board, the local chapter of the American Institute of Architects (AIA), and other organizations recommended that a City Planning Commission be officially created in order to zone Los Angeles.[55] In March 1920, the City Council voted to create such a Commission. The Realty Board, Chamber of Commerce, Fire Insurance Exchange, and a number of other business groups were well represented among the 51 city planning commissioners appointed by the mayor.[56]

With the gradual thawing of the real estate market in 1920 and the substantial increase in applications for building permits, considerations of proposed zoning changes quickly reached a stage of acute conflict. Differing groups of property owners on the west side alternately presented petitions, staged protests, and filed lawsuits as they vied for support from the City Council, some desiring to exclude apartments, some desiring to exclude stores, and others desiring to sell, build, and own or rent space in these controversial structures. In certain cases the City Council voted under the 1908 law to create new or uphold existing residential districts, in other cases granting "exceptions" and allowing for alternative developments and uses. Arguments raged within and between neighborhoods and organizations. The Realty Board, with the support of the Chamber of Commerce and the chairman of the new City Planning Commission, formed its own private committee to come up with a zoning plan for the city.[57]

Serious conflicts soon emerged, however, from within the Realty Board's own membership. When the Realty Board's Governing Committee proposed in May 1920 that the City Council immediately enact an emergency ordinance limiting almost the entire west side to single-family residences until a new zoning law could be enacted, some of the Realty Board's own members, "dealers in Wilshire District property," "protested against the proposed ordinance, stating that it was injuring their business" and "interfering with improvements contemplated by their clients."[58] The protesting realtors were generally smaller west side brokers battling against the big downtown brokers and the large-scale residential subdividers who dominated the Realty Board's Governing Committee. The Governing Committee wanted single-family residential zoning for the entire west side. The opposing realtors, who formed an organization called the Wilshire Improvement Association, wanted commercial development on all the main streets and higher density commercial and residential uses permitted in the Wilshire area.

Faced with this internal revolt, the Realty Board's Governing Committee quickly withdrew their proposal for an emergency zoning ordinance, "until such time as a scientific survey by a recognized City Planning expert can be made and a proposed ordinance or ordinances submitted to the City Council embodying the findings of such expert."[59] One month later the Realty Board sent an urgent telegram to Charles H. Cheney to come to Los Angeles. He was to be their expert.[60]

Charles Cheney arrived in Los Angeles in July 1920 with a reputation not only as a zoning expert, but as a strong advocate of the creation of exclusive single-family residence districts to encourage homeownership and property investment. He was wedded to the notion that Los Angeles should remain a city of large and small houses, and was strenuously opposed to apartment buildings.[61] Cheney hurriedly met with the zoning committees of the Realty Board, City Planning Commission, and City Council, and with a group of Wilshire District property owners which included the president, vice-president, and treasurer of the Los Angeles Realty Board and other leading realtors.[62] Despite his flurry of meetings, Cheney studiously avoided speaking with opponents of the Realty Board's zoning proposal.

Within a week of his arrival, Cheney delivered to the Realty Board's Governing Committee his completed "scientific" zoning report. Cheney's report addressed some of the objections of the Wilshire realtors who had protested the earlier Realty Board proposal. His recommendations, while mainly zoning the whole area for single-family residential use, did include several commercial zones on some of the major thoroughfares.[63] The Realty Board immediately presented Cheney's report to the City Council with a great deal of publicity, urging quick adoption by the Council.[64] The Board also suggested that the City Planning Commission hire Cheney as a consultant to zone the entire city.[65] The City Planning Commission agreed, and recommended that the City Council appropriate the funds to hire Cheney.[66] "The Realty Board was entirely satisfied with the services Mr. Cheney rendered in his survey of the Wilshire District," stated City Planning Commission Executive Committee member and Realty Board Vice-President Frank Ryan in his report to the City Council, "and we believe the Council should make effective its work by employing the services of an expert city planner."[67] Other business and civic leaders supported the hiring of Cheney, including the author of the 1908 zoning law, Judge Albert Lee Stephens, who spoke of the need to maintain Los Angeles' "enviable prestige of being the most desirable home city in America."[68]

In the months that followed, the zoning battle escalated as the Los Angeles Board of Public Works began to deny building permits to various proposed structures under the terms of the district ordinances. Attorneys for property owners argued that businesses had a right to expand to the west of downtown and that the new restrictions granted an artificial monopoly to the existing businesses and thus were clearly discriminatory. Legal actions and public protests were initiated by all sides in this dispute.[69] As a concession to this strong opposition, the City Council declined to appropriate funds to hire Charles Cheney, explaining that City Planning Commission Secretary Gordon Whitnall was capable of conducting the necessary zoning surveys, with the help of the City Engineer's Office.[70] The City Council also failed to adopt the Realty Board's Wilshire District zoning proposal due to vigorous opposition from Wilshire property owners and realty agents.[71] In the fall of 1920, the Realty Board and the Chamber of Commerce, concerned lest Los Angeles' reputation as a well-run city be tarnished by the controversy, joined forces again to push zoning forward.[72] Gordon Whitnall announced in October that the City Planning Commission would soon hold hearings to zone first Wilshire, then Hollywood, and eventually the entire city.[73]

It took another year before the Los Angeles City Council finally adopted the new zoning ordinance in October 1921.[74] The pressure of the depression which had set in across the nation the previous spring provided the final push.[75] All sides felt that the passage of a zoning law would remove some of the uncertainty hanging over property investment, with the issue still to be decided into which zone would properties be placed. The Realty Board, reflecting increasing nervousness, had escalated their advertising campaign in the spring of 1921, to "Own Your Own Home *and Build Now.*"[76] They also played a key role in establishing the All-Year Club to boost the city's economic fortunes by promoting both tourism and permanent population growth.[77]

The Los Angeles Realty Board won a significant victory with the passage of the new zoning law. The old residential district classification was now split into two separate zoning designations: an "A" Zone for single-family houses, and a "B" Zone for all other residential uses. The "C" Zone was for business or commercial uses, "D" Zone for "non-obnoxious" industry, and the "E" Zone was unrestricted. When the City Council passed the new zone law it also adopted actual zoning maps for five districts. Because Los Angeles was so huge, the City Planning Commission left 36 districts unmapped. These districts were to be covered under the old residential district ordinance until such time as the Council approved new zoning maps.[78]

Four of the five maps were for the Hollywood, East Hollywood, Wilshire, and West Lake sections, the very areas that had been the scene of the biggest controversies regarding the protection of these neighborhoods as "high-class residential districts." If one studies the maps, the surprising fact is how little of the land was placed in the "A" Zone. Except for some fairly well-developed deed-restricted areas of large, expensive homes, most of the interior land was placed in the "B" Zone and almost all of the major street frontage was zoned "C." The other district maps later adopted by the City Council consisted largely of industrial areas zoned "D" and "E," and residential areas zoned entirely for "B" and "C" uses. By the end of the decade the City of Los Angeles had 600 miles of street frontage zoned commercial ("C"), estimated to be more than enough land and building space to serve a population of 14 million people. The actual population in 1930 was 1.2 million. Many more miles were zoned for apartments and multiple dwellings (see chart 4.1).[79]

Los Angeles had once again established itself as a zoning pioneer by becoming the first large American city to create a separate category restricted solely to the construction and occupancy of single-family detached houses. Many of zoning's backers, the Realty Board among them, saw the legal fight to establish the validity of this type of land-use restriction as the most important goal behind the passage of the new law. The goal was accomplished within a few years when the California Supreme Court upheld the validity of this form of police power regulation in the Miller case in 1925, and the U.S. Supreme Court later concurred.[80]

The Realty Board and its allies, including the Chamber of Commerce, paid a price for this victory. To begin with, they did not succeed in holding back the tide of commercial decentralization; if anything, zoning in practice may have helped accelerate it. They also did not succeed in legally excluding housing from industrial zones, which became a source of irritation to manufacturers as the decade wore on. And while they won the battle for single-family zones and managed to help preserve a

CHART 4.1
RESULTS OF THE LOS ANGELES "USE OF PROPERTY"
SURVEY, 1926

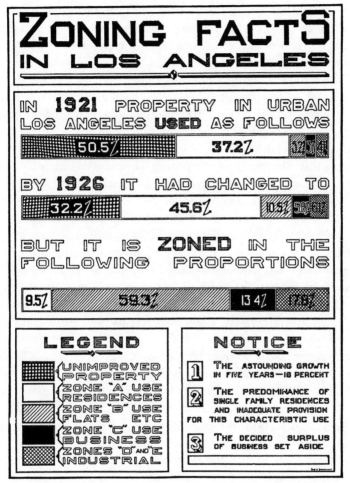

The above chart refers to the approximate two hundred square miles of urbanly developed Los Angeles that has been zoned for use since 1921. The remaining two hundred and fifty square miles of outlying areas now in process of being zoned are being given the advantage of previous experience.

The "13.4%" of "business" does not include the "downtown" area, which is found in the "17.8%" of "industrial." If the "business" occupancy in "industrial" classification were added to the "13.4%" it would bring the latter up to about 20%.

SOURCE: Gordon Whitnall, "Supply and Demand in Business Zoning," *The Community Builder*, I, 3, February 1928, p. 15.

few key residential enclaves, they failed utterly at zoning more than a small portion of the city in this category. In fact, it took more than two decades, after the Federal Housing Administration had significantly changed the rules of the game, before a majority of Los Angeles land was zoned "A" (by this time it was called "R-1"). As Huber Smutz, Los Angeles' longtime Zoning Administrator, observed about the compromise that led to the passage of the 1921 zoning law: "It was either a proposition of zoning the rabid speculator's property for the purpose for which he was holding it or having no zoning at all and hence no protection for residential districts."[81]

Perhaps this outcome is less surprising when one considers that for all its political power, economic resources, and media access, the Los Angeles Realty Board represented the interests of only a small minority of all the economic and political actors within the real estate business. In 1921 the Realty Board had fewer than 200 members, consisting of the oldest and largest real estate brokerage firms in Los Angeles, with the most employees and capital and the closest ties to builders, architects, engineers, subdividers, commercial developers, insurance companies, and financial institutions.[82] Real estate sales, however, was a highly competitive field with very easy entry and huge numbers of participants, especially in Los Angeles during the 1920s. Compared to other business sectors, such as the leading firms in finance, insurance, utilities, manufacturing, motion pictures, or oil, even the largest brokerage firms were fairly small-scale. The competitors of the Realty Board brokerage firms, though much tinier in size, were a great deal more numerous. In the fall of 1921 there were more than 1,200 real estate offices in Los Angeles and more than 33,000 people officially licensed to sell real estate.[83] Some of these salespeople worked for one of the nearly 200 Realty Board firms, but the overwhelming majority either worked for smaller brokers or for themselves. Real estate sales, speculation, and development was one of Los Angeles' largest industries in the 1920s, employing or self-employing a major portion of the working-age population on either a full- or part-time basis.[84]

Given this context, the "rabid speculator" who at first balked at zoning soon found it to be a very congenial ally, particularly as a tool for speculating in the purchase and sale of one or more of the hundreds of thousands of vacant lots that were rapidly being subdivided throughout the decade. As William Munro explained in 1931, zoning became the ultimate promotional device, a form of government-subsidized free advertising.[85] Vacant property zoned for "business" or "apartments" automatically took on added value as the purchaser either envisioned developing the land for an income-intensive use or of quickly passing it off to another more willing buyer for a substantially higher sales price:

> Zoning, however, quickly became popular. Hardly anything else in municipal administration has had so rapid a spread in the cities of the United States during the past fifteen years. And one of the principal reasons can be found in the fact that real estate agents and promoters throughout the country got behind the movement. They saw in it an opportunity to boom their business. With a city entirely zoned, they could assure purchasers of residential property that their neighborhoods would never be encroached upon by business, while on the other hand, zoning would give business property a touch of monopoly value. Accordingly the signs went up on vacant lots: "Zoned for business," or "Zoned for apartments," with the definite implication that such action on the part of the public authorities had resulted in giving the property a higher and more assured value than it would otherwise have.[86]

Zoning, by regulating the uses of a property, affected the income that could be derived from property. Unlike deed restrictions, however, zoning classifications and regulations could easily be changed by a majority vote of the City Council. Real estate values could therefore be manipulated by acquiring property with one zoning designation and having it changed to another, or by selling property with the implied promise that its current zoning designation could be changed. Throughout the decade of the 1920s, the Los Angeles City Planning Commission spent more than 80 percent of its time processing applications for zoning changes and exceptions. The great majority of them were granted. In some cases the City Planning Commission opposed a zoning change and was overruled by the City Council, but in most cases both bodies were amenable to all manner of pressure for accommodation. In built-up residential areas, people could occasionally be mobilized to successfully resist zoning changes, but since so much of Los Angeles was newly subdivided and sparsely developed the use of zoning as an aid to real estate promotion and speculation generally prevailed.[87]

Realty Board members were no less likely to seek individual zoning changes when it suited their client's interests. Since they were more able to exert power in the enactment of the initial maps, however, and were concerned to maintain stability and predictability in realty investment, they probably had less recourse to seeking zoning adjustments than the smaller speculators. Nevertheless, the manipulation of zoning could work just as easily to the benefit of the large developer as to the seller of an individual lot. A. W. Ross, through his enormous influence with the City Council and ownership of a few key parcels on a stretch of Wilshire Boulevard zoned entirely for single-family houses, was able to develop the "Miracle Mile" commercial strip to the exclusion of all competitors. His simple device was to get Council "spot zoning" changes from "A" to "C" every time he acquired one or more lots, while blocking efforts by anyone else to get zoning changes. Thus, without initially owning all the land, he succeeded in obtaining some of the vacant lots at "single-family" prices and then selling or leasing for a unified commercial development over which he exercised considerable control—thanks to zoning.[88]

In the battle for the Wilshire District, the Realty Board's governors were allied with the Chamber of Commerce, Merchants and Manufacturers Association, and Building Owners and Managers Association in combatting the decentralization of retail trade and commercial office space. These groups sponsored two ballot initiatives in 1924 and 1926 to halt the westward spread of commercial development along the Wilshire corridor. The 1924 referendum was soundly defeated. Two years later the downtown realtor-business coalition won the vote, but lost the zoning battle in the next four years through City Council "spot rezoning" of west Wilshire.[89]

In 1920 a Realty Board zoning committee, headed by Board president Otis A. Vickery, a leading downtown realtor, issued a statement that "We are in hearty accord with the protection of Wilshire Boulevard as one of the greatest show drives and thoroughfares of the city, and pledge ourselves to maintain it permanently as a residence district."[90] At the same time, however, many of the Realty Board's own members were strongly opposed to such a strategy and saw great potential and profit in developing Wilshire Boulevard as a magnificent suburban office and retail street for a wealthy west side clientele that no longer wished to travel all the way downtown. During the debate over Charles Cheney's zoning plan, one Wilshire District realtor asked the City Council to abolish the two-month-old Planning Commission and save the "needless expense."[91] The idea of zoning as *protection* (stabilizing of existing land-use patterns) was in direct conflict with the appeal of zoning as *promotion* (facilitating speculation, turnover, and changing patterns of land development). Both sides saw in public planning and zoning the possibility of controlling market competition and neighborhood externalities; but most of Los Angeles' numerous real estate operators were dealing with scattered lots in nearby locations, whereas the Realty Board leaders had a much larger vision of the degree of competition and the amount of territory they wished to control.

While the core of the exclusive single-family areas received protection under the Los Angeles zoning law, most of the major community builders operating in the high-income residential market adopted a strategy of subdividing in newer areas of the city using very strict deed restrictions, such as the Janss Company's development of Westwood Village, or in going outside the city limits to unincorporated areas or suburban municipalities where the local government was more amenable to the right kind of zoning. Beverly Hills, which successfully fought against annexation by Los Angeles, is a well-known example of the latter.[92]

The speculator's or curbstoner's notion that zoning should maximize property values at each individual location contradicted in practice the community builder's idea that through strict segregation and predictable public control of all specific land uses, zoning would maximize aggregate land values, and stabilize values at each location, but would not maximize values everywhere. The basis for zoning was, as the Los Angeles Realty Board told the City Council in 1920, "the greatest good to the greatest number."[93] Demonstrable losses might even be suffered by some property owners, which is why the legal battle to justify zoning as a reasonable exercise of the police power lent such critical importance to the contribution of "scientific city planning."

"Overzoning" and Land Economics: The Realty Board's Rezoning Campaign

An outstanding example of the advancement of city planning as "an exact science," to use Gordon Whitnall's phrase, was the 1926 Use of

Property Survey by the Los Angeles City Planning Commission.[94] (See chart 4.1.) The results of this survey were used as the opening volley in a political conflict concerning the extent to which Los Angeles was "overzoned." The concept of "overzoning" abandoned the legal justification for zoning as local government protection of the health, safety, and morals of the population. Instead, zoning was seen by both realtors and planners as "an exercise in land economics."[95] Gordon Whitnall defined zoning in 1926 "as a means that has been devised for furthering the highest utility of property and encouraging in the extreme the maximum development of that property."[96] "Overzoning," in Whitnall's opinion, stood in the way of this goal:

> Because of our over-doing a certain type of classification we fly right into the face of the eventualities of the law of supply and demand. Lack of proper zoning has made your investment a drug upon the market by reason of uncertainty. So, by giving substantially more of one classification to your city than is necessary for a given community, you create a degree of uncertainty which is sometimes spoken of by saying "the property is frozen." But zoning properly done and recognizing ratios of use will easily stabilize and encourage investment and development. That, if for no other reason, justifies zoning.[97]

During the speculative boom in Los Angeles from 1922 to 1924, nearly 4,000 new subdivisions were staked out and opened for sale.[98] A great number of people were buying lots in anticipation of selling for huge gains within a matter of weeks, and any zoning that could help push up the asking price was very much in demand. The two most favored categories were "B" and "C," income-producing uses of rental apartments and commercial structures. By 1924, however, as Whitnall put it, "the speculative gas seems to have been squeezed from the balloon."[99] In the mid-1920s one could travel for miles through Los Angeles and see occasional stores interspersed with acres of vacant lots growing weeds. In the interior between the major streets, one generally saw a sparse collection of small houses lived in by speculative lot owners, run-down rental houses, and more acres of weeded lots.[100] As the decade wore on, the real estate business began to thin its ranks as the effects of the realty recession spread.[101]

In the context of declining sales, the Los Angeles Realty Board launched a major campaign for "scientific" zoning and against "overzoning." In 1926 the Realty Board president was George Coffin, who as president of the Hollywood Chamber of Commerce fought to prevent the existing commercial center of the district from being eclipsed by new businesses springing up along nearby thoroughfares. The Realty Board under Coffin's leadership played a key role in inducing the City Planning Commission to undertake the Use of Property Survey. Coffin also led a publicity campaign on the economic effects of improper zoning which was echoed by a number of other Realty Board leaders in the ensuing decade.[102] Coffin's criticisms were sharp, as the following quote suggests:

It was a wise man who said, "You cannot make a silk purse out of a sow's ear." Neither can you make business property out of subdividers' illusions, deed restrictions, or zoning classifications. Sound economic forces create the relatively limited frontage of any city which can profitably be devoted to business use. Unfortunately, most of the so-called business frontage was born of the wedlock between ignorance and speculation, and the naked miles of vacant lots along our arteries of travel are mute testimony to an economic waste of such proportions that the imagination is startled at the farce of perpetuating this needless waste into the eternity of to-morrow.

I regret to state that much criticism must be directly charged to the greed of the property owners themselves, whether subdividers of large areas or individual lot owners, whose demands upon the authorities and the pressure used to enforce these demands have been of such magnitude as to force the dedicating of otherwise usable frontages to eternal wastage by improper zone classification, thus making it possible during an active real-estate market to exploit such land, pocket the false value created by the establishment of a business zone, and depart leaving a trail of depleted residential value in their wake.[103]

George Coffin initiated a two-pronged strategy by the Realty Board in attacking "overzoning." The first prong was to campaign for rezoning. This meant readjusting zoning categories to "unfreeze" properties in order to stimulate new sales and development, and to raise the value of existing built-up property in the older areas of the city. Coffin argued that the city's privately owned land should be rezoned "according to a comprehensive plan." "Scientific city planning," using the new principles of land economics, would be the best method of stimulating the overall real estate market. Gordon Whitnall acknowledged the political impact of the Realty Board's campaign for rezoning:

> That these conclusions are not purely theoretical is evidenced not alone by the actual studies that have been made, but is now being revealed with increasing frequency by the self-initiated moves on the part of property owners requesting that their heretofore "frozen" properties be "thawed" out by lending to it such protection as results from a reclassification into a zone use for which there is a demand and which, when so zoned, will have the protection of law with the consequent encouragement to immediate development.[104]

With the onset of the Great Depression and the virtual collapse of real estate activity, the Realty Board finally succeeded in overcoming the opposition to its rezoning proposal.[105] In 1930 the City Council adopted a new zoning ordinance. The new law added several use categories. The City Planning Commission was given responsibility to prepare a plan for rezoning major portions of Los Angeles. The new ordinance stated, however, that the City Council could only change a zoning designation to a more restrictive category if property owners representing 65 percent of the frontage signed a petition requesting the change. This requirement was put into the new ordinance at the insistence of the Realty Board, whose members were afraid that the City Council might eliminate *too much* land zoned for commercial use or for apartments.[106]

The second prong of the Realty Board's attack against "overzoning" was to argue for the reform of zoning administration. Beginning with George Coffin, a succession of Realty Board leaders consistently denounced the Planning Commission for not doing any "planning" and the City Council for being "corrupt" and for subjecting zoning to "politics."[107] In both cases the point of the criticism was that the Planning Commission and City Council were placing too much land in the wrong zoning category from the Realty Board's perspective, and that they were allowing too many and too frequent zoning changes. The latter included "spot zoning," in which small parcels or even a single lot were placed in a different and incompatible zone category with respect to the rest of the block or district.[108] At times the rhetorical flourishes became quite heated, as in this denunciation by the Realty Board's planning and zoning attorney, W. L. Pollard:

Political control of planning is a curse which has fastened itself upon
conditions in Southern California. Planning as it is generally known in Los
Angeles consists of zoning. There never was a subject more politically rid-
den or more politically controlled or more politically perverted than the
administration of zoning in the city of Los Angeles.[109]

The primary purpose of the Realty Board's denunciation of "politics"
was to use their own considerable political influence to reduce the ease
with which the smaller realty dealers, business proprietors, and property
owners could get zoning exceptions and amendments through the City
Council by "greasing" the appropriate palms of politicians and officials
or simply by mobilizing some electoral pressure on individual City Council
members. The new 1930 zoning law spelled out some required administrative procedures for the City Planning Commission designed to standardize the process of conducting investigations, holding hearings, and
granting or denying zoning variances and changing zoning classifications.[110] The Realty Board had for some time desired to create some
form of Board of Appeals to deal with zoning variances, and thus allow
the Planning Commission to do more "planning" and remove some
temptation from the City Council to engage in less "corruption."[111] With
the indictment of several councilmen and planning commissioners in the
late 1930s on charges of operating a zoning variance racket, and the
election of a new reform mayor in 1938, a civil service office of zoning
administration and a Board of Zoning Appeals were established in 1941.[112]
A new World War II-induced real estate boom was about to commence
in Los Angeles, and the Realty Board was poised to enter into a new
round of zoning controversies.

Conclusion

The longstanding Los Angeles love affair with single-family housing
set in beautiful surroundings is intimately tied to the history of its zoning
laws designed to separate business and industry from home "districts."
The community builders of the Los Angeles Realty Board played a major
role both in promoting the city's early and innovative zoning laws and
in establishing new standards of private land development and private

restrictions to further foster the suburban trend. Despite many obstacles during the 1920s boom, such as mixed uses and densities in the inner city and excessive and poor-quality subdividing on the urban fringe, by the 1940s boom the FHA had helped the Realty Board's community builders tip the balance such that fully developed and well-planned "neighborhood units" of owner-occupied houses became a reality for moderate-income workers and their families, and not just for the wealthy estate owners of the southern California "Riviera."

CHAPTER FIVE

THE CALIFORNIA
REAL ESTATE ASSOCIATION
AND
SUBDIVISION REGULATIONS

Introduction

T HIS CASE STUDY OF the California Real Estate Association (CREA) and subdivision regulations clearly demonstrates the important distinction between the three types of public-private planning for residential subdivision development: (1) *coordination,* (2) *design and engineering,* (3) *control.* Large community builders and smaller subdividers within CREA found common agreement on the need for coordinated public planning of traffic arteries and a host of other key elements of urban land-use and infrastructure development. They considered this form of public planning as a technical information service to help guide them in projecting market demand and development costs and thus enable them to create more profitable subdivisions. CREA actively promoted city and county planning expressly to make this service more effective and widely available.

The other two forms of planning created a greater degree of controversy. Community builders supported minimum design and engineering standards as a means of limiting competition from smaller subdividers, stabilizing market demand and realty values, and upgrading development standards. Many large developers were already utilizing deed restrictions that were far more drastic than anything the public sector might require.

Most smaller subdividers, however, vigorously opposed design and engineering regulations as needlessly adding to their development costs. Even community builders who could easily surpass any minimum requirements nevertheless feared that the exercise of arbitrary power by local planning commissions could reduce their flexibility and private initiative in planning new subdivisions. They therefore remained wary of local planning agencies and searched for other means of accomplishing their goal of standardizing and upgrading subdivision development.

Most realtors, including many small subdividers, were clearly in agreement on the need to exercise some form of control to prevent the "curbstone" or "bootleg" subdivider from wreaking havoc on the market for subdivision lots. The control issue was similar to the design and engineering controversy. The two questions constantly being debated by realtors were who would exercise such control and by what method could and should it be accomplished. A great deal of disagreement centered on the many answers to these questions. The community builders, again fearing the "meddling" of local planning commissions, continued to search for a way to exert control by some other method than local planning agency authority.

One method attempted by community builders was private control through CREA's Subdividers Code of Ethics, but when that experiment proved futile, two other avenues were explored: (1) private control through real estate lenders, title and property insurers, and utility companies (including water, power, and transit); (2) public control through the state licensing powers of the California Department of Real Estate. CREA leaders were still groping for solutions in 1934 when the Federal Housing Administration came along, and with the full cooperation of the community builders, FHA took charge of exercising market control and standardizing subdivision design and engineering, as well as encouraging local coordination-based compehensive land-use planning.

This case study also demonstrates the role of public opinion and legislative initiative by state and local elected officials, and the coalition nature of democratic politics. During more than a decade beginning in the middle 1920s, CREA was on the defensive in the face of the widely perceived waste and excess in both the public and private costs of the unregulated "curbstone" system of speculative subdividing. Only in responding to intense public pressure did community builders reluctantly move to shape the growing political debate and propose what they felt were appropriate governmental actions. CREA's political maneuvers were carefully worked out in discussions with a wide range of other constituency groups and public and private organizations. Even though CREA often appeared to have greater influence in state government than many of the other groups, the realtors still frequently found it necessary and prudent to compromise both on means and ends.

The outcome of such compromise was that by 1937 California had established an extensive network of city and county planning agencies based upon several important state enabling laws. Indeed, California led the nation in the number and authority of county planning commissions. The legal and administrative apparatus of state and local planning and regulation proved effective in supporting the efforts of America's most prodigious private developers of automobile-based suburban residential land for single-family homeownership, on a scale that had hardly seemed possible when the first California Map Act was passed in 1893.

Private Subdividing and "Uniform Boulevards"

Prior to 1893 California had no law concerning the filing of subdivision maps for official record. Maps could be filed with the county recorder, but would be considered in the same manner as the recording of any other legal document. In 1893, in the midst of a major national depression that caused financial chaos and a precipitous decline in real estate sales, the legislature passed a law requiring that anyone subdividing land in order to sell lots must first record an officially-approved subdivision map. Sale of subdivision lots from unrecorded maps or by reference to "metes and bounds" (natural boundaries) was made a misdemeanor offense. The purpose of this act was to restore some confidence on the part of purchasers as to accuracy and legality of title, and to simplify the work of title companies, lenders, and local governments.[1] After the Panic of 1907, which violently interrupted a major upswing in real estate activity, the newly formed California State Realty Federation (later called the California Real Estate Association) vigorously lobbied the state legislature to pass a new map act.[2] The 1907 law, reflecting the increasing importance of transportation and the accelerating trend of suburbanization, required that the subdivider submit a map to the local governing body which would have to certify the streets accepted for public dedication. The purpose of this action was to clarify confusion that often existed over which streets actually belonged in public ownership. The act did not give the local government any authority to tell the subdivider how to lay out the streets.[3]

Such additional power came in 1913, when the legislature authorized local governments to require that any streets accepted by them conform to the existing street system. It also set up a procedure for subdividers to issue street improvement bonds to be financed by special assessment of the property owners. Most significantly, the 1913 law repealed the 1893 Map Act, thus deregulating the prohibition against metes and bounds subdividing. A loophole that had previously been closed was now reopened.[4]

At the next legislative session, in 1915, an amendment to the Map Act was passed in conjunction with the passage of California's first City Planning Enabling Act. The support for this legislation came primarily from San Francisco's business and civic leaders from the Commonwealth Club, Chamber of Commerce, and Real Estate Board, from the League of California Municipalities, and from other government officials, business leaders, realtors, and community builders in the San Francisco Bay Area and Los Angeles metropolitan area.[5] The 1915 Map Act amendment required the local governing body to direct the subdivider to submit a proposed plat to a local city planning commission, where such body existed, or to the city engineer, to report on the suitability of the subdivision in relation to the city's development plans. Later, in 1921 and 1923, the Map Act was again amended to require the local government to examine not only the proposed streets but also the drainage, water supply, and other engineering features.[6]

The 1915 law was passed at the same time that the community builders among the realtors were beginning to work with the National Conference on City Planning (NCCP) to improve the development of residential subdivisions and devise new forms of municipal assistance in this process. Duncan McDuffie, one of California's most prestigious subdividers, was the vice-president of the California Conference on City Planning, which was formed in 1914 specifically to propose and lobby for the 1915 City Planning Act and Map Act amendment. McDuffie was a member of the newly created City Planning Committee of the National Association of Real Estate Boards (NAREB) that worked closely with a group of planners from the NCCP on a major study of "The Best Methods of Land Subdivision." As an example of the new American conception among the community builders of creating city planning commissions to coordinate public street plans with the regulation of private subdividing, the Los Angeles Realty Board formed a joint committee with the Chamber of Commerce in July 1915, just after the governor signed the Planning Act and Map Act amendment, to design "a plan for the construction of uniform boulevards within the city limits." The committee was chaired by Los Angeles' leading realtor and community builder, William May Garland. One of the other committee members from the Realty Board was Harry Culver, who was then in the process of subdividing and developing Culver City as a Los Angeles suburb.[7]

During the years from 1915 through 1921, residential building and subdividing activities were in the doldrums,[8] and very few city planning commissions existed in California.[9] This began to change in the early 1920s with the spread of zoning ordinances.[10] Los Angeles, for example, established a city planning commission in 1920 for the express purpose of designing and implementing a comprehensive zoning ordinance.[11] As subdivision activity began to heat up, particularly in southern California, a city planning process was at least formally in place to help shape future urban development. In point of fact, however, the planning agencies in most cases exercised very little control over the subdivision maps they were required to approve. The proximate reasons for the lack of any real planning presence during the biggest boom years of the decade were four-fold: (1) lack of a plan; (2) lack of staff resources; (3) the alternative of selling by metes and bounds; (4) lack of jurisdiction.

(1) Obviously the planning agency could only evaluate the subdivision in terms of the broader pattern of public and private urban development if it had some estimates of future trends and coordinated public plans prepared. Such a state of affairs was virtually nonexistent. Even major street traffic plans for such cities as Los Angeles, Oakland, and San Diego were not adopted until the mid-1920s.[12] Further, the planning commission was supposed to check to see that dedicated streets aligned with the existing street system. This was easily enough accomplished in densely

TABLE 5.1
Subdivisions Recorded in Los Angeles County,
1880–1935

Subdivisions Recorded Each Year:

Year	Tracts Recorded	Year	Tracts Recorded
1880	10	1908	347
1881	20	1909	377
1882	35	1910	544
1883	95	1911	593
1884	105	1912	646
1885	125	1913	500
1886	450	1914	228
1887	1350	1915	201
1888	400	1916	205
1889	130	1917	180
1890	70	1918	125
1891	75	1919	179
1892	80	1920	346
1893	85	1921	607
1894	110	1922	1020
1895	120	1923	1434
1896	125	1924	1306
1897	65	1925	684
1898	71	1926	599
1899	69	1927	529
1900	71	1928	382
1901	128	1929	269
1902	267	1930	171
1903	375	1931	92
1904	540	1932	67
1905	902	1933	55
1906	1146	1934	85
1907	545	1935	81

SOURCE: Charles D. Clark, "Subdivision Plotting and Map Filing," in Harrison R. Baker, ed., *Subdivision Principles and Practices* (Los Angeles: California Real Estate Association, 1936), Appendix B, p. 48.

built-up areas, but with the automobile facilitating the spread of subdivisions to far-flung farming areas, there were often no existing streets to align with.

(2) At the height of the boom in 1923, 1,434 subdivision maps were recorded in Los Angeles County, or 5½ maps per working day. (See table 5.1.) The local staff planning engineers were under intense pressure

TABLE 5.2
Metes and Bounds Subdividing
in Los Angeles County,
1920–1929

Year	Number of Metes and Bounds Subdivisions
1920	59
1921	44
1922	52
1923	69
1924	105
1925	103
1926	116
1927	88
1928	71
1929	71

SOURCE: *Annual Report*, Los Angeles Board of City Planning Commissioners, 1930, pp. 53–54.

to process these maps as quickly as possible, as speculative sales and avoidance of heavy carrying costs depended on quick approval. Many subdividers began taking orders for lot sales even before the maps were officially recorded. It was a true seller's market, and the local planning agency and local government had extremely limited resources with which to investigate abuses or even to enforce the laws and regulations it had on its books.[13]

(3) The "clouding" of private title had been the key problem that had led the 1893 legislature to outlaw metes and bounds subdividing. By 1913 the fast-growing private title insurance companies had solved most of the title problems, and metes and bounds subdividing was deregulated.[14] However, the speculative madness of the early 1920s, when tourists would be met at the train station and taken on a "free excursion" to some distant subdivision complete with Hollywood movie sets, led to new problems. Title companies very often refused insurance to "fly-by-night" tracts, and contract purchasers were left without title after having made substantial monthly payments. Yet so long as the alternative of metes and bounds was legal and marketable, subdividers could resist any efforts by public planners to control the ways they privately carved up the metropolitan landscape.[15] (See table 5.2.)

(4) The 1915 Map Act amendment and Planning Enabling Act required proposed subdivision maps to be submitted to the city planning commission for all tracts within 3 miles of a city's corporate boundaries. In some cases this led to jurisdictional disputes between two incorporated cities, or problems for subdividers who had to submit plats to two or three local governments—what the president of the Los Angeles Realty Board called "the very vicious law known as the Three Mile Limit."[16] Nevertheless, a large amount of subdividing in the 1920s was taking place in unincorporated areas outside of any city planning commission jurisdiction. The problem became so acute that the Los Angeles City Planning Commission joined together with other incorporated cities and lobbied the County Board of Supervisors to create the Los Angeles County Regional Planning Commission (LACRPC), the first of its kind in the nation. The LACRPC was responsible for helping coordinate planning between the various incorporated cities in the county and in unincorporated areas, for zoning the more urbanized portions of unincorporated land, for preparing master highway, park, and infrastructure plans, and for regulating the filing of subdivision maps of tracts located outside of any city's jurisdiction. LACRPC began operation in June 1923, and was immediately swamped with subdivision maps to review. It was constrained by all the problems just discussed, and as a consequence became one of the most active groups promoting stringent state legislation to control subdivision platting. Until 1929 only two other counties in California had established a planning commission, Santa Barbara in 1927 and San Francisco (where the city and county have identical boundaries) in 1917, so the twin problems of lack of jurisdiction by planning agencies and lack of coordination between planning agencies continued throughout the decade.[17]

In the first half of 1923 the subdivision boom in southern California, particularly in Los Angeles County, was reaching its peak of activity.[18] California led the nation in real estate profits that year,[19] and subdividing land was the most profitable end of the real estate business.[20] The larger subdivider-developers were beginning to build houses on their improved lots[21] and arrange mortgage financing for home and lot purchasers.[22] Real estate sales in Los Angeles during 1923 were estimated to exceed $500 million.[23] One Los Angeles realty operator claimed to have single-handedly sold $9 million worth of subdivision lots in 1923 at an average profit of 600 percent.[24]

Beginnings of Crisis in the Midst of a Boom

Despite the frenzy of activity, there were beginning to be signs that the subdivision market would soon be as shaky as a California earthquake fault. In December 1922, W. S. Clayton, president of the California Bankers Association and also a major San Jose realtor, sternly warned the annual convention of the California Real Estate Association that "sudden increases in population do not make sound value" if there is no corresponding increase "in profitable employment," and that the state's major banks were going to exercise caution in real estate lending. His hope was that financial conservatism in controlling the supply of mortgage money would "prevent any further booms and will prevent speculative values being developed."[25]

In February 1923, Colonel William May Garland of Los Angeles, former president of NAREB and California's most powerful realtor, warned that the subdivision boom in Los Angeles, with enough lots being subdivided to accommodate an immediate population influx of 10 million people, might soon crash like the 1887 southern California land boom did in 1888, which devastated the real estate market for a decade. He cited an example of one subdivision where all 150 lots sold immediately, and only 9 of the purchasers said they expected to build on the lots. The other 141 were "expecting to sell at a profit and are mortgaging other property to get the money with which to make these speculative buys."[26]

In January 1924, Henry Barbour, CREA's president, published his New Year's resolutions, including one which acknowledged concern over the market competition and overproduction problems in California's subdividing business, but still searched for private forms of control rather than public ones:

> Resolution #3: To amend the by-laws of your board and to provide immediately for a committee on subdivision, making it mandatory upon all members proposing to subdivide a tract of land for residential or indus-

trial purposes to submit a plat of the proposed subdivision for the approval of our committee and through it, of your board. Such committee to work in conjunction with the bank of the town or the clearing house of the city, all to the end that a stop may be put to reckless subdividing and the greedy, absolutely unnecessary, cutting up of good farm lands into diminutive, non-usable twenty-five foot lots, that not only the widow, the orphan and the financially non-competent may be protected, but that the values of legitimate subdivision and the development of our cities and towns may be better stabilized, the reputation of our state for conservatism preserved, and her real estate continue the synonym for confidence in the minds of the new settler and a joy and financial gain to the coming new investor.[27]

In May 1924, state Real Estate Commissioner Edwin Keiser issued a public warning against the sale of "wildcat lots" by "real estate tricksters," saying that a "number of complaints have recently been made to this department where persons entirely ignorant of county conditions" purchased lots fronting on rural boulevards and highways as "business property" at "five or six times their actual value." He warned licensed real estate brokers and salesmen against selling such property on behalf of these "unscrupulous" subdividers, or he might revoke their licenses.[28] The next month Keiser announced he was prosecuting three licensed real estate salesmen from southern California for making false statements in selling subdivisions. He stated that subdivision salesmen were getting desperate because of "the slowing up of the speculative demand in subdivision lots," that they were using high-pressure sales techniques to get people to put down their entire savings as a down payment on the promise of a quick resale.[29]

By December 1924, Commissioner Keiser had moved into the legislative arena to find a vehicle to stave off the rising tide of complaints coming into his office. He called on the incoming state legislature to pass a law requiring subdivision promoters to post a bond for the completion of promised improvements within a specified time. The state Real Estate Department would be the enforcement agency.[30] One month later Keiser called for legislation requiring that all subdivisions be submitted to his department for approval as to clear title and adequate financing, and requiring that subdividers make bonded guarantees to fulfill all promised or advertised improvements in connection with the sale of lots: "For it is the unfortunate knowledge of my office and of the Realtors of California that in many cases the subdivider is spending the payments from his purchasers on himself in a lavish fashion, while the purchasers are carrying water for household use several blocks despite the fact that when the subdivision was opened, water pipes and everything else were promised."[31]

Meeting in Los Angeles in February 1925, the CREA Legislative Committee decided to oppose Commissioner Keiser's proposal, stating that subdivision regulation should come under jurisdiction of the cities and counties, not the state Real Estate Department.[32] In fact, the CREA Legislative Committee opposed *all* state subdivision legislation during 1925: "As a direct result of active work by the association and boards against the ten or twelve proposed subdivision bills, the most important died in committee. Nevertheless, the State Association (CREA) legislative committee passed a resolution calling upon the Realtors of the state to propose a constructive subdivision law for 1927. The work can be done in cooperation with the City Plan Committee."[33] In the midst of this political turmoil, Edwin Keiser resigned as commissioner in early April and returned to the private real estate business.[34]

Among the bills CREA officially opposed was the Melville bill, coauthored by former state Assemblyman Hugh Pomeroy, who was secretary of the Los Angeles County Regional Planning Commission. LACRPC reviewed subdivision plats in unincorporated areas of the county, primarily to determine if the subdivision's street widths and alignment conformed with county street and highway plans. The Melville bill completely prohibited the sale of subdivision lots by metes and bounds description. Under this legislation all subdividers would be required to officially record their plats with the county recorder, after having first obtained approval from the city or county planning commission or engineer's office.[35] According to Hugh Pomeroy, many real estate operators opposed the Melville bill's attempt to close the loophole which allowed subdividers to "bootleg" their way around public regulation. (See table 5.2.) He also noted, however, that while the bill "failed of passage by reason of realty opposition, its strongest supporters were likewise Realtors."[36] Thus we see the beginning of an important trend—the split within CREA. While a majority of the Legislative Committee opposed the Melville bill, some of the bill's strongest supporters were realtors, particularly the leading community builders from CREA's Subdividers and Homebuilders Division. Many of the largest subdividers and bigger brokers wanted to outlaw "bootleg" subdivisions, and to require investigations as to title and financing, bonds to guarantee improvements, and public planning to secure proper street width and alignment and other design and engineering features of the plat. However, these leaders no longer had firm control over their fast-growing statewide organization. CREA was experiencing a great deal of both internal conflict and external pressure.

The new officers that took over CREA in January 1926 were headed by President Harry Culver, the developer of Culver City and one of the largest and most successful realtors in California. Culver, who was a member of the Major Highway Committee of Los Angeles and of the Los Angeles Traffic Commission, had chosen the sprawling barley fields of west Los Angeles as the site for Culver City because it "was accessible by boulevards."[37] He understood the need for highway and street planning, and as a leading community builder was desirous of regulating the small "curbstone" subdividers right out of the industry.[38] Culver appointed Fred Reed, one of Oakland's leading downtown realtors and a major residential subdivider, to head CREA's City Plan and Zoning Committee. Reed, who was also a NAREB vice-president and past CREA president, was a passionate advocate of city planning throughout his career, most famous for his frequent remark to real estate brokers that "City Planning is the production end of our business."[39] Reed immediately proceeded to organize the first NAREB-sponsored national conference on city planning in June 1926, and the largest statewide conference on city planning, held in California a month earlier.[40]

The CREA-sponsored California Conference on City Planning met at the Ambassador Hotel in Los Angeles, April 30 and May 1, 1926, in an atmosphere of mounting concern over the many problems of the subdivision market, especially in Los Angeles County. Nearly 400 realtors, bankers, public officials, planners, and leading citizens heard two days of speeches, the most important of which were on the subject of subdivision control.[41] The new California Real Estate Commissioner J. R. Gabbert opened his remarks by stating that the state Real Estate Department was being swamped with "hundreds of complaints" from "disappointed purchasers" of subdivision lots. He said that fraud in subdivision sales was the number one cause of real estate license revocations, involving 70 percent of the Department's complaint investigations. He noted that while in Los Angeles County during 1923–24 an average of five subdivision maps per day were officially recorded, the average had dropped to one per day.[42] Gabbert called, as did his predecessor, for the state Real Estate Department to issue permits before any subdivision lots could be sold in California:

> There is now a law which prohibits a subdivider from selling lots in a subdivision until a map is filed of record and yet there is hardly a subdivider in the state who observes it, for the reason that it is not made any official's duty to enforce it. . . . The problems are extremely difficult and the final draft of the law should be most carefully considered by successful subdividers who are familiar with all of the difficulties involved in such activities. The large (real estate) boards and the State Association (CREA), the banks, the escrow offices and trust companies should be carefully considered and consulted in working out details that will not be too drastic and yet will protect the investing public. . . . It should be of such form as to apply in every part of the state to any proposed new subdivision and should not encroach upon the work of city planning commissions, boards of supervision, and other local officials already established to take care of zoning, beautification and similar features.[43]

CREA President Harry Culver followed Commissioner Gabbert to the rostrum to announce his support for Gabbert's proposal, adding that subdivision regulation required expert technical knowledge of how to plan and build better communities and cities.[44] At the end of the two-day conference, the Resolutions Committee, consisting of five realtors and planner Hugh Pomeroy, unanimously adopted 12 resolutions, endorsing the outlawing of metes and bounds subdividing and the establishing of subdivision control both by the Department of Real Estate and by city, county, and regional planning commissions.[45]

Six months later CREA held a Subdividers and Homebuilders Conference as part of its November 1926 annual convention. Guy Rush of Los Angeles, one of California's largest subdividers[46] and a close ally of CREA President Harry Culver, called for statewide regulation of all subdivisions including minimum lot sizes, standard street widths, compulsory tree planting and reforestation, and reservation of parks and parking spaces. Rush, as chairman of CREA's Subdividers and Homebuilders Division, proclaimed that the land development industry should be restricted solely to genuine community builders: "If the business of subdividing is one which requires knowledge, capital, and vision, surely we are entitled to safeguard it as the physician or attorney guards his own, and we must make it increasingly difficult for the novice to enter our profession without having served his apprenticeship and qualified as a community builder."[47] The stage was set for Guy Rush to sit down with the CREA Legislative Committee and its attorney, Herbert Breed, to work out a plan for subdivision control to be introduced into the 1927 California Legislature.[48] CREA's newly elected president for 1927, Harry B. Allen, also chaired its Legislative Committee and served as the chief lobbyist for the realtors. Allen, a NAREB vice-president, developed the expensive Sea Cliff subdivision in San Francisco and was a well-known northern California community builder.[49]

Immediately following CREA's annual convention, the November statewide elections swept into office a new governor, C. C. Young, who as speaker of the State Assembly had been one of the sponsors of CREA's real estate license legislation from 1911 through 1917. Young was himself a realtor, as were a large number of other state and local politicians.[50] CREA realized that the incoming governor would be appointing a new real estate commissioner, and that J. R. Gabbert was on his way out. So for the second time in two years CREA decided to oppose any legislation giving the Real Estate Department authority to approve or deny all subdivision lot sales in California, deciding that such regulation "would be very drastic."[51]

CREA and State Government: Partners in Regulation

As negotiations proceeded within CREA's leadership during the months of December through March 1927, it became apparent that, rhetoric to the contrary, most subdividers would not agree to any measure that would significantly curtail their freedom of operation. But the pressure was on from the larger brokers, bankers, title companies, trust officers, and other

well as chairman of its City Planning and Zoning Committee, decided to follow up on CREA's successful 1926 city planning conference in Los Angeles with a bigger and better one for 1927 in his beloved hometown of Oakland. In order to boost attendance, Reed asked the League of California Municipalities to officially cosponsor the event, though CREA was still firmly in control. About 700 people attended, mostly from the San Francisco Bay area and the Los Angeles metropolitan area.[55] The Resolutions Committee of the CREA Oakland city planning conference adopted a resolution urging the consolidation of three different bills already introduced into the state legislature, which together would constitute "a complete city and regional plan act, practically identical with the standard city plan act recommended by Herbert Hoover and the United States Department of Commerce."[56] The "Hoover Act," still in draft, was modeled on the joint NAREB–American City Planning Institute statement on subdivision control adopted by NAREB in January 1927.[57] Fred Reed was an enthusiastic supporter of the NAREB-ACPI statement, and he brought back the gospel to California in the form of new comprehensive state planning enabling legislation.[58] Thus was born S.B. 585, the proposed California Planning Act of 1927. The endorsement of the Oakland conference gave a huge impetus to its legislative fortunes.[59]

Significantly, the Resolutions Committee did not endorse S.B. 645, because the Oakland conference was held before CREA had worked out a compromise with the Los Angeles County Counsel. One conference resolution, however, did assert the principle of preventing metes and bounds subdividing.[60] An important paper by Harry Culver on "Subdivision Control" was presented at the Oakland conference, and it indicated a significant backing off by the realtor-subdividers from strong public *control,* while simultaneously endorsing strong public *coordination.* Culver asserted that most responsible subdividers already exercised great control over their subdivisions through private deed restrictions and land planning, and implied that perhaps the buck should stop with the private sector after all. Culver, who was then serving as president of the Los Angeles Realty Board, reported that the "Subdividers Committee of the Los Angeles Realty Board has been considering for some years suggested recommendations for legislative action, but there has been a hesitancy to ask the enactment of laws governing acceptance of plats so drastic and hemmed in with so much detail that they might prove a deterrent to the community."[61] Culver's paper coincided with an announcement that the CREA Subdividers and Homebuilders Division, headed by Guy Rush and by Harrison Baker of Pasadena, was preparing a Subdividers' Code of Ethics to be administered privately through the local real estate boards.[62]

By 1927 CREA had become one of the more powerful lobbying groups in the state legislature. On matters of vital concern to the association, every bill CREA supported in 1927 passed, and every bill it opposed was defeated.[63] As a result of CREA's advocacy, S.B. 645, the subdivision control bill that outlawed metes and bounds subdividing in metropolitan areas, passed both houses of the state legislature unanimously. CREA, the Los Angeles Realty Board, Guy Rush, and "prominent subdividers throughout the state" made "strong appeals to the Governor to sign" S.B. 645.[64] S.B. 585, the California Planning Act that had received its impetus from the statewide city planning conference in Oakland and was strongly supported by the League of California Municipalities, also passed.[65] But CREA was beginning to have second thoughts about S.B. 585. "Opposition had arisen in Los Angeles," according to CREA's monthly magazine, because the subdivision control provisions of S.B. 585 seemed to conflict with the existing 1907 Map Act and with S.B. 645.[66] NAREB, from the national headquarters in Chicago, officially supported both bills, probably at Fred Reed's and Harry Allen's urging.[67]

The scene was now set for a bizarre political episode in the history of modern city planning. On June 3, the last day in which Governor C. C. Young could sign bills, only a week after both the State Senate and Assembly had unanimously passed S.B. 645, Governor Young pocket vetoed the measure.[68] Why? Because CREA asked him to do so, "owing to objections from prominent subdividers who felt that certain portions of it would affect their business seriously."[69] Specifically, Del Monte Properties, the developers of the massive and very exclusive 6,000-acre Pebble Beach residential community in Monterey, requested CREA to oppose S.B. 645 at literally the last minute when Del Monte's attorneys discovered that the bill's definition of a subdivision would have put Pebble Beach under public regulation.[70] (See exhibit 5.1.) Since CREA's ire was aimed at the "curbstone" subdividers and not at their colleagues, the realtors decided to scrap S.B. 645 and start over again when the state

EXHIBIT 5.1
"DEL MONTE PROPERTIES COMPANY APPRECIATES
ATTITUDE ON S. B. 645"

The following letter, received by officers of the California Real Estate Association from Jack Beaumont, of the Del Monte Properties Company, shows to some extent the appreciation felt by that organization on the attitude taken by the Association after opposition to Senate Bill 645, the metes and bounds measure, arose. The letter addressed to President Harry B. Allen and Secretary Glenn D. Willaman, follows:

Dear Harry and Glenn:

This note is addressed to you jointly for the purpose of expressing the deep appreciation of Del Monte Properties Company for the action taken by California Real Estate Association in the matter of Senate Bill 645.

Through our own negligence we found ourselves in the position that this bill was before the Governor for signature with strong backing, and only at the eleventh hour realized the extent of the burden which the bill placed on our Pebble Beach operations.

Goodfellow, Eells and Orrick, counsel for our company in San Francisco, after an examination of the bill, determined that through the inclusion of the words, "private roads," in Section 1 of the bill, the entire Pebble Beach area which includes some 150 miles of private roads and consisting of nearly 6,000 acres would come within the definition of subdivision, thereby presenting almost insurmountable obstacles to its further development and sale.

The basic idea behind Senate Bill 645 has the hearty approval of Del Monte Properties Company and we will gladly cooperate between now and the next session of the Legislature in the preparation of the bill which will accomplish the primary objects of Senate Bill 645 and overcome the objectionable features which we were so tardy in discovering.

We are convinced that we would have had practically no chance to induce the Governor to refrain from signing this bill if it had not been for the liberal attitude adopted by the officers of California Real Estate Association in suggestion to the Governor that the bill be allowed to go over for two years to avoid working the very great hardship on our company and the few other state association members similarly situated which must have ensued had Senate Bill 645 been approved by the Governor.

EXHIBIT 5.1 (*Continued*)

We particularly appreciate the help which we received at your hands in view of the fact that our belated appeal for assistance left you in a somewhat embarrassing position with both the Los Angeles County Counsel who very generously released you from your obligations to them when the situation was explained and the Governor who had shown throughout the session such a favorable attitude toward measures sponsored by the California Real Estate Association and who quite naturally believed that Senate Bill 645 had the undivided support of California Realtors as a substitute for their own measure 625 which had been allowed to die in committee.

SOURCE: *California Real Estate*, VII, 10, July 1927, p. 29.

legislature next met in 1929. For at least two more years metes and bounds subdividing would be legal and there would be no strong subdivision control. This would be true even though Governor Young signed S.B. 585, the California Planning Act. He did so with CREA's blessing, only because S.B. 585 was permissive legislation that realtors could block at the local government level if they chose.[71] Three other key planning measures to pass the 1927 legislature, a companion bill on map act regulations and two measures on building set-back lines, were also pocket vetoed by the governor on the last day, again with CREA's approval.[72] Charles Cheney, California's well-known planning consultant, tried to put the best possible face on the situation by wiring Governor Young his warm congratulations for signing S.B. 585, stating that the California Planning Act "will greatly help real estate development and increase its security as an investment."[73]

Controversy on All Sides

The debacle of the near-passage of the Subdivision Map Act combined with the actual signing of the California Planning Act set off political shock waves inside CREA and the local boards, particularly the Los Angeles Realty Board, which was by far the largest in the state (nearly 1,000 members). A virtual counterrevolution ensued against the benign rhetoric and ameliorative approach taken toward public regulation under the regime of Harry Culver in 1926 and Harry Allen in 1927. The new

CREA president for 1928, Hal Hotchkiss of San Diego, immediately sacked Fred Reed and Guy Rush. Hotchkiss appointed W. L. Pollard, an attorney for the Los Angeles Realty Board, to replace Fred Reed as chairman of CREA's City Planning and Zoning Committee.[74] The new chairman of CREA's Subdividers and Homebuilders Division, Harrison Baker of Pasadena,[75] launched a fervent crusade against the dangers of overregulation, speaking often of the abuses perpetrated by planning commissions and calling for elimination of red tape, sharply defined limits on city or county planning commission authority, and "provision for penal sums to be recovered by subdividers whose subdivisions have illegally been held up by public officials."[76] Many of the local boards began adopting the Subdividers' Code of Ethics, with the public relations argument that such action obviated the need for public control: "instead of passing laws to govern the subdividers, the subdividers themselves will adhere to the ethics of the national association."[77]

The third annual California Conference on City Planning held in Pasadena during April 1928 was sponsored solely by CREA.[78] The realtors had become angry at the League of California Municipalities over the subdivision planning issue; so angry, in fact, that Hugh Pomeroy, who as secretary of the Los Angeles County Regional Planning Commission had been a driving force behind map act reform both in 1925 and 1927, was forced to resign his position as California's leading county planner. Pomeroy appeared at the Pasadena conference in his new role as head of the Los Angeles Citizen's Committee on Parks, Playgrounds, and Beaches, and "in humorous vein, he attacked subdividers who are opposed to planning."[79] Harrison Baker, while supporting city and regional planning of streets, parks, and the like, also opined reassuringly that "the influence of city planning authority and governmental control practically stops entirely at the front property line. Beyond that the subdivider is in almost complete control." The solution to good overall development, according to Baker, was for the city to be "fortunate" in having subdividers who recognize that they are "city builders" rather than mere "sellers of land."[80]

The conference Resolutions Committee, which for the first time in the three conferences consisted exclusively of CREA members, was silent on the subdivision control issue; but they did resolve that "at least one Realtor with active subdivision experience should be appointed as a member of every City Planning Commission and Regional Planning Commission of California; and wherever possible a second Realtor with central business property experience be also appointed on such commissions."[81] Four months later a CREA survey revealed that more than 40 realtors were already serving on planning commissions in California, and on 8 commissions a CREA member was the chairman.[82]

Most of the members of CREA clearly wanted the public sector to socialize more of the costs of urban land development, whether it be roads, schools, parks, or water. Given that the local public sector was financed primarily through property taxes of one sort or another, they wanted public officials to better coordinate this socialized development and service provision so that the cost burden could be reduced and efficiency enhanced. They believed that the value of their private real estate could be substantially increased through this form of public action. Increasing private realty values was, for them, the very essence and purpose of "scientific city planning." They also understood that such public coordination of the uses of land and resources could not be successfully accomplished without the cooperation of the owners of private real estate in the community. Public-private cooperation in this vein also had their support, although more reluctantly, because it was but a short step from requesting their voluntary cooperation to requiring or coercing them to cooperate.[83]

The realtors knew that coordinated planning could not function properly if some key parties failed to cooperate, and they desired that those private owners who caused other real estate values to decline in pursuit of their own gain should somehow be constrained for the greater benefit of the rest of the real estate industry and property owners. They wanted to coerce others, but not be coerced themselves. They wanted to control the process of coercion and not be controlled by it. They wanted to limit the freedom of action of their "curbstone" competitors who destabilized local real estate markets, undermined confidence in the industry and caused property values in one or many locations to fall, but they did not want their own freedom of action to be limited. In short, they only desired regulations that would put them at a competitive advantage as individual entrepreneurs; any public action or regulation that threatened to put them at a competitive disadvantage vis-à-vis other entrepreneurs in real estate or in other sectors made them feel extremely ambivalent at best, if not downright hostile.

In the case of subdivisions, the subdividers wanted lot and home purchasers to feel confident that they would receive clear and unencumbered title, but they feared too much public interference in their financing arrangements and advertising. Subdividers wanted purchasers to be willing to pay more for a vacant lot in a "neighborhood" that would eventually contain all modern improvements, but they feared having to bear the cost of too many improvements themselves. They wanted coordinated public planning to ensure that the right amount of land in the right place would be set aside for streets and open space, but they did not want to be told how to plat their subdivisions for fear that public regulation would cut into their profits. Most of the larger real estate brokers and subdividers hoped that public subdivision controls would eliminate many of their competitors,[84] but they also feared it could eliminate them if they didn't proceed carefully and dominate the regulatory process as completely as possible. The local realty boards and CREA were the primary vehicles for attaining this collective domination.

The urban planners liked to point out to the real estate industry leaders that coordinated public planning, including subdivision controls, would actually cut private development costs, expand market demand for real property, stabilize private real estate markets, and overall be highly profitable to developers and brokers, lenders and insurers.[85] But the realtors feared that restrictions on the use of private property, particularly regulatory restrictions utilizing the public police power, could also wipe them out. "Scientific city planning" could make them richer *or* poorer, individually and collectively, depending on who did the planning and how it was done.[86]

However, the subdividers and the realty brokers and sales agents were sitting in the middle of an economic situation in 1928 where the demand for their product, once so clamorous, was rapidly vanishing. Both sales prices and the volume of subdivision sales transactions were declining, and new development was way down. The level of abuse and fraud over the boom period had been such that despite the best efforts of the realty boards and the Realtors' Code of Ethics, real estate was once again getting a bad name. Potential buyers either were afraid of getting conned or losing money in a sluggish market, or they had already been burned and thus were somewhere between "illiquid" and plain broke.

Public officials were caught in a tremendous fiscal squeeze as their budgets stretched to meet the infrastructure and service needs of the sprawling, half-occupied subdivision developments, while their revenues shrank as property owners began defaulting on property taxes and revolting against rapidly burgeoning special assessments. To forestall an impending budget and political crisis, local officials clamored for subdivision regulation.[87] Law enforcement agencies, facing angry citizens who had lost their savings speculating in real estate, also wanted new laws. Title insurance and trust companies wanted action to further standardize the subdivision map recording process. Institutional mortgage lenders solicited public assistance in their efforts to stabilize real estate markets. Homebuilders and commercial builders wanted stable and available building lots in improved locations, in order to stimulate demand for their own real estate products. Even major newspapers were caught in the subdivision dilemma, wanting advertising revenue from subdividers but not wanting to damage the paper's reputation.[88]

Most important of all, the continued discussions by Guy Rush and others concerning "standardization" by community builders[89] had made clear that the scale of land development and institutional involvement in real estate investment had taken a great leap forward since the Panic of 1907, when the last major California Map Act was passed. There was now too much at stake to leave private land-use to the vicissitudes of a "free market." Subdivider-imposed deed restrictions, formulated with encouragement from institutional mortgage lenders and title insurance and trust companies, were designed precisely to control and restrict market behavior.[90] The possibilities of controlling the market through public-private cooperation were now better than they had ever been. The leaders of CREA knew this, and felt all the pressures. They determined to stay in command of the city planning and subdivision regulation movement, despite, or perhaps because of, their ambivalence and their fears.

One excellent example of this seemingly contradictory attitude is that Jack Beaumont of Del Monte Properties, who caused the 1927 Map Act to be vetoed, now assumed a leading role in shaping CREA's proposed map act legislation for 1929.[91] Beaumont, having previously been caught napping on the public planning issue while he was busy planning the private paradise of Pebble Beach, actually became one of CREA's strongest city planning boosters. He was a catalyst in forming the new Monterey Peninsula Regional Planning Commission in 1928, and was appointed by Governor Young as chairman of the Commission.[92]

Another example of realtor ambivalence is that of Harrison Baker, chairman of CREA's Subdividers and Homebuilders Division and a member of the Pasadena City Planning Commission.[93] Baker, after announcing that "I am getting a little fed up on criticism of the subdivider and think it is about time to start a little program of glorification," took charge of CREA's efforts to secure new map act and city and regional planning legislation in the 1929 legislature.[94] At CREA's annual convention in October 1928, the discussion on city planning and subdivision legislation was held under the auspices of the Subdividers and Homebuilders Division.[95] At that session W. L. Pollard, chairman of CREA's City Plan Committee, announced that he was working with the Los Angeles County Counsel's office to repeal the 1927 California Planning Act and replace it with an entirely new state law.[96] Pollard told the realtors that the 1927 Planning Act was too broad and general in its scope to be practical:

> The authors of the bill attempted to include under its powers many conditions which, in the opinion of the real estate men, had no place in city planning legislation. Among other things, it provided for architectural control and had general provisions granting control on numerous other phases of urban life, which were so vague and uncertain that under them the commission could assume jurisdiction over anything having to do with subdivision building or general real estate activity.[97]

Pollard explained that many subdividers and title companies felt that the Planning Act conflicted with the existing 1907 Map Act, and that regulation of map filing concerning clarity of title, proper financing, and posting of improvement bonds should be handled separately from land-use planning: "A large number of the real estate fraternity have contended that the functions of city planning and map filing should be separated, and that the planning commission should have authority over map filing only when and as they have accomplished or done certain things."[98] In other words, subdividers only wanted city planning agencies to handle the *coordination* function—to prepare master land-use plans for public development and private zoning, and ensure that new subdivisions conform to those plans. *Design and engineering* would be handled primarily by the private subdividers, not the public planners. As to who would enforce *control*, CREA had yet to make up its mind. Baker and Pollard agreed to work together with CREA's Legislative Council to direct the lobbying effort on all bills concerning land-use planning and subdivision map regulation.[99] CREA Counsel Herbert Breed, author of the vetoed 1927 map bill, was kept at arm's length from this still sensitive area.

Compromise: The 1929 Planning and Map Filing Acts

W. L. Pollard then took the initiative in scheduling an early fourth annual CREA-sponsored California Conference on City Planning. The entire purpose of the two-day affair in mid-February in Fresno was to discuss "legislation pending before the Assembly and State Senate."[100] Pollard reported to the CREA magazine in January that he had assembled a committee of city planners to discuss with him and other realtors their views on how to amend or replace the 1927 Planning Act:

> The proposals originally put forth by the city planners were of such a nature that in many instances the real estate group could not accept them. These proposals, if enacted into the law, would have given to the city planning commissions throughout the state arbitrary power which the real estate group felt did not belong in the hands of such commissions. Many conferences have been held, both individual and joint, and as a result, compromise legislation is being submitted to Sacramento which, while not in all instances entirely acceptable to the real estate group, eliminates the dangers which the real estate operators saw in the city plan drafts.[101]

At the end of January, Los Angeles State Senator J. W. McKinley introduced two bills into the California Senate at the request of CREA. The bills took the existing California Planning Act and carved it in two. S.B. 614 dealt with subdivision control and map filing. S.B. 615 was concerned with city planning commissions and the preparation of master plans.[102] With regard to the potentially controversial S.B. 614, Pollard and Baker were anxious to avoid a repeat of the 1927 situation in which

the Los Angeles County Counsel had prepared a much stronger competing bill than their own Breed bill. This time the strategy was to line up
support from the Los Angeles County Counsel, Los Angeles County
Board of Supervisors, Los Angeles Chamber of Commerce, Los Angeles
City Attorney, the League of California Municipalities, the California
Land Title Association, and the "city planners' group" behind the CREA
legislation, to preclude the introduction of any competing bills before
the January legislative deadline. CREA focused almost exclusively on Los
Angeles, according to Pollard, because "Los Angeles County, having the
greatest subdivision activity of any county in the state, would have a
great interest in this type of legislation."[103]

In order to secure political support, however, Pollard and Baker were
forced to make a number of concessions that made many of the realtors
distinctly unhappy. Noting that city planners, city engineers, and county
surveyors generally approved of the first draft of the bill as introduced in
January, Pollard reported that the draft was "not quite acceptable to the
real estate group."[104]

> The real estate group in the main has contested the claim of the city
> planning group that this group should have the final say-so on map filing
> and city planning matters, the real estate group feeling that by placing the
> control of city planning and map filing in the hands of a city planning
> commission they would surrender to this commission control of the real
> property which they do not wish to surrender.
>
> One point for which the real estate group has definitely fought is a pro-
> vision which would allow the subdivision of property by metes and bounds.
> The planning group has fought this demand on the ground that if subdi-
> viding by metes and bounds were allowable, subdivisions would be put on
> the market which would not conform with the general plans in the city
> and county, and would disrupt and destroy the planning work carried on.
> This point will probably have to be fought out at the legislative meeting
> at Sacramento, but it is hoped that some compromise can be effected.[105]

The "compromise" that CREA lobbyists W. L. Pollard, Jack Beaumont, and Los Angeles Realty Board President Frank Brooks eventually
worked out with a long list of lobbyists and legislators after amending
S.B. 614 nearly 300 times, was that metes and bounds subdividing would
continue to be legal in California.[106] Pollard, noting that the working

out of this compromise "has been quite a storm center during the present session of the State Legislature," explained that:

> after many discussions the prohibition against metes and bounds subdivision was eliminated and under the bill as now amended, a subdivider has two courses to follow—one to sell from a recorded map, which map must meet with approval of the city planning commission and must conform to certain standards, or to sell by metes and bounds. However, he must submit his proposed layout and map to the city planning commission or city engineer or county surveyor and then wait thirty days. During this thirty-day period, the city planning commission has the right to check his map and determine wherein such map differs from their plan. If, however, the subdivider and the city planning commission have not reached an agreement at the expiration of thirty days, the subdivider is permitted to sell by metes and bounds description.
>
> Under this bill, the city planning commission is required to prepare and publish a set of definite regulations upon which it will accept subdivision maps. Inasmuch as this set of subdivision regulations must be approved by the city council or the board of supervisors, the subdivider will at all times know the exact rules governing subdivision requirements in the planning commission's office.[107]

S.B. 614, the Map Act, passed the Senate and Assembly unanimously. S.B. 615, the Planning Act, also passed the legislature unanimously, although it went through many amendments, mostly in response to concerns of title insurance companies, and to constitutionality problems related to intergovernmental division of powers between the state and counties and cities.[108] CREA, despite ambivalence about the metes and bounds issue, recognized that the *coordination, design and engineering, and control* functions of urban planning could not be completely separated, and therefore both a map filing act and a master planning act were needed: "These two bills are written in such a way that both should be passed and signed, in that the map filing act loses much of its force without the city planning act and without the city planning act, the map filing act would, in some instances, be ineffectual."[109] CREA wanted the planning commissions to adopt master plans, particularly major street plans, believing that the most important reason for public review of proposed subdivision plats was to assess them in the context of surrounding land uses and future development plans. Since the local planning commission was already responsible for preparing the zoning ordinance, it was the logical agency to review the interrelated pattern of private and public land uses.

The new planning law provided for a procedure under which city, county, or regional planning commissions could draw up major street plans as well as other elements of a master plan. It eliminated the extra-territorial three-mile rule for city subdivision control and replaced it with a requirement that all California counties must have planning commissions, so that either the county or a special regional planning commission would have jurisdiction over all unincorporated areas.[110] It included a provision for regional planning commissions to raise revenue through a small property tax levy. Most importantly, it gave the planning commission the authority to review proposed subdivisions, once it had drawn up a definite area plan and a set of regulations and procedures, and these had been approved by the local governing body.[111] California, drawing on the successful experiment with Los Angeles County planning, became a national leader in county land-use planning after 1929. By the mid-1930s, 34 California counties had planning commissions, zoning laws, and subdivision regulations.

S.B. 614 and S.B. 615 were signed together at a ceremony in Governor C. C. Young's office in Sacramento. One irony of the bill-signing ceremony is that at the final hearing in the governor's council room, as he deliberated whether or not to sign the bills, one of the principal proponents who put both bills "over the top" was Jack Beaumont, CREA vice-president and secretary of Del Monte Properties and the key opponent of the 1927 map bill. The other irony is that Charles Cheney, California's most distinguished city planning consultant and the author of the 1927 Planning Act, "wired from Oklahoma City urging" the governor to sign the bill repealing his proudest legislative achievement.[112]

After the passage of the master planning and subdivision control bills, CREA established a new committee headed by Walter H. Leimert, a prominent subdivider and realtor, to work with public officials, title companies, real estate brokers, and other interested parties to "standardize" local subdivision regulations.[113] At the fifth annual CREA-sponsored conference on city planning held at Santa Barbara in April 1930, a resolution was adopted that the new Map Filing and Planning Acts should not be amended in the legislature until 1933, so that they would be given a four-year period of trial, error, and evaluation.[114] The small group of planning consultants and local government planners readily agreed, as they were in no political position to press further demands and considered themselves fortunate to have passed any legislation at all.[115] This resolution was reaffirmed at the sixth annual CREA planning conference in Sacramento during February 1931.[116]

Real Estate Depression: The Search for Market Control

During the next few years, however, criticism of the sales practices of real estate agents intensified as large numbers of people who had purchased lots in new subdivisions in anticipation of profitable resale began defaulting on their mortgage loans and special tax assessments.[117] In the atmosphere of depression in real estate markets, CREA leaders became increasingly nervous about this rising tide of public criticism, and the California Real Estate Department was being attacked by state legislators as being ineffectual in regulating sales practices through its licensing authority. CREA's Harrison Baker issued an alarming report in August 1931, about the desperate need for "restoration of confidence in California real estate" and cited the example of how the state's building and loan associations had banded together to demand stricter state regulation to restore investor confidence after a major building and loan bankruptcy. However, neither Baker nor the real estate commissioner were willing to do anything other than study the problem.[118]

Baker enlisted W. L. Pollard to help the Subdividers and Homebuilders Division assess the need for new legislation, but by this point the Los Angeles real estate attorney was getting impatient with the reluctance of his realtor-clients to support any serious public action to rectify subdivision problems. Pollard no longer chaired CREA's City Planning Committee, though he represented CREA in a joint effort with the League of California Municipalities, the California Land Title Association, and other groups to agree on amendments to the planning and map acts for 1933. Pollard now openly endorsed making metes and bounds sales illegal, calling the 1929 planning and map filing laws "farcical in the extreme."

Thus we see that, while theoretically we have a Planning and a Map Filing Act, both of which are designed to protect the buying public from the operations of the unscrupulous, as a matter of fact both of these acts are practically worthless and serve no purpose except to create a uniformity of operation for that subdivider or seller of property who desires to obey the law and carry on a uniform program, which uniformity can be and is very readily upset by the nonconformist, who, after all, is the person whom such laws are designed to curb.[119]

What Pollard was pointing out was that public planning and subdivision review procedures, from the point of view of the real estate industry that had the most influential say in shaping the laws and administration, were designed primarily as a service to the more established community builders in order to stabilize their operations and socialize private costs along the lines of *coordination,* and *design and engineering,* rather than being a genuine attempt to directly regulate or *control* private market activity. Other structural means were developed within the private-public institutional framework to eliminate the competition of "fly-by-night" operators. The FHA mortgage insurance program of the 1930s became the primary vehicle for standardization and control, but even before then new methods were evolving. As L. Deming Tilton, the director of planning for Santa Barbara County, reported in 1930:

The sale of lots by metes and bounds is being more definitely curbed every year. Utility companies are making extra heavy charges for bringing service into such subdivisions; banks and money lending institutions are refusing to recommend loans on lots in such subdivisions, and title insurance companies and surveyors make extra charges for the increased work of running a title in such subdivisions. The lot purchaser finds it difficult to get streets paved for the delivery of material for his new home and suffers many annoyances and mental trials not encountered by the owner of a lot shown upon a recorded plat. These difficulties and sources of extra expense are being brought to the attention of the public through reports and newspaper articles prepared by planning agencies.[120]

As the deepening crisis in the world economy strained the nerves of California's shrinking body of solvent real estate entrepreneurs, divisions within the ranks of CREA again emerged over the subdivision regulation issue: large vs. small, northern California vs. southern California, subdividers vs. brokers, title companies and lenders vs. brokers and subdividers, community builders vs. curbstoners. W. L. Pollard was brought back to chair CREA's Planning and Zoning Committee in 1932 under the new regime of CREA President Peter Hanson, one of America's leading professional real estate appraisers.[121] In October 1932, Herbert Breed, still CREA's general counsel, announced that two positions regarding subdivision control were emerging for the 1933 legislative session, W. L. Pollard's and the real estate commissioner's.[122] Pollard, in conjunction with the League of California Municipalities, the California Land Title Association, the Los Angeles Chamber of Commerce, and representatives from city and county planning commissions, was drafting a revised map act that would outlaw metes and bounds sales as well as tightening other loopholes in the 1929 act.[123] The real estate commissioner, on the other hand, had finally reacted to the severe criticism of his department by proposing that the state Real Estate Department, under the license act, be given the power to regulate urban subdivisions.[124]

W. L. Pollard and his supporters, including many CREA members, opposed Real Estate Department regulation of subdivisions because they felt that regulation should be handled by local planning commissions, arguing that "a local body could more adequately and promptly perform this service than the State Division, and at the same or less cost."[125] Some real estate industry groups such as the title companies seemed to favor both approaches, as did a number of the ambivalent larger brokers within CREA. Many of the subdividers, wanting coordinated public planning services but no control, favored neither proposal. The city and county public officials wanted strengthened planning commission authority, although they were willing to support more state supervision as well. The situation on this issue was so divided and chaotic that Herbert Breed threw up his hands in frustration:

> For several sessions of the legislature I have been disappointed in the lack of agreement, not only among Association members, but among those who have sat together endeavoring to agree on strengthening 20a [state Real Estate Department supervision of subdivision financing, sales, and improvement practices]. The Association directors can hardly support legislation in the name of the Association approved by but a bare majority of directors or members. For its own sake, the Association should be substantially unanimous when publicly sponsoring legislation.[126]

Perhaps one indication of this split within CREA's ranks is that *California Real Estate* failed to report on the seventh annual CREA city planning conference organized by W. L. Pollard in June 1932.[127] But Pollard moved forward under at least the semiofficial blessing of one faction within CREA, and in conjunction with the other above-mentioned groups, he drafted a bill that was introduced into the 1933 California Legislature as S.B. 583. The bill made a number of changes to strengthen the 1929 Map Act, including bringing nearly all land subdividing under the legal definition of regulatory coverage. The key provision was the prohibition against metes and bounds subdivision lot sales.[128]

At the same time, S.B. 20 was introduced, which amended the Real Estate Act to require all subdividers to submit certain basic information and pay a fee to the Real Estate Department, which then would have the authority to conduct investigations if it so chose. If the subdivision appeared unsound or the sales campaign was based on fraudulent claims, the commissioner would have the power to issue a cease-and-desist order and block any further sales.[129]

CREA debated both of these measures for several months. In January the CREA magazine revealed that while Harrison Baker opposed both bills, "a referendum among state directors and among unaffiliated brokers showed a heavy trend for" S.B. 20.[130] At the CREA Board of Directors meeting on February 10, however, the Board voted to oppose S.B. 20, and to take no position on S.B. 583.[131] One month later, perhaps out of fear that S.B. 583 would gain too much support in the absence of any alternative, CREA's Board of Directors reversed themselves on March 25 and voted unanimously to endorse S.B. 20. They quickly followed this decision by holding "a meeting of leading Realtors in Los Angeles," who concurred in their endorsement.[132] Shortly thereafter the State Senate passed S.B. 20 by unanimous vote, and the Assembly did likewise, and the governor signed the measure into law.[133]

S.B. 583, the map bill drafted by W. L. Pollard, also passed both houses of the state legislature, though not unanimously.[134] CREA never officially took a position on the measure, because, while some of the main real estate boards in northern California such as San Francisco, Oakland, and San Jose supported the measure, there was "equally strong opposition" from key southern California boards such as the Los Angeles, Pasadena, and San Diego Realty Boards.[135] Since Los Angeles and

San Diego County were still the two fastest growing counties in the state and the Los Angeles Realty Board was the largest and most powerful in the U.S., their opposition carried more weight within CREA, and with the real estate commissioner and the governor.[136]

CREA directors who had supported S.B. 20 as the "lesser evil" to S.B. 583 were rewarded when state Real Estate Commissioner Joseph Smith asked Governor James Rolph to veto S.B. 583, arguing that "the new subdivision regulations in the real estate act will solve the problem." Governor Rolph agreed, vetoing W. L. Pollard's new Planning and Map Act.[137] The League of California Municipalities, bitterly disappointed over the governor's action, stated with confidence in the July issue of its magazine that the governor's veto would be overridden by the California Legislature during the July special session.[138] The League was wrong. Metes and bounds subdividing would live on for another four years, to be finally outlawed in 1937. Real Estate Department control over subdivision sales, the issue that had caused two real estate commissioners, Edwin Keiser and J. R. Gabbert, to lose their jobs in the mid-1920s, had now become CREA's salvation in the face of what they perceived to be a more drastic alternative, local planning commission subdivision control.[139]

Conclusion

Four years later Governor Frank Merriam, a Long Beach realtor and long-time leader of CREA, signed new California Planning Act and Map Act amendments. The 1937 laws eliminated metes and bounds subdividing, and added administrative strength to existing city and county master planning and to Real Estate Department enforcement of map filing and subdivision sales regulations.[140] Two years earlier the governor had signed legislation strengthening the Real Estate License Law and urban subdivision regulation. Together the three sets of laws were considered to be national models of *coordination* and *control*.[141] These subdivision laws also worked in cooperation with developer-imposed private deed restrictions enforced by civil courts. In fact, deed restrictions were strongly endorsed and encouraged by local planning commissions and by the Federal Housing Administration (FHA).[142] The FHA, which was insuring twice as many home mortgages in California than in any other state, had effectively imposed its own uniform subdivision *design and engineering* standards through its Land Planning Division. Adding it all together, a complicated four-way system of subdivision planning and co⁻trol had been worked out since the 1920s—(1) planning commissions, (2) Real Estate Department, (3) deed restrictions, (4) FHA—to the apparent satisfaction of most mortgage lenders, title companies, developers, public officials, and homebuyers.[143]

Beginning in 1939 southern California community builders began to develop large-scale residential subdivisions for middle-income workers clustering around the fast-growing aircraft industry. The rapid industrialization of Los Angeles provided the consumer market for a real estate boom in moderate-cost suburban housing tract development and sales. Hundreds of miles of wide, straight boulevards dedicated by private developers to public use, planned separation of private land uses, creation of adequate community facilities, the orderly extension of public utilities and improvements, miles of public beaches and ease of beach access, affordability of private housing and of public taxes—all these and other accomplishments of the 1940s, 50s, and 60s were the direct outgrowth of the multitiered planning system partially spawned and shaped by the activities, both in support and in opposition, of California's emerging residential real estate manufacturers and merchandisers—the community builders.

CHAPTER SIX

COMMUNITY BUILDERS
AND THE
FEDERAL HOUSING
ADMINISTRATION

Introduction

IN THE EARLY 1930s the community builders surveyed the land development and housebuilding industries and found them to be in a dis-
mal state. Land contracts, first and second mortgages, and real estate
bonds were all in widespread default, and little money was available from
lenders or investors for realty transactions. Potential customers were extremely wary of making new purchases with the collapse of the 1920s
speculative boom still so recent and readily apparent in falling property
values. The high level of tax delinquency, mortgage foreclosure, "frozen"
property, vacancies, wasted public and private infrastructure and utilities,
and the generally poor quality of much of the recent development all
pointed toward a reexamination of the existing subdivision and building
process. Never had community builders been more convinced of the need
for some new forms of planning and control.

At the same time, the earlier cooperation between the National Association of Real Estate Boards and the American City Planning Insti-
tute/National Conference on City Planning, manifested on the Advisory
Committee on City Planning and Zoning of the U.S. Department of
Commerce and in the NAREB-ACPI *Joint Statement on Subdivision Control,* had proven unsatisfactory to the community builders in the matter

of state and local planning legislation and implementation. Large residential subdividers, particularly in the big cities, found that zoning laws were administered in so promotional and unstable a fashion as to seriously undermine the degree of dependable protection that could be provided to their subdivisions and the surrounding neighborhoods. In addition, subdivision regulations were either nonexistent or very poorly enforced in most urbanizing areas. The overwhelming majority of metropolitan jurisdictions lacked long-range plans for major streets, parks, and other public investments, with virtually no land planning coordination between municipalities, unincorporated communities, and county governments. Where political movements were actively advocating the strengthening of land-use regulations, real estate boards generally feared such efforts, believing that local politicians and planning commissions could not be sufficiently trusted to exercise power in ways that would clearly benefit realty business interests.[1]

Accordingly, community builders, mortgage lenders, property and title insurers, brokers, and their allies searched for an appropriate vehicle to enforce strict land planning standards, curb speculative subdividing, and stabilize and protect long-term values for new residential developments. The mechanism they seized upon was the organization of the U.S. Federal Housing Administration (FHA) in 1934. Through the powerful inducement of mortgage insurance, FHA's Land Planning Division was able to transform residential development practices as well as play a key role in shaping and popularizing local land-use regulations.

FHA's underwriting standards and land planning policies were highly favorable to the community builders, enabling them to expand the scope of their businesses and capture a bigger market share by enhancing the financial feasibility and sales appeal of new, large-scale residential subdivision developments of single-family detached houses. FHA also helped put the 1920s-style "curbstone" subdividers and "jerry-builders" out of business, by imposing publicly advertised development standards and by denying mortgage insurance on properties located in subdivisions that failed to meet these standards.

This new federal agency, run to a large extent both by and for bankers, builders, and brokers, exercised great political power in pressuring local planners and government officials to conform to its requirements. By 1940, FHA had fully established the land planning and development process and pattern that a decade later captured media attention as "post-war suburbanization."

Searching for a Method

In early 1932 the President's Conference on Home Building and Home Ownership published the first of its 11 volumes of reports by committees of the conference. Volume 1, entitled *Planning for Residential Districts*, contained the reports of four committees: City Planning and Zoning, Subdivision Layout, Utilities for Houses, and Landscape Planning and Planting. It also contained two special reports—one on lot sizes, utilities and street costs, and the other on housing in unincorporated areas. The basic outlook of this remarkable document consisted of two primary elements: (1) that the future prospects for mass homeownership depended on large-scale, well-planned private development; and (2) that such private residential development could only succeed with the aid of large-scale public land development, coordination, and regulation.[2]

Of the various committees, one committee held special importance in considering the future prospects of land planning for community builders. The Committee on Subdivision Layout was heavily dominated by the Home Builders and Subdividers Division of the National Association of Real Estate Boards (NAREB). Of the 16 committee members, seven were community builders from NAREB, including two past NAREB presidents, the current NAREB president, and two future NAREB presidents. The committee was chaired by city planning consultant Harland Bartholomew, who at the time was NAREB's director of research in city planning, and it included five other planners, four of whom had long and close consulting relationships with NAREB subdividers.[3]

The principle concern of the Committee on Subdivision Layout was to eliminate curbstoner operations from the subdivision field, and to re-place speculative lot selling with stable, long-term "neighborhood unit" single-family housing development for the middle-income homebuyer. Much of the discussion in the committee report centered on principles of good subdivision design and engineering for greater attractiveness, market appeal, production efficiency, cost savings, and consumer safety. Other sections of the report focused on the need for master city plans to provide essential infrastructure and services and to coordinate individual private land and building developments with the overall urban pattern. Still other sections emphasized the need for public and private restrictions to rationalize land use and protect real property investment values from future instability. Finally, the report recommended procedures whereby local and regional planning commissions could control future subdividing to enforce minimum standards and curb wasteful, speculative, and destabilizing practices.[4]

Despite these recommendations, the NAREB leaders' lack of confidence in local planning commissions and fear of too much government control is clearly evident in this report. Community builders, even as they were supporting local and regional subdivision control, were also searching for an alternative and more acceptable means of achieving their planning goals for the land development industry:

> Subdivision control by public agencies has two purposes: to inform the subdivider of the city's requirements, and to check bad subdivision practices. The degree of control is increasing, and the extent to which it will go depends almost entirely upon the attitudes and actions of the subdividers. . . . The problem of excessive land subdivision is of paramount importance in the whole project of stimulating home building and home ownership. An unlimited subdivision boom absorbs in worthless lots the savings of thousands of prospective home owners, shatters their confidence and hope, and thereby, in the long run, greatly damages the home building movement and the subdivision business itself. Only the subdividers, by adjusting the amount and character of subdivisions to the real need, can obviate the necessity for public action to check this calamity.[5]

> • • •

> It is evident that a proper balance must be struck between, on the one hand, an unyielding detailed plan, drawn up on general principles for the general good but unnecessarily restraining private initiative and, on the other hand, a plan made flexible to allow the exercise of private initiative to such a point that broad general conceptions for the public good are unduly hampered in their accomplishment.[6]

The "subdividers," in this case the leading community builders in NAREB, never found a way to "obviate the necessity for public action." However, beginning in 1934 they discovered a method of striking what they considered to be "a proper balance" between "private initiative" and "the general good." The fulcrum of this balanced system of public-private cooperation and control was the newly created Federal Housing Administration .

FHA Is the Solution

The FHA was created in 1934 by Congressional passage of the landmark National Housing Act. The main purpose of the FHA was "to bring the home financing system of the country out of a chaotic situation."[7] Home mortgage lending by private financial institutions had slowed to a standstill by the early 1930s, with only the 1933 federal Home Owners' Loan Corporation (HOLC) providing liquidity for banks, insurance companies, and other holders of billions of dollars worth of delinquent home mortgages. New private lending, and consequently new housing starts, were relatively moribund. FHA's mutual mortgage insurance plan, by virtually eliminating the risk for lenders, acted as a powerful stimulus for reviving mortgage finance, sales of existing properties, and new construction. Through FHA's encouragement of the long-term, low interest, low down payment, self-amortizing first mortgage, prospective homebuyers were able to borrow the necessary funds to purchase a house, and repay the loan with regular and affordable monthly payments.

FHA was charged with maintaining the "economic soundness" of its mutual mortgage insurance system.[8] To protect against excessive losses, the Administration created an elaborate standardized appraisal procedure in which the borrower's income and employment prospects, the physical condition of the property, the characteristics of the neighborhood and its location in the metropolis, urban planning and land-use controls, deed restrictions, and market demand all entered into the "risk-rating" evaluation. Thus in the name of sound business practice, FHA was able to exercise an extraordinary degree of control over real estate development patterns.

The community builders who led NAREB enthusiastically welcomed FHA's powerful interventionist role. Their fear of local planning commissions did not translate into a similar anxiety over the potential intrusion of FHA into land planning. Basically there were two reasons for their favorable attitude: first, because FHA's financing policies promised to significantly widen the currently weak market for property develop-

ment and sales; and second, because FHA was largely run by representatives of the real estate and banking industries. The National Housing
Act was initiated and passed with the vigorous support of many of the
key trade associations in real estate finance, insurance, brokerage, construction, and materials and equipment manufacturing and distribution.
Houston community builder and NAREB President Hugh Potter, for
example, was a key lobbyist for the 1934 legislation.[9]

FHA's staff was recruited almost entirely from the private sector. Many
were corporate executives from a variety of different fields, but real estate
and financial backgrounds predominated. For example, Ayers DuBois,
who had been a state director of the California Real Estate Association,
was an assistant director of FHA's Underwriting Division. Fred Marlow,
a well-known Los Angeles subdivider, headed FHA's southern California
district office, which led the nation in insuring home mortgages. National figures associated with NAREB, such as real estate economist Ernest Fisher and appraiser Frederick Babcock, directed FHA operations in
economics and in underwriting.[10]

The extensive FHA *Underwriting Manual* lay at the heart of its entire
system of economic standardization. In order to justify the insuring of
80 percent loans for 20 years (soon increased to 90 percent for 25 years)
when the previous norm by commercial banks was 50 percent loans for
three years, FHA placed its faith on its detailed system of appraisal. The
complicated risk-rating procedures were designed to weed out loan re-
quests on properties that were either overinflated in value, or bad risks,
or both. Consequently in order to obtain FHA insurance, lenders, borrowers, subdividers, and builders were required to submit to the collective judgment of the Underwriting Division, who together with the
Technical Division determined minimum required property and neighborhood standards.[11]

Taking their cue from the recommendations of the 1931 Home Ownership conference, FHA's administrators made a commitment to promote moderate-cost housing production through large-scale building operations. FHA therefore made a special effort to enhance the position of
large-scale subdividers and single-family housing developers in the residential marketplace: "There exists, therefore, a natural union between the
operative builder and the Administration in bringing about improvement
in housing standards and conditions."[12] FHA had adopted the full agenda

of the community builders and was determined to make this still embryonic institutional form the preeminent approach to housing production.

> With these objectives in mind the Administration seeks to encourage that type of operative builder who looks upon the production of homes as a manufacturing and merchandising process of high social significance and who, preferably, assumes responsibility for the product from the plotting and development of the land to the disposal of the completed dwelling units.[13]

In order to fulfill this mandate, FHA promulgated a regulation called the "conditional commitment," which dramatically expanded the ability of community builders to successfully finance the production and sales of a large subdivision of houses and lots. Essentially, if the plans for land and housing development met FHA's underwriting standards, a conditional commitment could be made to an approved lender that FHA would insure all the home mortgages so long as the eventual borrowers were properly qualified. Armed with this commitment, a developer could obtain complete bank financing for land development and housing construction, and could be reasonably certain of being able to easily and profitably sell all of the completed product. The size of these commitments in dollars and in the number of individual mortgages was unlimited: Park Forest, Illinois, the famous suburb developed by American Community Builders, received FHA commitments to insure mortgages on 8,000 houses.[14] As an added incentive, since the FHA conditional commitments were based on the projected appraised value of the completed houses and lots, community builders who economized on construction costs through efficient large-scale operations could in some cases borrow more money from a bank or insurance company than it actually cost to acquire and develop the subdivision. The business advantages of this arrangement for large developers were quite intentional on FHA's part.[15]

FHA mortgage insurance was available to approved lenders for any operative builder who constructed one or more dwellings for rent or sale to others. The Administration's clear preference, however, was to use conditional commitments specifically to encourage large-scale producers of complete new residential subdivisions, or "neighborhood units." While

FHA might therefore insure separate blocks of housing produced by different operative builders within the same subdivision, the focus was nevertheless on privately controlled and coordinated development of whole residential communities of predominantly single-family housing on the urban periphery, based on a series of model design standards that FHA field staff adhered to with messianic fervor.

Accomplishing the Planning Goals

Officially the FHA did not assist in financing subdivision development. The mutual mortgage insurance applied only to individual properties within subdivisions. However, because FHA could refuse to insure mortgages on properties due to their location in neighborhoods that were too poorly planned or unprotected and therefore too "high-risk," it definitely behooved most reputable subdividers to conform to FHA standards. This put FHA officials in the enviable position, far more than any regulatory land planning agency, of being able to tell subdividers how to develop their land. Thus one of the three principal goals of the community builders, to find a method of shaping and standardizing the *design and engineering* features of new subdivisions, was achieved through the intervention of FHA.[16]

Under the leadership of Miles Colean, director of the Technical Division, FHA promulgated minimum requirements for the design and engineering of subdivisions, including provisions for street and lot layout and installation of necessary improvements. Not only did FHA establish minimum standards, but it also offered a free service to all subdividers: at the request of an approved lender, a subdivider could submit preliminary development plans to FHA, whose land planning consultants would evaluate the proposal and suggest methods of replanning in order to successfully meet FHA guidelines. The land planning consultants, in addition to their extensive field work with prospective subdividers, also held numerous conferences with subdivision developers, operative builders, and mortgage lenders to spread the gospel of good neighborhood design.[17]

By 1938 FHA's Land Planning unit had grown large enough to become a separate Division, headed by Seward Mott. Under Colean and

Mott's direction, FHA published four important sets of written guidelines and graphic suggestions: *Subdivision Development* (1935), *Planning Neighborhoods for Small Houses* (1936), *Planning Profitable Neighborhoods* (1938), and *Successful Subdivisions* (1940). The entire development pattern of modern American suburbia may be quickly and easily understood by reading these four remarkable documents.[18]

Perhaps even more revolutionary, FHA finally introduced the element of *control* of market competition that the community builders had been yearning for since their 1920s battles with the "curbstone" subdividers. FHA made a firm commitment to "postponing or abandoning the building up of subdivisions which are premature or plainly superfluous."[19] Unlike the local planning commission, which could only regulate the physical features of a subdivision, FHA introduced a new concept to be utilized in land-use regulation—market demand: "A subdivision might conform to the most rigid standards of location, design, and organization and yet present a critical degree of mortgage risk because of the absence of an effective demand for new property in the community."[20] Accordingly, the urban land economics skills of Ernest Fisher, Frederick Babcock, Homer Hoyt, Richard Ratcliff, Arthur Weimer and others were put to work devising analytical tests to determine how to limit the supply of new subdividing and maintain some balance with market demand. This research became an important part of the guidelines for real estate appraisal in the *Underwriting Manual,* and the land planning consultants emphasized market relationships in all their work with private developers: "One of the services rendered by the Land Planning Division is to discourage premature or unneeded subdivisions by pointing out the probable lack of a market."[21]

FHA's land planners also addressed the third major planning goal of community builders—the public *coordination* of private subdivision development. Land-use restrictions, modern planning and improvements, transportation accessibility, and availability of utilities, schools, and public services were all important criteria for risk-rating in FHA's *Underwriting Manual.* For new or relatively undeveloped subdivisions, FHA required the following:

> (4) Wherever the undeveloped subdivision, or any part of it, falls within the jurisdiction of a city, county, or regional plan or of subdivision regu-

lations promulgated thereunder by any duly authorized public agency, the design and development shall comply with such plans and regulations.

(5) Zoning and deed restrictions, if present, shall be appropriate to the type of anticipated development, with particular reference to permitted uses of lots, restrictions on types of buildings, and building lines. In general, undeveloped subdivisions should be protected by municipal zoning or by effective deed restrictions, or preferably both, before properties can be considered to be eligible for insured mortgages.[22]

FHA considered zoning restrictions to be an essential prerequisite for insuring a home mortgage on any property, whether in a new subdivision or a fully developed neighborhood. Their goal was to use zoning to *protect* whole neighborhoods of middle-income single-family houses, rather than the "overzoning" that was commonly used in the 1920s to *promote* property speculation and higher density apartment building and commercial development. For community builders such as the leaders of the Los Angeles Realty Board, FHA provided the necessary political leverage to force recalcitrant public officials to rezone areas of cities that were "overzoned," to make zoning more comprehensive (including restrictions on use, height, and bulk), and to eliminate "spot zoning" and variance rackets. For example, with FHA's prodding, the Oakland (California) City Council finally passed a comprehensive zoning ordinance in 1935, after 15 years of conflict between the prozoning Oakland Realty Board and the antizoning mayor. Oakland's City Planning Commission publicly acknowledged that the basic purpose of the new zoning law was to make property loans in the city eligible for FHA mortgage insurance.[23] Seward Mott, FHA Land Planning Director, emphasized the importance of zoning at a NAREB conference in 1938:

> We found in small towns we were unable to insure loans because there was no zoning protection. We are asked how this situation can be remedied. The best advice we can give these communities is that they organize and establish their own commission and thus gain proper control over the growth of the town, and get subdivision regulations. We will be glad to come down and tell you how to go about organizing a City Planning Commission, and what are the various methods of protecting residential areas that we feel should be covered in a zoning ordinance.[24]

In relatively new subdivisions, which were the primary beneficiaries of FHA mortgage insurance, zoning was considered to be vital as a protection of the border areas, to be supplemented inside the newly subdivided neighborhood by private deed restrictions. FHA recommended that restrictive covenants cover a wide range of physical planning issues that zoning laws did not address, including placement of the house on the lot, property maintenance, and architectural design.[25] In most cases, FHA also encouraged covenants to maintain racial exclusion.[26] Seward Mott outlined the relationship of zoning and deed restrictions in a question-and-answer session at the NAREB conference:

Q: I would like to ask you how you give effect to the zoning or restrictions in your risk rating. How far do you go in examining the property for proper restriction?

MOTT: We give a very careful inspection. It is one of the most heavily weighted factors in locating rating.

Q: What do you examine?

MOTT: We examine the effectiveness of the zoning ordinance. For instance, just because there is a zoning ordinance does not necessarily mean that it gives full protection. It may be subject to political pressure. There may be a Board of Appeal that is authorized to change the ordinance. We would then have to depend more on the restrictions than on zoning. Each situation is to be investigated separately.[27]

FHA's Land Planning Division played a critical role in organizing and restructuring local land-use planning in the United States. In 1938 FHA was authorized by Congress to insure mortgages for up to 90 percent of value, amortized for 25 years at a maximum 4½ percent interest plus ½ percent mortgage insurance premium. With the improvement of the economy in 1939, demand from lenders and borrowers for FHA mortgage insurance greatly increased.[28] FHA assumed the vital national role of promoting local planning as a prerequisite to making loan insurance available. In 1939 the Land Planning Division held 86 conferences with local officials "in regard to the preparation of city plans and zoning ordinances."[29] By 1940 the number of such conferences had increased to 221.[30]

The following year a well-known urban planner, Earle Draper, was appointed assistant administrator of FHA, and the Land Planning Division initiated several key projects to guide local planning. One such project was a pilot program to establish and coordinate land-use planning

among several growing towns in a small metropolitan area.[31] Together
with similar efforts by the National Resources Planning Board, the work
of FHA's Land Planning Division clearly served as the basis for the au-
thorization of federal assistance to local planning under Section 701 of
the 1954 National Housing Act.[32] James S. Taylor, an FHA official who
had searched for a method of promoting urban planning in his earlier
role as chief of the U.S. Department of Commerce's Division of Building
and Housing in the 1920s, was probably pleased that FHA, which succeeded where President Hoover had failed, nevertheless remained true to
Hoover's stated policy preference for voluntary public-private cooperation.

The "Carrot" Is Mightier Than the "Stick"

The genius of the FHA system and its popularity with lenders, borrowers, brokers, builders, and subdivision developers is that mortgage
insurance fit the American image of voluntarism. Unlike direct government police power regulations, FHA always appeared to be noncoercive
to the private sector. FHA was generally perceived as engaging in a simple business proposition—to insure only low-risk mortgages with a sound
economic future. The extensive requirements in the *Underwriting Manual,* including the property standards and neighborhood standards, were
considered by the general public to be wise businesslike protections, rather
than coercive intrusions. Despite the fact that FHA was a government
agency, its operations were considered to be more in the nature of private marketplace activity. Property owners and real estate entrepreneurs
viewed FHA rules and regulations as similar to deed restrictions—private
contracts which were freely entered into by willing parties—rather than
as similar to zoning laws, which were sometimes seen as infringing on
constitutional liberties.

FHA officials were always very careful to cultivate and preserve the
image of voluntarism. For example, consider the following statement from
FHA's 1935 booklet prescribing standards for subdivision development:

> The Administration does not propose to regulate subdividing through-
> out the country, nor to set up stereotype patterns of land development. It

does, however, insist upon the observance of rational principles of development in those areas in which insured mortgages are desired.[33]

Whenever an FHA land planning consultant would replan a subdivision for a prospective developer, printed on the new design would be an FHA disclaimer stating that "This study is simply a suggestion to assist the developer in planning his property." The developer was urged to hire a "competent subdivision designer," and was informed by FHA officials that following the land planning consultant's "suggestions" was not officially required, nor would it guarantee the issuance of a conditional commitment for mortgage insurance. The game of noncoercion was played to the hilt.[34]

Beneath the surface, of course, FHA officials and their clients in the real estate finance and development business were quite well aware of the tremendous power of the "carrot" of mortgage insurance to shape the American housing industry, particularly during the Great Depression when the banking and real estate sectors were in almost total collapse. FHA Administrator James Moffett clearly recognized this power during a confidential meeting of his newly formed Housing Advisory Council in January of 1935:

> Make it conditional that these mortgages must be insured under the Housing Act, and through that we could control over-building in sections, which would undermine values, or through political pull, building in isolated spots, where it was not a good investment. You could also control the population trend, the neighborhood standard, and material and everything else through the President.[35]

The underlying degree of FHA control of residential development was underscored by an example cited in the *Annual Report* for 1937:

> In the case of one subdivision in a large city in the Middle West, examination by the Federal Housing Administration office revealed that the proposed homes were deficient in plans and in quality of construction. All plans for it were rejected. The mortgagee (lender) then discussed the proposed development again with the subdivider. Following the conference, a competent architect was employed to design new plans with adequate specifications. The result was satisfactory Federal Housing Administration commitments and prompt sale of all the homes.[36]

The president and his FHA administrator were able to exert tremendous authority in the housing field through the simple expedient of making an offer that was difficult to refuse. For lenders concerned about risk, the insurance feature was most welcome. Later as the system became more established, and particularly after the creation of a secondary market (FNMA) in 1937, the liquidity of FHA-insured mortgages became an added advantage for lenders. For borrowers, the longer terms, lower down payments, and lower interest rates were an unbeatable attraction. For brokers and builders, stimulating the flow of mortgage money was the key incentive. Finally, for operative builders and subdivision developers, FHA's conditional commitment was a godsend. Within a few short years of the program, FHA's economic power, and thus its ability to affect urban land planning, grew rapidly:

> The Administration's efforts in this direction, especially in insisting on competent lay-out and reasonable neighborhood protection for new subdivisions, have been more effective than ever before, because of the large increase in the number of new homes financed with insured mortgages.[37]

When FHA was created in 1934, no state banking laws permitted the FHA program, so it took approximately a year before most state legislatures had made the necessary changes. However, even in 1935 FHA insured nearly $100 million in new mortgages, while private noninsured mortgage lending fell by nearly one billion dollars from its low 1934 level.[38] By 1938 FHA was insuring the mortgages on nearly one-third of all new dwelling units started in the U.S. during that year, and the figure remained at slightly over one-third for each succeeding year until 1942, when FHA began to totally dominate private war housing production (nearly 80 percent of all private housing starts in 1943). After the war these percentages dropped, but FHA was at one-third again in 1950.[39]

Creating the Modern Residential Subdivision

Although FHA was authorized to insure rental housing and had a division headed by Miles Colean to promote large-scale rental construction in big cities, the Administration's overall community building bias toward suburban-style subdivisions was quite pronounced. In 1940, for example, of the total new dwelling units financed by FHA mortgage insurance, less than two percent were for rental housing. All the rest were one-to-four family homes, mostly single-family. Rental housing also represented less than two percent of the dollar value of all mortgages insured by FHA in 1940, and less than one percent of the total number of insured mortgages. In addition, most of the rental housing mortgages that were insured were for new garden-type apartments in suburban subdivisions.[40]

The 1940 pattern was typical of the general FHA performance during this entire period. California was FHA's leading state with more than twice the volume of insured mortgages than any other state: 83 percent of these mortgages were on newly constructed single-family houses.[41] FHA proudly reported for 1940 that:

> The steadily increasing reliance of the home building industry upon the neighborhood-planning principles fostered by the Administration since the start of the FHA program was reflected during 1940 by the fact that in some cities approximately 70 percent of the new homes financed under the FHA plan were located in new subdivisions planned and developed from the beginning in cooperation with the FHA.[42]

The creation of the modern residential subdivision was further underscored by FHA's report that of the 2,680 subdivisions analyzed by the Land Planning Division in 1940, approximately 70 percent were new subdivisions, a 30 percent increase from 1939. Rather than just trying to replan or accommodate the sparsely developed subdivisions left from the boom of the 1920s, FHA was now making its mark on a completely new framework for land development. Reinforcing the Administration's own bias, FHA reported that an incredible 98 percent of the 2,680 subdivisions were restricted solely to single-family detached houses. Noting an important trend toward the development of subdivisions of smaller, moderate-cost homes for middle-income purchasers, FHA stated that 36 percent of the 2,680 subdivisions were selling houses costing under $4,000. The study also revealed that "the trend toward more generous home sites is continuing."[43] Most importantly, FHA reviewed the successful transformation in the residential development industry that the Land Planning Division and mortgage insurance had helped foster: "more and more real estate developers are becoming home builders rather than distributors of speculative and unneeded lots."[44]

FHA's program of conditional commitments to promote large-scale subdividing and homebuilding was also having a considerable impact by the late 1930s. A U.S. Department of Labor survey of 72 cities in 1938 concluded that large-scale operative builders dominated construction of "medium-cost" single-family houses. While less than two percent of the nearly 14,000 builders took out permits to build more than 25 single-family houses in a particular city during 1938, these larger builders accounted for 30 percent of the total permits. The study stated that "a firm erecting 15 or more houses a year can buy more cheaply and operate more efficiently in many respects than an individual building a single house."[45]

The Department of Labor revealed some striking statistics about community builders—those firms who built more than 100 houses a year in a single city. While only 33 of the nearly 14,000 builders fit this category, these 33 accounted for 11 percent of the total number of houses. All of these 33 operated in cities with more than 500,000 in population, and nearly all of the houses produced by these builders were valued at between $2,500 and $7,500, the "middle-priced" range. In cities such as New York, Philadelphia, Baltimore, and San Francisco, the handful of community builders accounted for one-quarter or more of the total number of new houses. In Los Angeles, less than one percent of the builders took out permits for nearly 15 percent of the houses.[46]

Conclusion

FHA had cast the die. All of the elements that constituted what many have referred to as "postwar suburbanization" were firmly in place by prewar 1940. The real estate industry, particularly in the sectors of finance and development, had undergone a remarkable transformation. While the first Levittown was not built until after World War II, the Levitt family firm was already engaging in large-scale FHA-financed subdivision and building operations by the early 1940s.[47]

Most of the goals that J. C. Nichols outlined in 1916, for public and private land-use planning and regulation to aid the residential development industry, were basically achieved by 1940. The Urban Land Institute (ULI) formed the Community Builders' Council four years later, and the National Association of Home Builders (NAHB) was just on the brink of organizing its 10,000 members as a separate trade association, finally parting ways in 1942 with its parent organization, NAREB.[48] The American Institute of Planners had many members in high positions or working as consultants with FHA, with the private developers who worked with FHA, and with the local planning agencies who worked with the private developers.[49]

NAREB's community builders of the 1920s and early 1930s, who had feared the potential power of local planning commissions even as they lobbied in support of land-use regulations, found the perfect vehicle for subdivision and real estate market *control* in 1934 through the creation of a highly supportive federal real estate agency, the FHA, with its "noncoercive" methods of enforcing subdivision standards and restrictions. Landscape architect S. Herbert Hare, who designed the Country Club District in Kansas City for J. C. Nichols, summarized in 1938 the effectiveness of FHA's approach to guiding subdivision development and urban land-use:

> While this method of control is indirect, it has probably been more effective in many cases than the strictest regulations of local governmental units because it has established an advantage or a disadvantage in relation to other properties for conformance or nonconformance with the requirements, and at the same time has had no element of compulsion. . . . The greatest value of the Federal Housing Administration regulations has been in raising the standards of design in districts for less expensive houses.[50]

FHA's minimum property and neighborhood standards were subject to criticism, particularly as the general quality of urban development increased. Critics such as Charles Abrams charged in *The Future of Housing* that FHA was generally too lenient with builders and subdividers. Yet even Abrams acknowledged the impact of FHA: "A larger measure of control over building operations than heretofore existed is a by-product of the FHA scheme."[51] Whether stricter requirements could have or should have been imposed as Abrams advocated was a controversial

CONCLUSION

MODERNIZING
THE REAL ESTATE INDUSTRY

A SOPHISTICATED WEB OF institutional changes brought about a dramatic transformation in the decades after 1940: the suburbanization of America. The transition from subdivider of raw lots to land developer to home builder to community builder was facilitated by the 1930s federal intervention that spawned a virtual revolution in housing finance. Another important though less well-known revolution was in urban planning: private site planning, public land planning, and public-private land-use regulation. Zoning laws, subdivision regulations, deed restrictions, master highway and park plans, set-back lines, official maps, and an array of other tools became an essential component of the residential development process that was rapidly occurring at the periphery of America's central cities.[1]

In reviewing this revolutionary change, several points need emphasizing. The first point is simple but often overlooked: the creation of the modern residential subdivision was a remarkable accomplishment. In 1915, when NAREB's City Planning Committee and the professional planners from the NCCP collaborated on their landmark study of "The Best Methods of Land Subdivision,"[2] it was by no means obvious that four decades later private developers would be producing affordable houses in attractive, well-planned neighborhoods for nearly two-thirds of the American population. Such a result was achieved through a carefully interwoven network of private and public institutional innovations. The dream that skilled workers could own and live in "a decent home and a suitable living environment" was realized through intentional cooperative effort.[3] The vision of working toward such a goal was nicely expressed by Miles Colean during the inaugural meeting of FHA's Housing Advisory Council Planning Committee in January 1935:

> The function of government is to make it possible for private enterprise, both from a capital and construction point of view, to produce the best results. I think we have an instrument here that if followed through to its ultimate end, can pretty well do that. I don't think we have accomplished it at the moment, but I think the possibilities are there.[4]

The key point to emphasize is that "the possibilities" in historical action do not simply refer to a passive determinism based on technological innovations and macroeconomic cycles. Technological and institutional changes, government and industry policies, were consciously created and shaped with the purpose of achieving the goal of community building. Real estate developers and urban planners cooperated in designing new approaches to private and public land planning to facilitate this new pattern of urbanization. Many other actors, from bankers to bricklayers to building inspectors to block clubs, also played important roles in fostering debate and taking actions to produce a vision of the future and turn the vision into reality. In the process of the ongoing debates a great deal of conflict emerged. Such conflict was an essential element of the decision-making structures. The existence of conflict should not be used to mask the underlying cooperation that was a prerequisite for the orderly and complete development of modern residential subdivisions.

A related point is that a great deal of the debate centered around designing new forms of organization. The main internal economic problem in the residential real estate sector was one of industrial organization—the extreme fragmentation among the numerous private actors in the development process. What the rise of the community builders provided, with the assistance of government agencies, was a vital degree of administrative coordination. Such coordination was made possible by a substantial increase in the scale of operations, as well as a transformation in the structure of operations through increased integration of previously separate and uncoordinated activities. The coordination and control of supply factors by both public and private entities, combined with coordination and control of demand factors through the federal intervention in housing finance, allowed for: (1) the partial elimination of market destabilizing overcapacity and excess supply, (2) the introduction of considerable production cost efficiencies, including timeliness and simplification of transactions and flows, and (3) the ability to better manage the positive and negative effects of externalities in the urban built environment.

The "miracle" of Levittown in 1947 exemplified this structural shift. Large-scale producers of suburban houses, while relatively small in number, garnered an increasingly bigger and more profitable market share in the 1940s and 1950s. Four percent of all builders and developers constructed 45 per cent of the new dwelling units in the U.S. in 1949, with just 720 firms building 24 percent of all new houses in that year. These figures represented dramatic advances by large subdivision developers and homebuilders over the previous decade.[5] Though community builders by no means operated on a scale comparable to Fortune 500 manufacturing corporations, the insights of Alfred Chandler concerning the special importance of administrative coordination are nevertheless highly relevant to producers in the housing sector. Chandler argues that

administrative coordination helps to account for a significant segment of what economists have defined as a residual, that is, the proportion of output that cannot be explained by the growth of input. Certainly the speed and regularity with which goods flow through the processes of production and distribution and the way these flows are organized affect the volume and unit cost. Until economists analyze the function of administrative coordination, the theory of the firm will remain essentially a theory of production. The institution through which the factors of production are combined, which coordinates current flows, and which allocates resources for future economic activities in major sectors of the economy deserves more attention than it has yet received from economists.[6]

The planning system, including deed restrictions, zoning and subdivision regulations, master plans, and agency review, all represented a newly designed system of administrative coordination.[7] Similarly, the primary role of the developer, or community builder, was to serve as a systems integrator and administrator for the complex processes and multitude of separate business and government transactions involved in urban land development. Other institutions, from title insurance and trust companies to the FHA, also performed important coordinating functions. The rise, decline, and changing nature of private and public institutions, including firms, agencies, and trade associations, is a vital aspect of the story of the community builders. A great deal of further research by historians, planners, and business and policy analysts is called for in the area of institutional change and its effects on urban land development.[8]

As we are now living through a whole new set of significant changes, most notably the deregulation of financial institutions, it would be worthwhile to take a long and deep look backward to better understand this complicated and fascinating process. Such research may help us both to comprehend what may be in store for us in the decades ahead and to formulate and act upon a renewed vision.

NOTES

PROLOGUE

1. Hugh R. Pomeroy, "The Realtor in Regional Planning," *California Real Estate Directory-Bulletin*, Supplement, V, 2, December 1924 (Sacramento: California State Printing Office, 1924), p. 73.
2. Hugh R. Pomeroy, "Subdivision in Relation to Community Building," *Annals of Real Estate Practice*, Volume III, Home Building and Subdividing (Chicago: National Association of Real Estate Boards, 1925), p. 263.
3. Fred E. Reed, "Realtors and City Planning Progress," *City Planning*, 4, 3, July 1928, p. 213.

1. BUILDING COMMUNITIES

1. More than any other source, the book that was most influential in shaping my approach to this topic is the brilliant synthesis by Thomas Adams, *The Design of Residential Areas* (Cambridge: Harvard University Press, 1934). Several other books were critical in helping form my basic outlook: Charles Mulford Robinson, *City Planning, with Special Reference to the Planning of Streets and Lots* (New York: Putnam, 1916); Helen C. Monchow, *The Use of Deed Restrictions in Subdivision Development* (Chicago: Institute for Research in Land Economics and Public Utilities, 1928); Ernest M. Fisher, *Advanced Principles of Real Estate Practice* (New York: MacMillan, 1930); A. D. Theobald, *Financial Aspects of Subdivision Development* (Chicago: Institute for Economic Research, 1930); John M. Gries and James Ford, eds., *Planning for Residential Districts*, vol. 1, President's Conference on Home Building and Home Ownership (Washington, D.C.: National Capital Press, 1932); National Resources Committee, *Urban Planning and Land Policies* (Washington, D.C.: U.S. Government Printing Office, 1939); Miles L. Colean, *American Housing: Problems and Prospects* (New York: Twentieth Century Fund, 1944); Community Builders' Council (Seward Mott, Max Wehrly, and Harold Lautner, eds.), *The Community Builders Handbook* (Washington, D.C.: Urban Land Institute, 1947); Leo Grebler, *Production of New Housing* (New York: Social Science Research Council, 1950); Sherman J. Maisel, *Housebuilding in Transition* (Berkeley: University of California Press, 1953); Richard L. Nelson and

Frederick T. Aschman, *Real Estate and City Planning* (Englewood Cliffs, N.J.: Prentice-Hall, 1957); Sam Bass Warner, Jr., *Streetcar Suburbs: The Process of Growth in Boston, 1870–1900* (Cambridge: Harvard University Press, 1962); Kevin Lynch, *Site Planning* (Cambridge: MIT Press, 1962); Edward P. Eichler and Marshall Kaplan, *The Community Builders* (Berkeley: University of California Press, 1967); Robert A. M. Stern, *The Anglo-American Suburb* (London: Architectural Design, 1981); Ned Eichler, *The Merchant Builders* (Cambridge: MIT Press, 1982); Kenneth T. Jackson, *Crabgrass Frontier: The Suburbanization of the United States* (New York: Oxford University Press, 1985).

2. Harrison R. Baker, "Subdivision Practices," in Harrison R. Baker, ed., *Subdivision Principles and Practices* (Los Angeles: California Real Estate Association, 1936), p. 7.

3. On Levittown, see Kenneth Jackson, *Crabgrass Frontier*, ch. 13; Barry Checkoway, "Large Builders, Federal Housing Programs, and Postwar Suburbanization," *International Journal of Urban and Regional Research*, 4, 1, March 1980; Herbert J. Gans, *The Levittowners: Ways of Life and Politics in a New Suburban Community* (New York: Knopf, 1967); Alfred S. Levitt, "A Community Builder Looks at Community Planning," *Journal of the American Institute of Planners*, 17, 2, Spring 1951.

4. Clarence Stein to Alfred K. Stern, September 15, 1930 (Presidential Papers Subject File—Better Homes, Box 74, Herbert Hoover Presidential Library). On Radburn, see also Henry Wright, "How Long Blocks Cut Down Street Costs, and other Economies of Modern Planning," and Alexander M. Bing, "Community Planning for the Motor Age," in *Annals of Real Estate Practice* (Chicago: National Association of Real Estate Boards, 1929); Clarence S. Stein, *Toward New Towns for America* (New York: Reinhold, 1957); Henry Wright, *Rehousing Urban America* (New York: Columbia University Press, 1935); Thomas Adams, *Design;* Daniel Schaffer, *Garden Cities for Tomorrow: The Radburn Experience* (Philadelphia: Temple University Press, 1982); Eugenie L. Birch, "Radburn and the American Planning Movement: The Persistence of an Idea," *Journal of the American Planning Association*, 46, 4, October 1980.

5. Federal Housing Administration, *Successful Subdivisions*, Land Planning Bulletin No. 1 (Washington, D.C.: U.S. Government Printing Office, 1940). See also FHA, *Planning Profitable Neighborhoods*, Technical Bulletin No. 7 (Washington, D.C.: U.S. Government Printing Office, 1938); National Association of Home Builders, *Home Builders Manual for Land Development* (Washington, D.C.: NAHB, 1950); Urban Land Institute, *Community Builders Handbook.*

6. On deed restrictions, see chapter 3; and Helen Monchow, *Deed Restrictions.*

7. The phrase "municipal assistance" is a quote from J. C. Nichols, "Financial Effect of Good Planning in Land Subdivision," *Proceedings of the Eighth National Conference on City Planning* (New York: Douglas C. McMurtrie, 1916), p. 100. For a thorough discussion of the community builders' perspective on urban planning and J. C. Nichols' speech, see chapter 3.

8. Theodora Kimball Hubbard and Henry Vincent Hubbard, *Our Cities To-Day and To-Morrow* (Cambridge: Harvard University Press, 1929), p. 293.

9. Ernest M. Fisher, "Speculation in Suburban Lands," and Herbert D. Simpson, "Real Estate Speculation and the Depression," *American Economic Review*, 23, 1, Supplement, March 1933; Charles D. Clark, "Penalties of Excess Subdividing," *City Planning*, 10, 2, April 1934; Philip H. Cornick, *Premature Subdividing and its Consequences* (New York: Institute of Public Administration, 1938). Also see chapter 3.

10. For the national history of subdivision regulation in the U.S., see chapter 3.

11. Walter H. Leimert, "Selection of Property: Improvement and Development Program," in Harrison Baker, *Subdivision*, p. 30.

12. J. Mortimer Clark, "Subdivision Control Under the California Real Estate Act," in Harrison Baker, *Subdivision*, p. 54. On J. Mortimer Clark's career as a realtor, see *California Real Estate*, XIV, 11, August 1934, p. 12; *California Real Estate*, VII, 1, October 1926, p. 58.

13. Charles D. Clark, "Subdivision Plotting and Map Filing," in Harrison Baker, *Subdivision*.

14. *California Real Estate*, VII, 1, October 1926, p. 58.

15. On the state laws for Wisconsin and Washington, see John Nolen, *Replanning Small Cities: Six Typical Studies* (New York: B. W. Huebsch, 1912), pp. 172–177. On California, see chapter 5.

16. Charles Clark, "Subdivision," p. 42. Charles Clark later directed FHA's Land Planning Division in southern California. See Charles D. Clark, "Federal Housing Administration Standards for Land Subdivision," *The Planners' Journal*, 4, 5, September–October 1938. See also chapters 5 and 6.

17. Herbert U. Nelson, "How Good is Zoning?," *Headlines*, 14, 37, September 15, 1947 (Chicago: National Association of Real Estate Boards, 1947), p. 1. The standard interpretation of zoning fits Herbert U. Nelson's statement. See Seymour I. Toll, *Zoned American* (New York: Grossman, 1969); John Delafons, *Land-Use Controls in the United States* (Cambridge: MIT Press, 1969); Richard F. Babcock, *The Zoning Game* (Madison: University of Wisconsin Press, 1966); Constance Perin, *Everything in Its Place* (Princeton: Princeton University Press, 1977).

18. For example, urban planner Charles H. Cheney, in a letter describing the deed restrictions of the famous Palos Verdes Estates he designed with Frederick Law Olmsted, Jr., says, "The type of protective restrictions and the high class scheme of layout which we have provided tends to guide and automatically regulate the class of citizens who are settling here. The restrictions prohibit occupation of land by Negroes or Asiatics. The minimum cost of house restrictions tends to group the people of more or less like income together as far as it is reasonable and advisable to do so." Quoted in Robert M. Fogelson, *The Fragmented Metropolis: Los Angeles, 1850–1930* (Cambridge: Harvard University Press, 1967), p. 324 fn.

On race restrictions, see Clement E. Vose, *Caucasians Only: the Supreme Court, the NAACP, and the Restrictive Covenant Cases* (Berkeley: University of California Press, 1959); Thomas Lee Philpott, *The Slum and the Ghetto* (New York: Oxford University Press, 1978), ch. 8; Herman H. Long and Charles S. Johnson, *People vs. Property* (Nashville: Fisk University Press, 1947); Charles Abrams, *Forbidden Neighbors* (New York: Harper, 1955).

19. Barbara J. Flint, "Zoning and Residential Segregation: A Social and Physical History, 1910–1940" (Ph.D. diss., Department of History, University of Chicago, 1977), p. 215. On the national debate about "overzoning" and "rezoning," in addition to the many references that I cite in chapter 4, see also Harland Bartholomew, *Urban Land Uses* (Cambridge: Harvard University Press, 1932); Coleman Woodbury, "The Size of Retail Business Districts in the Chicago Metropolitan Region," and Orman S. Fink and Coleman Woodbury, "Area Requirements of Cities in the Region of Chicago," in *Journal of Land and Public Utility Economics,* 4, 1, February 1928, and 4, 3, August 1928; and the important *Proceedings of the National Zoning Conference,* Chicago, December 12–14, 1937 (Washington, D.C.: National Resources Committee, 1938). The best document on zoning from this period, cited in chapter 4, is W. L. Pollard, ed., *Zoning in the United States,* Annals of the American Academy of Political and Social Science, 155, II, May 1931.

20. On Berkeley's zoning law, see Marc A. Weiss, "Urban Land Developers and the Origins of Zoning Laws: The Case of Berkeley," *Berkeley Planning Journal,* III, 1, 1986.

21. On FHA, see chapter 6.

22. For background, see chapter 2.

23. On regional planning in the U.S. in the 1920s, see Hubbard and Hubbard, *Our Cities.* On California, including the Los Angeles County Regional Planning Commission, see chapter 5. Also see James Charles Stephens, "The Development of County Planning in California" (M.A. thesis, Department of Political Science, University of California, Berkeley, 1938).

24. Fred E. Reed, "Realtors and City Planning Progress," *City Planning,* 4, 3, July 1928, p. 208.

25. Hubbard and Hubbard, *Our Cities,* p. 71. On the annual California Conferences on City Planning, see chapter 5.

26. For historical background, see Hubbard and Hubbard, *Our Cities;* Robert A. Walker, *The Planning Function in Urban Government* (Chicago: University of Chicago Press, 1950); Russell Van Nest Black, *Planning and the Planning Profession* (Washington, D.C.: American Institute of Planners, 1967); Mel Scott, *American City Planning Since 1890* (Berkeley: University of California Press, 1969); John W. Reps, *The Making of Urban America: A History of City Planning in the United States* (Princeton: Princeton University Press, 1965); Donald A. Krueckeberg, ed., *The American Planner* (New York: Methuen, 1983); idem, ed., *Introduction to Planning History in the United States* (New Brunswick, N.J.: Center for Urban Policy Research, 1983); Laurence C. Gerckens, "Historical Development of Amer-

ican City Planning," in Frank S. So, ed., *The Practice of Local Government Planning* (Washington, D.C.: International City Management Association, 1979); Peter Marcuse, "Housing in Early City Planning," *Journal of Urban History*, 6, 2, February 1980; Eugenie L. Birch, "Advancing the Art and Science of Planning: Planners and their Organizations, 1909–1980," *Journal of the American Planning Association*, 46, 1, January 1980; David A. Johnson and Daniel Schaffer, eds., "Symposium: Learning from the Past—The History of Planning," *Journal of the American Planning Association*, 51, 2, Spring 1985; M. Christine Boyer, *Dreaming the Rational City* (Cambridge: MIT Press, 1983); Richard E. Foglesong, *Planning the Capitalist City* (Princeton: Princeton University Press, 1986).

27. See Pearl Janet Davies, *Real Estate in American History* (Washington, D.C.: Public Affairs Press, 1958); Garnett Laidlaw Eskew, *Of Land and Men: The Birth and Growth of an Idea* (Washington, D.C.: Urban Land Institute, 1959); Michael Sumichrast and Sara A. Frankel, *Profile of the Builder and His Industry* (Washington, D.C.: National Association of Home Builders, 1970); Joseph B. Mason, *History of Housing in the U.S., 1930–1980* (Houston: Gulf, 1982).

28. For a good summary of this accomplishment, see Joseph Laronge, "The Subdivider of Today and Tomorrow," *Journal of Land and Public Utility Economics*, 18, 3, August 1942. On Park Forest, see William H. Whyte, Jr., *The Organization Man* (New York: Simon and Schuster, 1956), part 7.

2. The Rise of the Community Builders

1. *Real Estate*, II, 9, June 1913, p. 240.

2. *Ibid.*, II, 10, July 1913, p. 292.

3. C. W. Taylor, "History of the California Real Estate Association" (Los Angeles, unpublished manuscript in the library of the California Association of Realtors, 1955).

4. Frederick E. Case, *Real Estate Brokerage* (Englewood Cliffs: Prentice-Hall, 1965); Sherman J. Maisel and Albert H. Schaaf, *Characteristics and Performance of Real Estate Brokers and Salesmen in California*, Research Report Number 9, Real Estate Research Program (Berkeley: Bureau of Business and Economic Research, University of California, October 1956).

5. Peter Wolf, *Land in America* (New York: Pantheon, 1981); Aaron M. Sakolski, *The Great American Land Bubble* (New York: Harper, 1932); Charles N. Glaab and A. Theodore Brown, *A History of Urban America* (New York: Macmillan, 1983).

6. Record and Guide, *A History of Real Estate, Building and Architecture in New York City* (New York: The Real Estate Record Association, 1898); Richard M. Hurd, *Principles of City Land Values* (New York: Record and Guide, 1903); Stanley L. McMichael and Robert F. Bingham, *City Growth and Values* (Cleveland: The Stanley McMichael Publishing Organization, 1923); Helen C. Monchow, "Finding a Base-Year for the Study of Urban Problems," *The Journal of*

Land and Public Utility Economics, V, 3, August 1929; Eugene Rachlis and John E. Marqusee, *The Land Lords* (New York: Random House, 1963); Richard A. Walker, "The Transformation of Urban Structure in the Nineteenth Century and the Beginnings of Suburbanization," in Kevin R. Cox, ed., *Urbanization and Conflict in Market Societies* (Chicago: Maaroufa Press, 1978); Raymond A. Mohl, *The New City: Urban America in the Industrial Age, 1860–1920* (Arlington Heights, Ill.: Harlan Davidson, 1985); David R. Goldfield and Blaine A. Brownell, *Urban America: From Downtown to No Town* (Boston: Houghton Mifflin 1979); Kenneth T. Jackson, *Crabgrass Frontier: The Suburbanization of the United States* (New York: Oxford University Press, 1985).

7. Adna Ferrin Weber, *The Growth of Cities in the Nineteenth Century* (New York: MacMillan, 1899); Ernest M. Fisher, *Real Estate Subdividing Activity and Population Growth in Nine Urban Areas,* Michigan Business Studies, I, 9 (Ann Arbor: School of Business Administration, University of Michigan, July 1928); Manuel Gottlieb, *Long Swings in Urban Development* (New York: National Bureau of Economic Research, 1976).

8. Pearl Janet Davies, *Real Estate in American History* (Washington, D.C.: Public Affairs Press, 1958), pp. 36–52.

9. A leading California real estate broker and government official stated in the 1930s, "Prior to the creation of the State Real Estate Department, it was common practice for a man who was a total failure in all other lines of endeavor, to go into the real estate business. The result was that a large number of people called themselves real estate agents, who were totally unfit, either by training or experience, to assume the serious responsibility of advising others how to invest their money in real estate." J. Mortimer Clark, "Subdivision Control Under the California Real Estate Act," in Harrison R. Baker, ed., *Subdivision Principles and Practices* (Los Angeles: California Real Estate Association, 1936), p. 52.

10. Discussing one such crisis period, urban planner Charles Cheney declared: "Suspicion of real estate as an investment, on the part of the general public, has been prevalent since the panic of 1907. Tabulations of the losses incurred in the various cities of this country and Canada are only beginning to be available, but sufficient evidence exists to show that a number of the main causes of suspicion and uncertainty can be removed." *California Real Estate,* IX, 4, January 1928, p. 24.

11. Pearl Davies, *Real Estate,* pp. 55–56.

12. *San Francisco Real Estate Board Bulletin,* IV, 2, February 15, 1918, p. 2. The highly competitive real estate market was characterized by frequent and extreme cyclical fluctuations. The classic work on real estate cycles is Homer Hoyt, *One Hundred Years of Land Values in Chicago* (Chicago: University of Chicago Press, 1933). Research into the nature and timing of real estate cycles covers a wide area of statistical information. Since the latter part of the 1920s a fairly substantial body of literature has been published based on research analyzing the pattern of real estate cycles in the U.S. Prior to the advent of academic research, newspapers and periodicals, industry trade journals, business information companies such as

F. W. Dodge or S. W. Straus, and public agencies all routinely documented the ups and downs of the real estate business. The Indexes were created to numerically record the monthly and annual variations in sales prices for various types of property, volume of realty transactions and deeds recorded, value and number of building permits, new construction starts, the number of subdivision plats recorded and the number of new subdivision lots, rent levels, assessed valuation of real property, amount of new mortgage lending, number of mortgage foreclosures, prices of building materials, cost of construction labor, and other statistical time series. Four broad categories of data are discernible: (1) realty transactions; (2) new construction; (3) new subdividing; and (4) debt financing. In each case both the volume and value were calculated where possible. See Homer Hoyt, *Prices of Building Materials,* War Industries Board Price Bulletin No. 6 (Washington, D.C.: U.S. Government Printing Office, 1919); John H. Cover, "Building Permits as a Basis for Analyzing Building Activity," *Journal of the American Statistical Association,* XXVII, 177A, Supplement, March 1932; Corrington Gill, "Construction Statistics," *Journal of the American Statistical Association,* XXVII, 181, March 1933; Roy Wenzlick, "The Problem of Analyzing Local Real Estate Cycles," *Journal of the American Statistical Association,* XXVIII, 181A, Supplement, March 1933; John R. Riggleman, "Building Cycles in the United States, 1875–1932," *Journal of the American Statistical Association,* XXVIII, 182, June 1933; U.S. National Recovery Administration, *Chronological History of the Construction Industry, 1920 to 1934,* mimeo, Division of Research and Planning, 1934; William H. Newman, *The Building Industry and Business Cycles,* Studies in Business Administration, V, 4 (Chicago: University of Chicago Press, 1935); Roy Wenzlick, *The Coming Boom in Real Estate* (New York: Simon & Schuster, 1936); Lowell J. Chawner, "Economic Factors Related to Residential Building," *Annals of the American Academy of Political and Social Science,* 190, March 1937; Clarence D. Long, Jr., *Building Cycles and the Theory of Investment* (Princeton: Princeton University Press, 1940); David L. Wickens, *Residential Real Estate* (New York: National Bureau of Economic Research, 1941); Walter Isard, "A Neglected Cycle: The Transport-Building Cycle," *The Review of Economic Statistics,* XXIV, 4, November 1942; Arthur F. Burns and Wesley C. Mitchell, *Measuring Business Cycles* (New York: National Bureau of Economic Research, 1946), pp. 418–27; Miles L. Colean and Robinson Newcomb, *Stabilizing Construction: The Record and the Potential* (New York: McGraw-Hill, 1952); Leo Grebler, David M. Blank, and Louis Winnick, *Capital Formation in Residential Real Estate* (Princeton: Princeton University Press, 1956); Alvin H. Hansen, *Business Cycles and National Income* (New York: Norton, 1964), pp. 39–52; Manuel Gottlieb, *Long Swings;* Alan Rabinowitz, *The Real Estate Gamble* (New York: AMACOM, 1980); Leo Grebler and Leland S. Burns, "Construction Cycles in the United States Since World War II," *Journal of the American Real Estate and Urban Economics Association,* 10, 2, Summer 1982. On cycles in subdividing activity, see note 40 in chapter 3.

13. NAREB was originally called the National Association of Real Estate Exchanges, but changed its name to "Boards" in 1916. Pearl Davies, *Real Estate,* pp.

56–62. For a detailed analysis of one local board that parallels the NAREB experience, see Everett Cherrington Hughes, *The Chicago Real Estate Board: The Growth of an Institution* (Chicago: The Society for Social Research of the University of Chicago, 1931). For an excellent history of a trade association in another industry (cotton textiles), see Louis Galambos, *Competition and Cooperation: The Emergence of a National Trade Association* (Baltimore: Johns Hopkins University Press, 1966); for general background, see Robert F. Himmelberg, *The Origins of the National Recovery Administration: Business, Government, and the Trade Association Issue, 1921–1933* (New York: Fordham University Press, 1976); and Thomas K. McCraw, ed., *Regulation in Perspective: Historical Essays* (Cambridge: Harvard University Press, 1981).

14. Pearl Davies, *Real Estate*, pp. 63–64.

15. Ibid., p. 102.

16. Ibid., pp. 114–15; Herbert U. Nelson, *The Administration of Real Estate Boards* (New York: MacMillan, 1925), pp. 126–43, 219–32; Michael Terence Carney, "Real Estate Brokerage Commission Rates: Price Fixing in Home Brokerage" (Ph.D. diss., Department of Economics, University of California at Los Angeles, 1981), pp. 4–28.

17. Pearl Davies, *Real Estate*, pp. 110–14. In 1917 the newly-appointed Realtor Committee of the Los Angeles Realty Board concluded that "the use of the title 'Realtor'—rather than 'Real Estate Broker,' or 'Real Estate Operator,' or 'Real Estate Agent'—or such, would, in itself, tend to a certain distinction, and might prove advantageous to those who are entitled to style themselves, 'Realtors.' " See letter from D. F. McGarry to the Governing Committee of the Los Angeles Realty Board, June 19, 1917, p. 1; C. N. Chadbourn, the Minneapolis realtor who invented the word, noted in 1924 that "Babbit, the hero of Sinclair Lewis' latest novel, is a Realtor who is fairly well described by the author in conformity with the above definition. Babbitt is a prominent member of the local board and of the state association, and the definition is as accurate as one would expect in a book written in the ironic vein of the author of *Main Street*." *California Real Estate*, IV, 5, February 1924, p. 44; Sinclair Lewis, *Babbitt* (New York: Harcourt Brace, 1922), ch. 13.

18. Pearl Davies, *Real Estate*, pp. 97–103; Herbert Nelson, *Administration*, pp. 167–75, 203–9.

19. Pearl Davies, *Real Estate*, pp. 103–10; 164–65.

20. "Summary of the Proceedings of the States Council," *Annals of Real Estate Practice* (Chicago: National Association of Real Estate Boards, 1930), p. 763. Approximately 20 percent of all the licensed brokers and salesmen in the U.S. were in the state of California in 1930, and earlier percentages were even higher. See *California Real Estate Directory-Bulletin*, XI, 1 (Sacramento: California State Printing Office, 1930).

21. A. D. Theobald, "Real Estate License Laws in Theory and Practice," *Journal of Land and Public Utility Economics*, VII, 1, February 1931; Joseph K. Brittain, "Real Estate License Laws, Report of the President," *Annals of Real*

Estate Practice, I, General Real Estate Topics (Chicago: National Association of Real Estate Boards, 1925); Glenn D. Willaman, "Real Estate License Law and Enforcement," *Annals of Real Estate Practice* (Chicago: National Association of Real Estate Boards, 1928); Nathan William MacChesney, *The Principles of Real Estate Law* (New York: MacMillan, 1927); N. B. Nelson, *Law of Real Estate Brokerage* (New York: Prentice-Hall, 1928).

22. *California Real Estate,* VIII, 8, May 1928, p. 34.

23. "The organized real estate groups have on the whole favored the general principles of real estate license laws." A. D. Theobald, "License Laws," p. 19.

24. "Meeting of National Association of License Law Officials," *Annals of Real Estate Practice,* I, General Real Estate Topics (Chicago: National Association of Real Estate Boards, 1925), pp. 299–396.

25. C. W. Taylor, "History," ch. 7, p. 1; *California Real Estate,* IV, 1, October 1923, p. 42.

26. C. W. Taylor, "History," ch. 7, pp. 1, 9; on licensing figures and CREA convention proceedings, see successive volumes of the *California Real Estate Directory-Bulletin* (on CREA 1927 membership, see VIII, 2, supplement, September 15, 1927, p. 442); For the history of one large California realty brokerage firm, see Jo Ann L. Levy, *Behind the Western Skyline: Coldwell Banker, The First 75 Years* (Los Angeles: Coldwell Banker, 1981).

27. Pearl Davies, *Real Estate,* p. 104.

28. *Survey of Real Estate Business* (Chicago: National Association of Real Estate Boards, August 1933), p. 1.

29. *Real Estate Agencies and Brokerage Offices,* 1935 Census of Business, U.S. Department of Commerce (Washington, D.C.: U.S. Government Printing Office, 1937), Table I, pp. 1–4. (I am using data from the 1930s because it is the best early data available. This is true for several other sections of this chapter. The organization of the real estate and homebuilding industry did not make an impact on social science data collection by government agencies, business trade associations, or university researchers until the latter half of the 1920s.) On NAREB membership, see *California Real Estate,* VII, 5, February 1927, p. 17.

30. Ibid., p. vi.

31. Ibid., p. 1; *Survey,* pp. 3–4.

32. NAREB, *Survey,* p. 4; U.S. Census, *Real Estate,* p. iii.

33. Pearl Davies, *Real Estate,* pp. 128–37. The chairman of NAREB's War Service Board was J.C. Nichols of Kansas City. See letter from NAREB President William May Garland to Los Angeles Realty Board, May 9, 1919. See also chapter 3.

34. William Lindus Cody Wheaton, "The Evolution of Federal Housing Programs" (Ph.D. diss., Department of Political Science, University of Chicago, 1953); Pearl Davies, *Real Estate,* pp. 172–88.

35. U.S. National Recovery Administration, *Proposed Code for the Real Estate Business,* Code Number 392, submitted by the National Association of Real Estate Boards, August 30, 1933 (Washington, D.C.: U.S. Government Printing Office,

1933). On the NRA, see Ellis W. Hawley, *The New Deal and the Problem of Monopoly: A Study in Economic Ambivalence* (Princeton: Princeton University Press, 1966); Louis Galambos, *Competition;* Robert Himmelberg, *Origins.*

36. Ibid., p. v (Letter of Transmittal).

37. U.S. National Recovery Administration, *Code of Fair Competition for the Real Estate Brokerage Industry,* Approved Code Number 392, as approved on April 9, 1934 (Washington, D.C.: U.S. Government Printing Office, 1934), pp. 259–71.

38. Blake Snyder, ed., *Real Estate Handbook* (New York: McGraw-Hill, 1925); Ernest M. Fisher, *Principles of Real Estate Practice* (New York: MacMillan, 1923); idem, *Advanced Principles of Real Estate Practice* (New York: MacMillan, 1930); Philip A. Benson and Nelson L. North, *Real Estate Principles and Practices* (New York: Prentice-Hall, 1922); John B. Spilker, *Real Estate Business as a Profession* (Cincinnati: Stewart Kidd, 1923); Felix Isman, *Real Estate In All Its Branches* (New York: D. Appleton, 1926); Albert G. Hinman and Herbert B. Dorau, *Real Estate Merchandising* (Chicago and New York: A. W. Shaw, 1926); Herbert B. Dorau and Albert G. Hinman, *Urban Land Economics* (New York: MacMillan, 1928); Arthur M. Weimer and Homer Hoyt, *Principles of Urban Real Estate* (New York: Ronald Press, 1939); Charles Abrams, *Revolution in Land* (New York: Harper, 1939); Frederick Morrison Babcock, *The Appraisal of Real Estate* (New York: MacMillan, 1924); Karl Scholz, ed., *Real Estate Problems, Annals of the American Academy of Political and Social Science,* 148, I, March 1930; Richard U.Ratcliff, *Urban Land Economics* (New York: McGraw-Hill, 1949); Paul F. Wendt, *Real Estate Appraisal* (New York: Henry Holt, 1956); Michael Doucet and John Weaver, "The North American Shelter Business, 1860–1920: A Study of a Canadian Real Estate and Property Management Agency," *Business History Review,* 58, Summer 1984.

39. Ibid.; see successive annual papers of the Home Builders and Subdividers Division conferences in NAREB, *Annals of Real Estate Practice,* passim.

40. Robert F. Bingham and Elmore L. Andrews, *Financing Real Estate* (Cleveland: Stanley McMichael, 1924); Grebler, Blank and Winnick, *Capital;* Raymond W. Goldsmith, *Financial Intermediaries in the American Economy Since 1900* (Princeton: Princeton University Press, 1958); J. E. Morton, *Urban Mortgage Lending: Comparative Markets and Experience* (Princeton: Princeton University Press, 1956); John H. Gray and George W. Terborgh, *First Mortgages in Urban Real Estate Finance* (Washington, D.C.: The Brookings Institution, 1929); Samuel N. Reep, *Second Mortgages and Land Contracts in Real Estate Financing* (New York: Prentice-Hall, 1928); William N. Loucks, *The Philadelphia Plan of Home Financing* (Chicago: Institute for Research in Land Economics and Public Utilities, 1929); A. D. Theobald, *Financial Aspects of Subdivision Development* (Chicago: Institute for Economic Research, 1930); John M. Gries and James Ford, eds., *Home Finance and Taxation,* (Washington, D.C.: The National Capital Press, 1932); idem, *Home Ownership, Income and Types of Dwellings* (Washington, D.C.: The National Capital Press, 1932); David L. Wickens, *Financial Survey of Urban Housing,* U.S. Department of Commerce (Washington, D.C.: U.S. Government Printing Office, 1937); Ernest M. Fisher, *Urban Real Estate Markets: Characteris-*

tics and Financing (New York: National Bureau of Economic Research, 1951); Alan Rabinowitz, *Real Estate Gamble.*

41. Bureau of the Census, *Mortgages on Homes,* U.S. Department of Commerce (Washington, D.C.: U.S. Government Printing Office, 1923), pp. 41–45.

42. Grebler, Blank and Winnick, *Capital,* p. 163.

43. Ibid., p. 441; U.S. Census, *Mortgages,* pp. 46, 120–21.

44. Grebler, Blank and Winnick, *Capital,* p. 192.

45. Morton Bodfish and A.D. Theobald, *Savings and Loan Principles* (New York: Prentice-Hall, 1938), pp. 49–57; H. Morton Bodfish, ed., *History of Building and Loan in the United States* (Chicago: United States Building and Loan League, 1931).

46. J. E. Morton, *Urban,* p. 37; Horace F. Clark and Frank A. Chase, *Elements of the Modern Building and Loan Associations* (New York: MacMillan, 1925); H. Morton Bodfish, *Money Lending Practices of Building and Loan Associations in Ohio* (Columbus: Ohio State University Press, 1927); Wilfred George Donley, "An Analysis of Building and Loan Associations in California, 1920–1935" (Ph.D. diss., Department of Economics, University of California, Berkeley, 1937); Grebler, Blank and Winnick, *Capital,* pp. 197, 203–4; Raymond Goldsmith, *Financial,* pp. 176–77.

47. Bodfish and Theobald, *Savings,* p. 58.

48. William Wheaton, "Evolution," pp. 8–37; Gries and Ford, *Home Finance,* pp. 98–101.

49. Grebler, Blank and Winnick, *Capital,* pp. 195–99.

50. John Lintner, *Mutual Savings Banks in the Savings and Mortgage Markets* (Boston: Harvard University Press, 1948).

51. Carl F. Behrens, *Commercial Bank Activities in Urban Mortgage Financing* (New York: National Bureau of Economic Research, 1952); Grebler, Blank and Winnick, *Capital,* pp. 197, 201–3; American Institute of Banking, *Home Mortgage Lending* (New York: American Bankers Association, 1938); on NAREB lobbying for federal banking laws to permit and encourage real estate lending, see Pearl Davies, *Real Estate,* pp. 87–95, 139–43, 157–59, 172–80; William Wheaton, *Evolution.*

52. Grebler, Blank and Winnick, *Capital,* p. 197.

53. R. J. Saulnier, *Urban Mortgage Lending by Life Insurance Companies* (New York: National Bureau of Economic Research, 1950), pp. 9–15.

54. Ibid.; Harold J. Hoflich, "The Investments of Life Insurance Companies Since 1906" (Ph.D. diss., Department of Economics, University of California, Berkeley, 1933); Lester E. Wurfel, "Life Insurance Service as Reflected in Mortgage Loans," *Annals of Real Estate Practice,* IV, Real Estate Finance, (Chicago: National Association of Real Estate Boards, 1926); Arthur J. Mertzke, "Mortgage Investments of Life Insurance Companies, 1915–1928," *Annals of Real Estate Practice* (Chicago: National Association of Real Estate Boards, 1929); Grebler, Blank and Winnick, *Capital,* pp. 199–201.

55. Elias Henry Wrenn, Jr., "Charting the Organization of the Mortgage and Loan Department," and Louis Kahn, "Records of the Loan Department," in

Annals of Real Estate Practice, IV, Real Estate Finance (Chicago: National Association of Real Estate Boards, 1926); L. K. Boysen, "Safe Mortgage Banking," *Annals of Real Estate Practice,* V, Real Estate Finance (Chicago: National Association of Real Estate Boards, 1927); Samuel Reep, *Second Mortgages;* Grebler, Blank and Winnick, *Capital,* pp. 204–6.

56. Pearl Davies, *Real Estate,* pp. 185–88.

57. Mortgage bonds were a major feature of the speculative real estate boom in large office and apartment buildings in the latter part of the 1920s. Most of the bonds defaulted during the 1930s and the ensuing scandals caused real estate mortgage bond dealers to disappear from the market for more than 40 years. According to Leo Grebler, "Apartment house construction during the middle and late twenties was greatly fostered by the urge of financing houses issuing mortgage bonds to maintain a high level of operations, and the product almost became an outlet for the execution of a particular financing scheme." Leo Grebler, *Production of New Housing* (New York: Social Science Research Council, 1950), p. 103. See also S. W. Straus, "Real Estate Mortgage Bonds and What They Have Done for Real Estate," *Annals of Real Estate Practice,* I, General Real Estate Topics (Chicago: National Association of Real Estate Boards, 1925); Robert Alexander Halliburton, "The Real Estate Bond House" (Ph.D. diss., Faculty of Political Science, Columbia University, 1939); Ernest Allan Barbeau, *The Mortgage Bond Racket* (Albany, N.Y.: Real Estate Bond Research Bureau, 1932); Alan Rabinowitz, *Real Estate Gamble;* Coleman Woodbury, *The Trend of Multi-Family Housing in Cities in the United States* (Chicago: Institute for Economic Research, 1931).

58. Pearl Davies, *Real Estate,* pp. 155–59; Ernest Fisher, *Principles,* pp. 152–75; "More Helpful Loans Needed," *California Real Estate,* II, 3, December 1921, p. 20.

59. R. J. Saulnier, *Urban;* Grebler, Blank and Winnick, *Capital,* p. 206.

60. Lawrence G. Holmes and Carrie Maude Jones, eds., *The Real Estate Handbook* (New York: Prentice-Hall, 1948), pp. 311–15, 500; N.R.A., Code 392, *Proposed Codes of Fair Competition for the Real Estate Mortgage Business,* pp. 17–21; also see note 55.

61. Leo Grebler, *Production,* p. 72.

62. Herbert D. Simpson, "Real Estate Speculation and the Depression," *American Economic Review,* XXIII, 1, supplement, March 1933, p. 164.

63. U.S. Census, *Real Estate,* p. 22.

64. NAREB, *Survey,* pp. 1–4.

65. For example, NAREB's Proposed NRA code was for the "Real Estate and Insurance Brokerage Business," NRA, *Proposed Code,* pp. 5–9; and the 1935 *Census of Real Estate Agencies and Brokerage Offices* covered 21,567 "Insurance and Real Estate Offices," pp. i–v; see also Ernest Fisher, *Principles,* pp. 53–71; Benson and North, *Real Estate;* John Spilker, *Profession;* Raymond Goldsmith, *Financial.*

66. Los Angeles Realty Board, Minutes of the Governing Committee, August 4, 1903, p. 1.

67. NAREB, *Survey,* p. 2; U.S. Census, *Real Estate,* p. 1; Holmes and Jones, *Handbook,* p. 502.

68. Leslie C. Rogers, "Advantages of Title Insurance to the Investor," *Annals of Real Estate Practice,* V, Real Estate Finance (Chicago: National Association of Real Estate Boards, 1927); Daniel D. Gage, *Land Title Assuring Agencies* (San Francisco: Recorder, 1937); Ernest Fisher, *Advanced Principles.*

69. Holmes and Jones, *Handbook,* p. 499; see for example the "California Title Men's Department," *California Real Estate,* III, 2, November 1922, pp. 16–23, including the important letter on page 23 from the president of the California Land Title Association urging close cooperation with the California Real Estate Association "in all matters of mutual interest," stating that "The influence of the two (associations) combined is very powerful." He also noted that title insurance companies were "few in numbers" compared to real estate brokers, a good indication of the oligopoly status of the industry as exemplified by such large institutions as the Chicago Title and Trust Co., or the Title Insurance and Trust Co. of Los Angeles.

70. Holmes and Jones, *Handbook,* p. 501. On commercial buildings, see Cecil C. Evers, *The Commercial Problem in Buildings* (New York: Record and Guide, 1914); Reginald P. Bolton, *Building for Profit* (New York: De Vinne Press, 1922); Charles H. Lench, *The Promotion of Commercial Buildings* (New York: Architectural Economics Press, 1932). NAREB cooperated with NABOM, as well as with the National Association of Apartment House Owners, in the preparation of its proposed NRA code for the "Real Estate Building Management Business," see NRA, *Proposed Code,* p. 15.

71. A quick glance through any issue of a real estate journal, such as the *National Real Estate Journal, California Real Estate,* or the *Los Angeles Realtor,* will yield numerous examples. The battle by CREA for private transit extensions and more permissive state regulation of fare increases is typical of this relationship. See *California Real Estate,* III, 2, November 1922, p. 4.

72. John M. Gries, "Construction," in President's Conference on Unemployment, *Recent Economic Changes in the United States,* I (New York: McGraw-Hill, 1929); Bureau of the Census, Fifteenth Census of the United States: 1930, *Construction Industry* (Washington, D.C.: U.S. Government Printing Office, 1933); William Haber, *Industrial Relations in the Building Industry* (Cambridge: Harvard University Press, 1930); the editors of "Fortune," *Housing America* (New York: Harcourt, Brace, 1932); Southgate Haynie, *The Construction Industry,* U.S. National Recovery Administration, Evidence Study Number 7, June 1935; Arthur Holden, "The Construction Industries," in George B. Galloway, ed., *Industrial Planning Under Codes* (New York: Harper, 1935); David T. Rowlands and Coleman Woodbury, eds., *Current Developments in Housing, Annals of the American Academy of Political and Social Science,* 190, March 1937; U.S. Congress, Hearings before the Temporary National Economic Committee, Investigation of Concentration of Economic Power, Part 11, *The Construction Industry,* June 27–29, July 6–7 and 11–14, 1939 (Washington, D.C.: U.S. Government Printing Office, 1940); U.S. Congress, Temporary National Economic Committee, Mono-

graph Number 8, *Toward More Housing* (Washington, D.C.: U.S. Government Printing Office, 1940); U.S. National Resources Planning Board, *Housing: The Continuing Problem* (Washington, D.C.: U.S. Government Printing Office, 1940); Thurman Arnold, *The Bottlenecks of Business* (New York: Reynal & Hitchcock, 1940); Miles L. Colean, *American Housing: Problems and Prospects* (New York: Twentieth Century Fund, 1944); Charles Abrams, *The Future of Housing* (New York: Harper, 1946). For analysis of a somewhat later period, see Sherman J. Maisel, *Housebuilding in Transition* (Berkeley: University of California Press, 1953); Leo Grebler, *Production;* James Gillies and Frank Mittelbach, *Management in the Light Construction Industry,* (Real Estate Research Program, University of California at Los Angeles, 1962); Ned Eichler, *The Merchant Builders* (Cambridge: MIT Press, 1982). For a view of an earlier period, see Sam Bass Warner, Jr., *Streetcar Suburbs: The Process of Growth in Boston, 1870–1900* (Cambridge: Harvard University Press, 1962); Gwendolyn Wright, *Moralism and the Model Home: Domestic Architecture and Cultural Conflict in Chicago, 1873–1913* (Chicago: University of Chicago Press, 1980); Olivier Zunz, *The Changing Face of Inequality: Urbanization, Industrial Development, and Immigrants in Detroit, 1880–1920* (Chicago: University of Chicago Press, 1982), ch. 6; Michael J. Doucet and John C. Weaver, "Material Culture and the North American House," *Journal of American History,* 72, 3, December 1985.

73. Census of Construction, 1930, pp. 20–23.

74. U.S. Department of Labor, Bureau of Labor Statistics, "Builders of 1-Family Houses in 72 Cities," *Monthly Labor Review,* 51, 3, September 1940; idem, "Operations of Urban Home Builders," *Monthly Labor Review,* 52, 5, May 1941.

75. Census of Construction, 1930, p. 21.

76. U.S. TNEC, *Toward More Housing,* pp. 33–34.

77. Census of Construction, 1930, p. 3; Ernest Fisher, *Principles,* pp. 133–52. Sherman Maisel, *Housebuilding,* p. 71, and Leo Grebler, *Production,* p. 72, also make this point.

78. Ibid., p. 23.

79. Ernest M. Fisher, *Advanced Principles;* idem, "Speculation in Suburban Lands," *American Economic Review,* XXIII, 1, Supplement, March 1933; idem, "Expansion of the Urban Land Area," in R.D. McKenzie, *The Metropolitan Community* (New York: McGraw-Hill, 1933), pp. 199–212; Helen Corbin Monchow, *Seventy Years of Real Estate Subdividing Activity in the Region of Chicago* (Chicago: Northwestern University Press, 1939). On page 152, Monchow says, "Like so many other devices of the real estate market, the option is said to have been first used extensively in 1890."

80. Ibid.; A.D. Theobald, *Financial Aspects of Subdivision Development;* Ann Durkin Keating, "From City to Metropolis: Infrastructure and Residential Growth in Chicago," *Infrastructure and Urban Growth in the Nineteenth Century,* Essays in Public Works History, Number 14 (Chicago: Public Works Historical Society, 1985); Roger D. Simon, *The City-Building Process: Housing and Services in New Milwaukee Neighborhoods, 1880–1910* (Philadelphia: American Philosophical Society,

1978). Interview with Fred W. Marlow, former partner, Marlow-Burns Development Company, one of California's leading subdividers, on subdivision practice in southern California since the early 1920s, Los Angeles Board of Realtors, December 6, 1982.

81. Ibid. According to Pearl Davies, *Real Estate,* p. 133, in 1918 "Subdividers at this time were only beginning to be home builders. Construction of houses was still largely on order, or by small unorganized builders. In some cities the operative builders felt themselves to be on the opposite side of the table from brokers selling houses. Indeed in some cities they were not eligible to be members of the real estate board." See also Guy T. O. Hollyday, "Making Use of the Broker in Subdivision Selling," *Annals of Real Estate Practice* (Chicago: National Association of Real Estate Boards, 1929).

82. A.D. Theobald, *Financial,* p. 54; H. M. Seldon, "Stabilizing the Subdivision Business," *Annals of Real Estate Practice* (Chicago: National Association of Real Estate Boards, 1928), p. 607.

83. Ernest Fisher, *Advanced Principles,* p. 190; Pearl Davies, *Real Estate,* p. 70; William E. Harmon, "Suburban Real Estate—Financing, Developing and Selling," *Annals of Real Estate Practice,* Home Builders and Subdividers (Chicago: National Association of Real Estate Boards, 1924); William E. Harmon, "Playgrounds in New Land Subdivisions," *City Planning,* 2, 2, April 1926.

84. Stanley L. McMichael, "Trends in Urban Real Estate Values, Past and Future," *Annals of the American Academy of Political and Social Science,* 148, I, March 1930, p. 174; Fred T. Wood, "Selling Subdivisions," *Annals of Real Estate Practice,* III, Home Building and Subdividing (Chicago: National Association of Real Estate Boards, 1925); L. H. Mills, "Fundamentals of the Business of Home Building," *Annals of Real Estate Practice* (Chicago: National Association of Real Estate Boards, 1929); Harrison R. Baker, "The Broker's Interest in the Subdivision," *California Real Estate,* XI, 2, November 1930, p. 53; idem, "How To Stimulate Selling Through a Homeownership Campaign," *California Real Estate,* X, 5, February 1930, p. 35. For a later view, see Joseph Laronge, "The Subdivider of Today and Tomorrow," *Journal of Land and Public Utility Economics,* 18, 4, November 1942; Stanley L. McMichael, *Real Estate Subdivisions* (New York: Prentice-Hall, 1949). For an early view, see Anne Bloomfield, "The Real Estate Associates: A Land and Housing Developer of the 1870s in San Francisco," *Journal of the Society of Architectural Historians,* 37, 1, March 1978.

85. Hearings, U.S. TNEC, *Construction Industry,* p. 4998.

86. In 1930, the chairman of NAREB's Home Builders and Subdividers Division, a former president of the Washington, D.C. Real Estate Board, said "The Real Estate Board has not until very recently allowed 'lot sellers' to become members, because we have frowned upon their practice generally; but now that the subdivider is taking on the modern point of view, he is looked upon more favorably than before; and we have allowed him to come in as a member of our Board." W.C. Miller, "Modern Trends in Subdividing," *Annals of Real Estate Practice* (Chicago: National Association of Real Estate Boards, 1930), p. 296; H.

Morton Bodfish, "The 'Free-Lot' Subdivider: His Method of Operation and the Available Methods of Control," *Journal of Land and Public Utility Economics*, V, 2, May 1929, and V, 3, August 1929. Particularly once real estate license laws were established, most of the larger subdividers, by virtue of their sales operations, were licensed brokers, and by virtue of their need to be in good standing with other brokers and the general real estate fraternity, and to avail themselves of the multiple listing system, were active members of real estate boards.

87. See chapters 3 through 5.

88. NAREB, *Survey*, p. 1; Pearl Davies, *Real Estate*, pp. 68–71, 159–60.

89. Pearl Davies, *Real Estate*, p. 155; I have determined this by counting the annual NAREB Division membership rosters for 1928–30 in *Annals of Real Estate Practice*. The Brokers Division was the largest.

90. Southgate Haynie, *Construction*, p. 60.

91. Pearl Davies, *Real Estate*, pp. 196–205; Holmes and Jones, *Handbook*, pp. 501–2.

92. Leo Grebler, *Production*, p. 62.

93. Irenaeus Shuler, "Subdivisions," in Blake Snyder, *Real Estate Handbook*; idem, "Selecting, Planning, and Developing Subdivisions," *Annals of Real Estate Practice*, III, Home Building and Subdividing (Chicago: National Association of Real Estate Boards, 1927); Helen C. Monchow, *The Use of Deed Restrictions in Subdivision Development* (Chicago: Institute for Research in Land Economics and Public Utilities, 1928); J.C. Nichols, "A Developer's View of Deed Restrictions," *Journal of Land and Public Utility Economics*, V, 2, May 1929; Harrison Baker, *Subdivision Principles and Practices*.

94. Ernest Fisher, *Principles*, p. 211; Irenaeus Shuler, "Subdivisions," pp. 103–5; *California Real Estate*, VII, 2, November 1926, p. 26; Hugh Pomeroy, "Subdivision in Relation to Community Building," *Annals of Real Estate Practice*, III, Home Building and Subdividing (Chicago: National Association of Real Estate Boards, 1925); Harrison R. Baker, "Subdividing and City Planning," *California Real Estate*, VIII, 9, June 1928, p. 158; Hal G. Hotchkiss, "The Annual City Planning Conference of the California Real Estate Association," *The Community Builder*, I, 3, February 1928; Hugh Evans, "The Subdivider Speaks," *The Community Builder*, II, 2, July 1928; *The Community Builder* was published in Los Angeles. For discussion of a later period, see also Edward P. Eichler and Marshall Kaplan, *The Community Builders* (Berkeley: University of California Press, 1967).

95. Community Builders' Council, *The Community Builders Handbook* (Washington, D.C.: Urban Land Institute, 1947); Holmes and Jones, *Handbook*, p. 506. On the history of ULI, see Garnett Laidlaw Eskew, *Of Land and Men: The Birth and Growth of an Idea* (Washington, D.C.: Urban Land Institute, 1959).

96. J. C. Nichols, *Real Estate Subdivisions: The Best Manner of Handling Them* (Washington, D.C.: American Civic Association, 1912), p. 6; also see idem, "Suburban Subdivisions With Community Features," *Annals of Real Estate Practice*, Home Builders and Subdividers (Chicago: National Association of Real Estate Boards, 1924); *California Real Estate*, III, 12, September 1923, p. 14; the special issue on J. C. Nichols and the Country Club District, *National Real Estate Jour-*

nal, 40, 2, February 1939; Mark H. Rose, "There is Less Smoke in the District: J. C. Nichols, Urban Change, and Technological Systems," *Journal of the West,* 25, 1, January 1986.

97. E. H. Bouton, "The Financial Effect of Good Planning in Land Sub-Division," *The City Plan,* II, 3, October 1916.

98. *California Real Estate,* VI, 4, January 1926, p. 8; Harry H. Culver, "How We Built Up Our Subdivision Business," *Annals of Real Estate Practice,* General Sessions (Chicago: National Associaton of Real Estate Boards, 1924); also see chapter 5.

99. *California Real Estate,* I, 9, August–September 1921, p. 14.

100. Community Builders' Council, *Handbook;* G. L. Eskew, *Land and Men;* the information on NAREB presidents comes from analyzing the membership roster and list of officers of the Home Builders and Subdividers Division in *Annals of Real Estate Practice.* The NAREB presidents from the Home Builders and Subdividers Division during this period were: Irving B. Hiett (1922), Robert Jemison, Jr. (1926), Henry G. Zander (1928), Harry H. Culver (1929), Leonard P. Reaume (1930), Harry S. Kissell (1931), Lawrence T. Stevenson (1932), W. C. Miller (1933), and Hugh Potter (1934). On NAREB's role in the shaping of national housing policy in the 1930s, see Pearl Davies, *Real Estate;* William Wheaton, "Evolution"; and chapter 6.

101. Herbert Nelson, *Administration;* Everett Hughes, *Chicago; Real Estate,* III, 6, May 1914, p. 144; letter from the Membership Committee to the Governing Committee, Los Angeles Realty Board, March 9, 1921.

102. On the National Conference of Subdividers, see J. C. Nichols, "Town Planning," in Blake Snyder, *Real Estate Handbook,* p. 359. In Los Angeles there was an organization called the Associated Subdividers of Southern California, and its members were also licensed realtors who belonged to the Los Angeles Realty Board and the California Real Estate Association. See Los Angeles Realty Board, Minutes of the Governing Committee, September 18, 1919, p. 1; *California Real Estate Directory-Bulletin,* II, 1, October 15, 1921 (Sacramento: California State Printing Office, 1921), pp. 5, 190, 194, 224, 230.

103. Herbert Nelson, *Administration,* p. 12 (see also pp. 15, 83–4).

104. E. H. Bouton, "Financial," p. 9. See also idem, "Development of Roland Park, Baltimore," *Annals of Real Estate Practice,* Home Builders and Subdividers (Chicago: National Association of Real Estate Boards, 1924); Hugh R. Pomeroy, "The Realtor in Regional Planning," *California Real Estate Directory-Bulletin,* V, Supplement, December 1924 (Sacramento: California State Printing Office, 1924).

3. COMMUNITY BUILDERS AND URBAN PLANNERS

1. The classic statement of this approach was made by Charles Mulford Robinson in his *Modern Civic Art, or the City Made Beautiful* (New York: Putnam, 1904), and his *The Improvement of Towns and Cities* (New York: Putnam, 1907).

The best summaries of this period in planning are: George B. Ford, ed., *City Planning Progress in the United States* (Washington, D.C.: American Institute of Architects, Committee on Town Planning, 1917), and Theodora Kimball, *Municipal Accomplishments in City Planning and Published City Plan Reports in the United States* (Boston: National Conference on City Planning, 1920). For a look at some representative plans, see John Nolen, *Replanning Small Cities: Six Typical Studies* (New York: B. W. Heubsch, 1912).

2. For example, see Judd Kahn, *Imperial San Francisco: Politics and Planning in an American City, 1897–1906* (Lincoln: University of Nebraska Press, 1979); and William H. Wilson, *The City Beautiful Movement in Kansas City* (Columbia: University of Missouri Press, 1964).

3. On New York, see S. J. Makielski, Jr., *The Politics of Zoning: The New York Experience* (New York: Columbia University Press, 1966); "Shall We Save New York," *The City Plan*, II, 1, April 1916, p. 9. On the 1909 Chicago plan, see Walter D. Moody, *What of the City?* (Chicago: A. C. McClurg, 1919); Robert A. Walker, *The Planning Function in Urban Government* (Chicago: University of Chicago Press, 1950); and Michael Patrick McCarthy, "Businessmen and Professionals in Municipal Reform: The Chicago Experience, 1887–1920" (Ph.D. diss., Department of History, Northwestern University, 1970). On Chicago zoning and the Real Estate Board, see Charles M. Nichols, *Zoning in Chicago*, Final Report of the City Planning and Zoning Committee (Chicago: Chicago Real Estate Board, 1923); Everett Cherrington Hughes, *The Chicago Real Estate Board: The Growth of an Institution* (Chicago: The Society for Social Research of the University of Chicago, 1931); Andrew Jay King, "Law and Land Use in Chicago: A Prehistory of Modern Zoning" (Ph.D. diss., Department of History, University of Wisconsin, 1976); and Barbara J. Flint, "Zoning and Residential Segregation: A Social and Physical History, 1910–1940" (Ph.D. diss., Department of History, University of Chicago, 1977). The quote from Everett Hughes is on page 99, see also pages 83 and 96–100.

4. Thomas S. Ingersoll, "How the Real Estate Man Can Help," *Proceedings of the Ninth National Conference on City Planning* (New York: Douglas C. McMurtrie, 1917), p. 139.

5. NAREB's original City Planning Committee, chaired by Lee J. Ninde, consisted of Edward H. Bouton, Paul A. Harsch, Robert Jemison, Jr., Duncan McDuffie, J. C. Nichols, and King G. Thompson, all of whom were leading residential subdividers. See *Proceedings of the Seventh National Conference on City Planning* (Cambridge: Harvard University Press, 1915), pp. 71–87, 241–46.

6. "Science of City Planning Applied to Real Estate Business in California," *Real Estate*, III, 6, May 1914, pp. 153–54.

7. Harrison R. Baker, "The Broker's Interest in the Subdivision," *California Real Estate*, XI, 2, November 1930, p. 53.

8. See note number 5 in this chapter.

9. John Nolen, "Real Estate and City Planning," *The City Plan*, II, 1, April 1916, pp. 3–4. The term "progressive" is Nolen's, referring to J. C. Nichols on page 3.

10. Russell Van Nest Black, *Planning and the Planning Profession: The Past Fifty Years, 1917–1967* (Washington, D.C.: American Institute of Planners, 1967). Black lists the 52 founders of ACPI. On Lee Ninde, see Albert H. Schaaf, "A State Campaign for City Planning," *Proceedings of the Ninth National Conference on City Planning*, pp. 133–38.

11. Paul A. Harsch, "Land Subdivision: The Point of View of the Real Estate Developer," *The City Plan*, I, 3, October 1915; the advertisement for Ottawa Hills is on the inside front cover of *The City Plan*, II, 1, April 1916; King G. Thompson, "Discussion of Point of View of the Real Estate Developer," *Proceedings of the Seventh National Conference on City Planning*; Alexander S. Taylor, "Districting through Private Effort," *Proceedings of the Eighth National Conference on City Planning* (New York: Douglas C. McMurtrie, 1916); Pearl Janet Davies, *Real Estate in American History* (Washington, D.C.: Public Affairs Press, 1958), pp. 58–80, 145–49. On Duncan McDuffie, see Marc A. Weiss, "Urban Land Developers and the Origins of Zoning Laws: The Case of Berkeley," *Berkeley Planning Journal*, III, 1, 1986.

12. See "Best Methods of Land Subdivision," *Proceedings of the Seventh National Conference on City Planning*, pp. 42–106, 241–73; also E. P. Goodrich, "Best Methods of Land Subdivision," *The City Plan*, I, 3, October 1915; Paul A. Harsch, "Land Subdivision"; John Nolen, "The Subdivision of Land," and Edward Henry Bouton, "Local and Minor Streets," in John Nolen, ed., *City Planning* (New York: Appleton, 1916).

13. See *Proceedings of the Eighth* and *Ninth National Conference on City Planning*, p. 273 (1916) and pp. 302–3 (1917); Pearl Davies, *Real Estate*, pp. 128–37, 146. On the importance of wartime cooperation for business-government relations in the 1920s and 30s, see Ellis W. Hawley, *The Great War and the Search for a Modern Order* (New York: St. Martin's, 1979); William E. Leuchtenburg, "The New Deal and the Analogue of War," in John Braeman, Robert H. Bremner, and Everett Walters, eds., *Change and Continuity in Twentieth-Century America* (Columbus: Ohio State University Press, 1964).

14. Pearl Davies, *Real Estate*, pp. 128–37. On World War I housing, see Edith Elmer Wood, *Recent Trends in American Housing* (New York: MacMillan, 1931); Miles L. Colean, *Housing for Defense* (New York: Twentieth Century Fund, 1940).

15. Frederick Law Olmsted, Jr., "Planning Residential Subdivisions," *Proceedings of the Eleventh National Conference on City Planning* (Cambridge: Harvard University Press, 1919), pp. 14–15; on the planners and the war, see also U.S. Department of Labor, Bureau of Industrial Housing and Transportation, *Report of the United States Housing Corporation, II, Houses, Site-Planning, Utilities* (Washington, D.C.: U.S. Government Printing Office, 1919); "War Housing," *Proceedings of the Tenth National Conference on City Planning* (Cambridge: Harvard University Press, 1918); "City Planning and the War," *The City Plan*, III, 2, August 1917; "Community Planning for War-Time Industries," *The City Plan*, III, 4, April 1918. For some of Olmsted's earlier views on city planning, see Flavel Shurtleff and Frederick Law Olmsted, Jr., *Carrying Out the City Plan* (New York: Survey

Associates, 1914); Frederick Law Olmsted, Jr., "Land Subdivision from the Point of View of a Development Company," *Proceedings of the Fourth National Conference on Housing* (New York: National Housing Association, 1915).

16. The earliest sophisticated statements on the coming of a new era in residential subdivision planning were J. C. Nichols, *Real Estate Subdivisions: The Best Manner of Handling Them* (Washington, D.C.: American Civic Association, 1912), and Charles Mulford Robinson, *The Width and Arrangement of Streets* (New York: Engineering News, 1911). Also see Robinson's revised edition, *City Planning, with special reference to the Planning of Streets and Lots* (New York: Putnam, 1916). The best overview of the history of American suburbanization is Kenneth T. Jackson, *Crabgrass Frontier: The Suburbanization of the United States* (New York: Oxford University Press, 1985). See also the review essay by Michael H. Ebner, "Re-Reading Suburban America: Urban Population Deconcentration, 1810–1980," *American Quarterly*, 37, 3, Bibliography 1985.

For an interesting anaysis of physical changes in subdivision development patterns, see Robert Luther Williams, "Eighty Years of Subdivision Design: An Historical Evaluation of Land Planning Techniques in San Mateo County, California" (M.C.P. Thesis, Department of City and Regional Planning, University of California, Berkeley, 1952); Elizabeth Kates Burns, "The Process of Suburban Residential Development: The San Francisco Peninsula, 1860–1970" (Ph.D. diss., Department of Geography, University of California, Berkeley, 1974); and John Beatty Dykstra, "History of the Physical Development of Oakland, 1850–1930" (M.C.P. Thesis, Department of City and Regional Planning, University of California, Berkeley, 1967); Joel A. Tarr, "Transportation Innovation and Changing Spatial Patterns: Pittsburgh, 1850–1934," *Essays in Public Works History*, Number 6 (Chicago: Public Works Historical Society, 1976). For an analysis that ties the spatial changes more closely to economic, political, and social trends and conflicts, see Richard A. Walker, "A Theory of Suburbanization: Capitalism and the Construction of Urban Space in the United States," in Michael Dear and Allen Scott, eds., *Urbanization and Urban Planning in Capitalist Society* (New York: Methuen, 1981); and Matthew Edel, Elliott D. Sclar, and Daniel Luria, *Shaky Palaces: Homeownership and Social Mobility in Boston's Suburbanization* (New York: Columbia University Press, 1984).

17. *Proceedings of the Seventh National Conference on City Planning*, pp. 97–98.

18. See Frank Backus Williams, "Public Control of Private Real Estate," in John Nolen, *City Planning;* Alexander Taylor, "Districting"; John Nolen, "Real Estate"; "The First Meeting of the American City Planning Institute," *The City Plan*, III, 3, December 1917; Lawrence Veiller, "Protecting Residential Districts," *Proceedings of the Sixth National Conference on City Planning* (Cambridge: Harvard University Press, 1914); idem, "Districting by Municipal Regulation," *Proceedings of the Eighth National Conference on City Planning;* Lawson Purdy, "Districting and Zoning of Cities," and Charles H. Cheney, "Districting Progress and Procedure in California," in *Proceedings of the Ninth National Conference on City Planning*. The phrase "Building for Permanency" comes from Charles H.

Cheney, "Building for Permanency," in *Planning Problems of Town, City, and Region* (Philadelphia: Wm. F. Fell, 1928).

19. See note number 40 in this chapter, and note number 12 in chapter 2.

20. *Real Estate*, IV, 12, November 1915, p. 388.

21. Ibid.

22. *Proceedings of the Seventh National Conference on City Planning*, p. 87. The subdivision that King Thompson is discussing is Upper Arlington in Columbus. See his lavish prospectus, *The Country Club District* (Columbus: The King Thompson Company, 1914). John Nolen and Henry Vincent Hubbard later made the identical argument as King Thompson about the advantages of good planning both for the private *and* public sectors: "From all our study we have come to a firm conviction that parkways, properly designed in their relation to all the needs of a considerable population, will be worth their expense and that their value will be reflected in the taxable values of property so that, in truth, the community as a business will be better off financially on account of the parkway because it will ultimately be receiving annually in taxes more than the annual charge to the community for creating and maintaining the parkway." John Nolen and Henry V. Hubbard, *Parkways and Land Values* (Cambridge: Harvard University Press, 1937).

23. J. C. Nichols, "Financial Effect of Good Planning in Land Subdivision," *Proceedings of the Eighth National Conference on City Planning*; John Nolen, "Real Estate." On Nichols' 1912 NAREB speech, see chapter 2.

24. Ibid., p. 92.

25. Ibid., p. 100.

26. Ibid., p. 101.

27. Ibid., pp. 101–2.

28. Ibid., pp. 105–6. For additional views by J. C. Nichols on urban planning and development, see J. C. Nichols, "Housing and the Real Estate Problem," in Carol Aronovici, ed., *Housing and Town Planning* (Philadelphia: American Academy of Political and Social Science, 1914); idem, *Real City Planning Results and What They Mean to Property Owners*, Bulletin Number 3 (San Francisco: California Conference on City Planning, 1918); idem, "Zoning as Applied to Subdivision Development," *Annals of Real Estate Practice*, Home Builders and Subdividers (Chicago: National Association of Real Estate Boards, 1923); idem, "When You Buy a Home Site," *Good Housekeeping*, 76, February 1923; idem, "Responsibilities and Opportunities of Real Estate Boards in Building Cities," *National Real Estate Journal*, 25, 13, June 30, 1924; idem, "Town Planning," in Blake Snyder, ed., *The Real Estate Handbook* (New York: McGraw-Hill, 1925); idem, "The Responsibilities of Realtors in City Planning," *City Planning*, I, 1, April 1925; idem, "The Planning and Control of Outlying Shopping Centers," *Journal of Land and Public Utility Economics*, II, 1, January 1926; idem, "A Developer's View of Deed Restrictions," *Journal of Land and Public Utility Economics*, V, 2, May 1929.

29. Advisory Committee on Zoning, U.S. Department of Commerce, *A Standard State Zoning Enabling Act* (Washington, D.C.: U.S. Government Printing

Office, 1924); Advisory Committee on City Planning and Zoning, U.S. Department of Commerce, *A Standard City Planning Enabling Act* (Washington, D.C.: U.S. Government Printing Office, 1928). The other key works of the Advisory Committee were *A Zoning Primer* (1922), *A City Planning Primer* (1928), *The Preparation of Zoning Ordinances* (1931), and *Model Subdivision Regulations* (1932). The Division of Building and Housing of the U.S. Department of Commerce also published a great deal of mimeographed literature on zoning and city planning, including their popular, annually updated *Zoning Progress in the United States*. See Division of Building and Housing, Bureau of Standards, U.S. Department of Commerce, *Publications Relating to Zoning and City Planning*, mimeo, June 2, 1930.

30. Of the 11 volumes published by the President's Conference on Home Building and Home Ownership, it is notable that volume 1, the first in the series, was John M. Gries and James Ford, eds., *Planning for Residential Districts* (Washington, D.C.: National Capital Press, 1932). This volume contained the reports of the committees on: (1) City Planning and Zoning, (2) Subdivision Layout, (3) Utilities for Houses, (4) Landscape Planning and Planting. Another important book in this series was volume 3, *Slums, Large-Scale Housing and Decentralization*. A summary of all the Conference recommendations is contained in volume 11, *Housing Objectives and Programs*. For the active participants, see *The President's Conference on Home Building and Home Ownership*, Directory of Committee Personnel, December 2–5, 1931 (Washington, D.C.: U.S. Department of Commerce, 1931). For a description of the Conference, see William Lindus Cody Wheaton, "The Evolution of Federal Housing Programs" (Ph.D. diss., Department of Political Science, University of Chicago, 1953), pp. 8–14. On the further codification of subdivision standards following the President's Conference Committee Report on Subdivision Layout, see American Society of Civil Engineers, Committee of the City Planning Division on Land Subdivision Manual, *Land Subdivision* (New York: American Society of Civil Engineers, 1939). The 1931 Conference Subdivision committee and the 1939 ASCE committee were both chaired by the same person, planner Harland Bartholomew, NAREB's director of research in city planning. See *Annals of Real Estate Practice* (Chicago: National Association of Real Estate Boards, 1930), p. 480.

31. Thomas Adams, *The Design of Residential Areas* (Cambridge: Harvard University Press, 1934); on the greenbelt towns, see Joseph L. Arnold, *The New Deal in the Suburbs* (Columbus: Ohio State University Press, 1971); and Zane L. Miller, *Suburb: Neighborhood and Community in Forest Park, Ohio, 1935–1976* (Knoxville: University of Tennessee Press, 1981). On Radburn, see Thomas Adams, *Design;* Eugenie Ladner Birch, "Radburn and the American Planning Movement: The Persistence of an Idea," *Journal of the American Planning Association*, 46, 4, October 1980; Daniel Schaffer, *Garden Cities for America: The Radburn Experience* (Philadelphia: Temple University Press, 1982); Roy Lubove, *Community Planning in the 1920s* (Pittsburgh: University of Pittsburgh Press, 1963); Henry Wright,

Rehousing Urban America (New York: Columbia University Press, 1935); Clarence S. Stein, *Toward New Towns for America* (New York: Reinhold, 1957); Clarence Arthur Perry, *Housing for the Machine Age* (New York: Russell Sage Foundation, 1939). Little-known primary sources on Radburn are Henry Wright, "How Long Blocks Cut Down Street Costs, and other Economies of Modern Planning," and Alexander M. Bing, "Community Planning for the Motor Age," in *Annals of Real Estate Practice* (Chicago: National Association of Real Estate Boards, 1929). Another important source on various examples of large-scale residential subdividing is Arthur C. Comey and Max S. Wehrly, "Planned Communities," in National Resources Committee, *Urban Planning and Land Policies* (Washington, D.C.: U.S. Government Printing Office, 1939). On FHA's Land Planning Division, see chapter 6. For an example of FHA codification of the basic community builder planning and design principles in creating the modern residential subdivision, see FHA, *Successful Subdivisions*, Land Planning Bulletin Number 1 (Washington, D.C.: U.S. Government Printing Office, 1940). Seward Mott, as Executive Director of ULI, coedited *The Community Builders Handbook* with ULI's Assistant Director, Max Wehrly (author of the 1939 "Planned Communities" study), and Harold Lautner (author of *Subdivision Regulations*). See Community Builders' Council, *The Community Builders Handbook* (Washington, D.C.: Urban Land Institute, 1947). On the history of ULI, see Garnett Laidlaw Eskew, *Of Land and Men: The Birth and Growth of an Idea* (Washington, D.C.: Urban Land Institute, 1959). For an overview of the history of residential subdivision design, see Robert A. M. Stern, *The Anglo-American Suburb* (London: Architectural Design, 1981).

32. George B. Ford, "City Planning and the Outlying Unbuilt Areas," *Annals of Real Estate Practice*, III, Home Building and Subdividing (Chicago: National Association of Real Estate Boards, 1925), p. 247; J. C. Nichols, "Financial," p. 105.

33. Helen C. Monchow, *The Use of Deed Restrictions in Subdivision Development* (Chicago: Institute for Research in Land Economics and Public Utilities, 1928); J. C. Nichols, "Developer's View."

34. J. C. Nichols, *Real Estate Subdivisions*, p. 7.

35. The best source is Arthur Comey and Max Wehrly, "Planned Communities"; on Duncan McDuffie, see *Real Estate*, III, 5, April 1914, p. 128; and Marc Weiss, "Urban Land Developers." On the pioneer, see John Emerson Todd, *Frederick Law Olmsted* (Boston: Twayne, 1982).

36. John Nolen, "Real Estate," p. 6.

37. J. C. Nichols, "The Planning and Control of Outlying Shopping Centers."

38. Lawson Purdy, "Districting and Zoning of Cities," pp. 173–74. J. C. Nichols made the same point eight years later: "Due to the familiarity of the realtor with the creation and maintenance of property values through privately restricted areas primarily in residential properties, he has been a real asset to zoning throughout the city as a whole." J. C. Nichols, "The Responsibilities of Realtors in City Planning," p. 36.

39. Edward M. Bassett, in advocating the need for public regulations, frequently would begin his argument by pointing out some of the inadequacies of private restrictions. For example, see Edward M. Bassett, *Zoning* (New York: National Municipal League, 1922), p. 317; and *Pacific Municipalities*, 36, 2, February 1922, p. 55.

40. Homer Vanderblue, "The Florida Land Boom," *Journal of Land and Public Utility Economics*, III, 2, May 1927, and III, 3, August 1927; Ernest M. Fisher, *Real Estate Subdividing Activity and Population Growth in Nine Urban Areas*, Michigan Business Studies, I, 9, July 1928 (Ann Arbor: University of Michigan, 1928); idem, "Speculation in Suburban Lands," *American Economic Review*, XXIII, 1, Supplement, March 1933; idem, and Raymond F. Smith, *Land Subdividing and the Rate of Utilization*, Michigan Business Studies, IV, 5 (Ann Arbor: University of Michigan, 1932); Lewis A. Maverick, "Cycles in Real Estate Activity," and "Cycles in Real Estate Activity: Los Angeles," *Journal of Land and Public Utility Economics*, VIII, 2, May 1932, and IX, 1, February 1933; Homer Hoyt, *One Hundred Years of Land Values in Chicago* (Chicago: University of Chicago Press, 1933); Helen Corbin Monchow, *Seventy Years of Real Estate Subdividing in the Region of Chicago*, (Chicago: Northwestern University Press, 1939); Charles Henry Wray, *Real Estate Subdividing in New Jersey*, Bulletin of the Bureau of Business and Economic Research, III, 1 (New Brunswick: Rutgers University, 1932); Herbert D. Simpson and John E. Burton, *The Valuation of Vacant Land in Suburban Areas* (Chicago: Institute for Economic Research, 1930); Herbert D. Simpson, "Real Estate Speculation and the Depression," *American Economic Review*, XXIII, 1, Supplement, March 1933; Philip H. Cornick, *Premature Subdivision and Its Consequences* (New York: Institute of Public Administration, 1938); Charles D. Clark, "Penalties of Excess Subdividing," *City Planning*, 10, 2, April 1934; A. M. Hillhouse, *Municipal Bonds: A Century of Experience* (New York: Prentice-Hall, 1936), pp. 67–87.

41. Irenaeus Shuler, "Subdivision Control and Standards," *Annals of Real Estate Practice*, III, Home Building and Subdividing (Chicago: National Association of Real Estate Boards, 1925), p. 241; "Detroit Meeting of the Institute," *City Planning*, I, 2, July 1925, p. 126; Flavel Shurtleff, "Institute Meeting at Detroit on Subdivision Regulation," *City Planning*, I, 3, October 1925, pp. 198–200; *California Real Estate*, V, 10, July 1925, p. 23. One sign of the growing cooperation is that in 1925, three NAREB leaders, Robert Jemison, Jr., Nathan William MacChesney, and Irenaeus Shuler, were elected to the Board of Directors of the National Conference on City Planning. J. C. Nichols was already a director.

42. *California Real Estate*, V, 6, March 1925, p. 27; Irenaeus Shuler, "Subdivision Control," p. 241. Shuler was a leading community builder, head of Shuler & Cary, one of the biggest real estate brokerage and land development firms in Omaha, Nebraska. Shuler & Cary specialized in expensive, high-quality residential subdivisions, similar to J. C. Nichols' Country Club District. Shuler, in addition to his role in NAREB (he was vice-president as well as chairman of the Home Builders and Subdividers Division), was also president of the Omaha Real

Estate Board in 1920, chairman of the Omaha City Planning Commission from 1923 on, and on the Board of Directors of the National Conference on City Planning from 1925 through 1928. Shuler's views on subdividing were summarized in a 1927 NAREB speech: "Planning and developing the modern subdivision (the new community), means much more than merely engineering, platting and building. Successful planning and developing requires the united efforts of the city planner, the landscape architect, the engineer, the building architect, and the Realtor. The city planner is consulted to determine the best available use to which the land may be put. . . . The farsighted Realtor-subdivider will generally secure such advice, especially in the larger community developments. The subdivision should be planned as a part of a community and if this thought is kept in mind, the subdivision will be more likely to fit in a general plan and an increase in values is much more likely to occur." See Irenaeus Shuler, "Selecting, Planning and Developing Subdivisions," *Annals of Real Estate Practice*, III, Home Building and Subdividing (Chicago: National Association of Real Estate Boards, 1927), pp. 103–4; and idem, "Subdivisions," in Blake Snyder, *The Real Estate Handbook*.

43. Irenaeus Shuler, "Subdivision Control," p. 239.

44. Ibid., p. 240.

45. Ibid., p. 242.

46. N. P. Dodge, "Report of the Committee on Legislation," *Annals of Real Estate Practice*, 1925, pp. 302–3.

47. Ibid., p. 301. See chapters 1 and 5.

48. On deliberations and approval, see Morris Knowles, "Subdivision Control," *Annals of Real Estate Practice*, III, Home Building and Subdividing (Chicago: National Association of Real Estate Boards, 1926); Hugh Pomeroy, "How Should the Platting of Suburban Territory be Controlled," H. W. Elmore, "Regulations of the Offering and Sale of Subdivisions," Axel Lonnquist, "The Subdividers' Code of Ethics," and Irenaeus Shuler, "Subdivision Control," *Annals of Real Estate Practice*, III, Home Building and Subdividing (Chicago: National Association of Real Estate Boards, 1927); Theodora Kimball Hubbard, "Survey of City and Regional Planning in the United States," *City Planning*, 2, 2, April 1926, p. 102; Flavel Shurtleff, "Florida Conference," *City Planning*, 2, 3, July 1926, pp. 217–19; Irving C. Root, "Joint Committee on Subdivision Control," *City Planning*, 2, 4, October 1926, p. 304; "The Annual Meeting of the A.C.P.I.," *City Planning*, 3, 3, July 1927; Irving C. Root, "Regulating Land Subdivision—A Progress Report," *Planning Problems of Town, City and Region* (Philadelphia: Wm. F. Fell, 1926); Morris Knowles, "Subdivision Control—A Report by a Committee of the American City Planning Institute," *Planning Problems of Town, City, and Region* (Philadelphia: Wm. F. Fell, 1927). The complete statements are published in Shuler, "Subdivision Control," 1927, pp. 325–34, and Knowles, "Subdivision Control," 1927, pp. 194–201. The disputed word "all" is missing from Shuler, p. 329, and included in Knowles, p. 197.

On the issue of voluntary or mandatory dedication of parks, see the argument for voluntary private land dedication and public planning, development, and maintenance by C. C. Hieatt, "Planning Play Areas in New Real Estate Subdivisions," *City Planning*, 4, 1, January 1928, p. 74. Hieatt was president of NAREB and a member of the Louisville City Planning and Zoning Commission in 1927. On parks and playgrounds, see also William E. Harmon, "Playgrounds in New Land Subdivisions," *City Planning*, 2, 2, April 1926; "The Harmon Foundation Announces $40,000 in Awards," *The Community Builder*, II, 3, August 1928; "Five Percent for Parks in Oklahoma City Subdivisions," *City Planning*, 4, 4, October 1928, p. 305; "Dedication of Leimert Park to City of Los Angeles," *California Real Estate*, XI, 4, January 1931, p. 36; S. Herbert Hare, "Acquisition of Park Land in Connection with Real Estate Subdivisions," *City Planning*, 9, 1, January 1933. On follow-through by NAREB, see Guy M. Rush and W. Sumner Holbrook, Jr., "Subdivision Control Methods: A Nation-Wide Survey," *National Real Estate Journal*, 29, July 23, 1928, pp. 42–45; and the creation by NAREB's Home Builders and Subdividers Division of a subdivision Consultation Bureau and a system of Subdivision Certificates of Approval. See "Raising the Standards of Subdivisions," *City Planning*, 5, 2, April 1929, p. 114. The NAREB Consultation Bureau, according to 1931 NAREB President Harry S. Kissell, was designed "to protect the public against the land butcher, not only those who sell unusable lots but those in every community who have a semblance of respectability but sell lots which never will have improvements, which never can get utilities, and in many cases have titles that are not marketable." See Pearl Davies, *Real Estate*, pp. 159–60. Two influential articles among realtors were H. Morton Bodfish, "The 'Free-Lot' Subdivider: His Method of Operation and The Available Methods of Control," and Coleman Woodbury, "Some Suggested Changes in the Control of Urban Land Development," *Journal of Land and Public Utility Economics*, V, 3, August 1929.

On follow-up by ACPI, see the very important supplementary statement on "Control of Land Subdivision and Building Development," *City Planning*, 4, 3, July 1928, pp. 251–55. This statement, drawn up by a separate committee somewhat more dominated by architects than the committee predominantly made up of engineers and lawyers that drew up the ACPI-NAREB compromise statement, is more far-reaching and socially oriented than the earlier joint effort. Frederick Bigger, the committee's chairman, reprints the 1928 ACPI statement in his manual on "Site Planning," in *Housing: The Continuing Problem*, National Resources Planning Board (Washington, D.C.: U.S. Government Printing Office, 1940).

49. Theodora Kimball Hubbard, the librarian of the American City Planning Institute (and the School of Landscape Architecture and Department of City and Regional Planning, Harvard University), wrote in April 1928: "An event of 1927 which promises far-reaching results in the wise development of suburban lands is the adoption jointly by the National Association of Real Estate Boards and the American City Planning Institute of a report on subdivision control, endorsing the preparation of an official master plan and the control of platting of subdivisions by local planning commissions. *The principles thus endorsed have already been*

embodied in the Standard City Planning Enabling Act of the Department of Commerce . . ." (emphasis added). Theodora Kimball Hubbard, "Annual Survey of City and Regional Planning in the United States, 1927," *City Planning,* 4, 2, April 1928, p. 117.

A NAREB press release described the effect of the recommendations of the NAREB-ACPI *Joint Statement on Subdivision Control* thusly: "They thenceforth became a nationally accepted platform for sound subdivision development, particularly for areas outside a city's corporate limits. The principle which they enunciated for such control is recognized in the so-called Hoover Model City Planning Enabling Act." *California Real Estate,* IX, 9, June 1929, p. 380. Henry Vincent Hubbard and Theodora Kimball Hubbard, in their book *Our Cities To-Day and To-Morrow* (Cambridge: Harvard University Press, 1929), p. 9, call the work of the Hoover Advisory Committee "The most potent single recent influence on city planning in the United States." For a later discussion of the "Hoover Act," see T. J. Kent, Jr., *The Urban General Plan* (San Francisco: Chandler, 1964).

The Advisory Committee on City Planning and Zoning, using the impetus of the NAREB-ACPI statement, not only published the Standard Act and *A City Planning Primer* in 1928 but prepared *Model Subdivision Regulations* in 1932. Unfortunately, the mimeographed manuscript was circulated but not printed before President Roosevelt terminated the Advisory Committee upon assuming office in March 1933. The *Model Subdivision Regulations* were rescued and later "reproduced and distributed," without alteration, by the U.S. National Resources Committee in December of 1936. The story is explained by Charles W. Eliot, 2d, in his Preface on page i. See the Advisory Committee on City Planning and Zoning, U.S. Department of Commerce, *Model Subdivision Regulations: A Guide for Local Planning Commissions in the Preparation of Local Regulations Governing the Subdivision of Land* (Washington, D.C.: National Resources Committee, 1936). Two members of the Advisory Committee also published their own version of the state and local recommendations. See Edward M. Bassett, Frank B. Williams, Alfred Bettman, and Robert Whitten, *Model Laws for Planning Cities, Counties, and States— Including Zoning, Subdivision Regulations, and Protection of Official Map* (Cambridge: Harvard University Press, 1935); Edward M. Bassett, *The Master Plan* (New York: Russell Sage Foundation, 1938); idem, *Zoning* (New York: Russell Sage Foundation, 1936); Alfred Bettman, *City and Regional Planning Papers,* edited by Arthur C. Comey (Cambridge: Harvard University Press, 1946). For the further evolution, see Russell Van Nest Black, *Building Lines and Reservations for Future Streets* (Cambridge: Harvard University Press, 1935); idem, and Mary Hedges Black, *Planning for the Small American City* (Chicago: Public Administration Service, 1938); Harold S. Buttenheim, "Urban Land Policies," in National Resources Committee, *Urban Planning;* Ladislas Segoe, ed., *Local Planning Administration* (Chicago: Institute for Training in Municipal Administration, 1941); Harold W. Lautner, *Subdivision Regulations* (Chicago: Public Administration Service, 1941); Robert E. Merriam, *The Subdivision of Land: A Guide for Municipal Officials in the Regulation of Land Subdivision* (Chicago: American Society of Planning Officials,

1942). Harold Lautner was assistant director of the Urban Land Institute until March 1946, and he helped prepare *The Community Builders Handbook.* See Garnett Eskew, *Land and Men,* p. 106.

For the impact of the NAREB-ACPI statement and subsequent "Hoover Act" on California, see chapter 5. Also see Fred E. Reed, "Realtors and City Planning Progress," *City Planning,* 4, 3, July 1928; *California Real Estate,* VII, 7, April 1927, p. 27; *Pacific Municipalities,* 41, 7, July 1927, pp. 233–34, and 42, 3, March 1928, p. 85.

50. *Planning Problems of Town, City, and Region,* 1926, p. 51 (Bassett), p. 38 (president of FSAREB). In addition to some of the sources cited above, others that indicate the new interest in metropolitan regional master plans and land-use regulations include George B. Ford, *The Newer City Planning* (Washington, D.C.: American Civic Association, 1928); Harlean James, *Land Planning in the United States for the City, State and Nation* (New York: MacMillan, 1926); idem, "The Cost of Regional Planning," *Journal of Land and Public Utility Economics,* V, 3, August 1929; Thomas Adams, Edward M. Bassett, and Robert Whitten, "Problems of Planning Unbuilt Areas," in *Neighborhood and Community Planning* (New York: Regional Survey of New York and its Environs, 1929); and the newly added chapter on "Regional Planning" by John Nolen in the second edition of his classic, John Nolen, ed., *City Planning* (New York: Appleton, 1929). Another indication of the growing metropolitan-suburban-regional trend is the publication in 1932 of the first special U.S. Census of Population report on this subject. See U.S. Department of Commerce, Bureau of the Census, *Metropolitan Districts: Population and Area,* Fifteenth Census of the United States, 1930 (Washington, D.C.: U.S. Government Printing Office, 1932).

4. The Los Angeles Realty Board and Zoning

1. Robert M. Fogelson, *The Fragmented Metropolis: Los Angeles, 1850–1930* (Cambridge: Harvard University Press, 1967); Carey McWilliams, *Southern California: An Island on the Land* (Santa Barbara: Peregrine Smith, 1973); Remi Nadeau, *Los Angeles* (New York: Longmans, Green, 1960); Frederic Cople Jaher, *The Urban Establishment* (Urbana: University of Illinois Press, 1982), pp. 577–709; Glenn S. Dumke, *The Boom of the Eighties in Southern California* (San Marino: The Huntington Library, 1944); William L. Kahrl, *Water and Power* (Berkeley: University of California Press, 1982); Mel Scott, *Metropolitan Los Angeles* (Los Angeles: The Haynes Foundation, 1949); Robert Gottlieb and Irene Wolt, *Thinking Big* (New York: Putnam, 1977); Frank L. Beach, "The Transformation of California, 1900–1920: The Effects of the Westward Movement in California's Growth and Development in the Progressive Period" (Ph.D. diss., Department of History, University of California, Berkeley, 1963); Mark Stewart Foster, "The Decentralization of Los Angeles During the 1920s" (Ph.D. diss., Department of History, University of Southern California, 1971).

2. Los Angeles Realty Board, Minutes of the Governing Committee (Archives of the Los Angeles Board of Realtors), July 31, 1903, p. 1; August 4, 1903, p. 1; September 1, 1903, p. 1; November 3, 1903, pp. 1–2; December 15, 1903, p. 2; January 5, 1904, p. 1; Richard Pierce, "A History of the Los Angeles Board of Realtors" (Los Angeles Board of Realtors, undated); C. W. Taylor, "History of the California Real Estate Association" (manuscript in the library of the California Association of Realtors, 1955); Charles Mulford Robinson, *Los Angeles, California: The City Beautiful,* Report of the Municipal Art Commission for the City of Los Angeles (Los Angeles: William J. Porter, 1909); *Los Angeles Examiner,* December 19, 1910, p. 11; Arthur S. Bent, "Discussion," *Economic Height of Buildings,* Civic Development Department (Washington, D.C.: Chamber of Commerce of the United States, 1927), pp. 22–25. In a speech to the Los Angeles Realty Board on April 16, 1915, Henry W. O'Melveny, the most powerful corporate attorney in Los Angeles and a principal with the Title Insurance and Trust Company, said: "A friend of mine described the chief business of Los Angeles to be that of manufacturing homes, and when you come to think about it he is right. People are flocking here from all parts of the world to make this their home. We have the raw material and the finished product. A home presupposes the ownership of a tract or parcel of land. This presupposes the sale by some one, of course, and a majority of those transactions are handled through [realty] agents. This makes your profession, for it is a profession, a very important part in this community. You play a very important part in the largest manufacturing industry in this country. . . . We all know that many of the allusions that are made to real estate agents are ill-founded. The same remarks can be made of doctors, or of ministers, or of lawyers, or of bankers." Henry W. O'Melveny, "What a Realty Broker Owes to His Client, and His Legal Rights," *California Real Estate Directory-Bulletin,* I, 1, April 1, 1920 (Sacramento: California State Printing Office, 1920), p. 300.

3. Los Angeles City Ordinance Number 17136 N.S., Section 2.

4. Los Angeles City Ordinance Number 17135 N.S.

5. Lewis A. Maverick, "Cycles in Real Estate Activity: Los Angeles," *Journal of Land and Public Utility Economics,* IX, 1, February 1933, pp. 523–26; Harrison R. Baker, ed., *Subdivision Principles and Practices* (Los Angeles: California Real Estate Association, 1936), p. 48; *California Realty Bulletin,* 1, 1, May 1908, p. 3; Margaret S. Gordon, *Employment Expansion and Population Growth* (Berkeley: University of California Press, 1954), pp. 112–20; Frank L. Kidner, *California Business Cycles* (Berkeley: University of California Press, 1946); Harold U. Faulkner, *The Decline of Laissez Faire, 1897–1917* (New York: Rinehart, 1951), pp. 22–32; Glenn Dumke, *Boom;* Frank Beach, "Transformation," pp. 212, 225–28; Carey McWilliams, *Southern California,* pp. 118–34.

6. Dana W. Bartlett, *The Better City* (Los Angeles: Neuner Press, 1907), pp. 19, 70.

7. Ray E. Nimmo, "Accomplishing the Segregation of Industries," *The California Outlook,* XV, 10, September 6, 1913, p. 8.

8. *Los Angeles Times,* July 24, 1909, Section II, p. 2.

9. Gottlieb and Wolt, *Thinking Big;* Frank Beach, "Transformation," pp. 223–25.

10. Los Angeles City Ordinance Number 17136 N.S., Section 5; W. L. Pollard, "Outline of the Law of Zoning in the United States," *Annals of the American Academy of Political and Social Science,* 155, II, May 1931, pp. 15–33; Rollin L. McNitt, *The Law of Zoning* (San Francisco: A. Carlisle, 1926); Jefferson M. Hardin, "The Present Status of Municipal Zoning in the Law," *Pacific Municipalities,* 42, 7, July 1928, pp. 235–45, 251; 42, 8, August 1928, pp. 274–76, 289.

11. Ray Nimmo, "Accomplishing," p. 8.

12. Los Angeles City Ordinance Number 17135 N.S., Preamble.

13. Ray Nimmo, "Accomplishing," pp. 8–9; Judith Norvell Jamison, "Administration of City Planning in Los Angeles" (M.A. thesis, Department of Political Science, University of California at Los Angeles, June 1947), p. 44; John E. Roberts, "Cases Preliminary to Comprehensive Zoning Wherein Certain Near Nuisances Have Been Prohibited Within Certain Districts," Office of the Zoning Administrator, Department of City Planning, City of Los Angeles, September 1946.

14. W. L. Pollard, "Outline," p. 17.

15. Paul Ong, "An Ethnic Trade: The Chinese Laundries in Early California," *Journal of Ethnic Studies,* 8, 4, Winter 1981, pp. 95–113; W. L. Pollard, "Outline"; Gordon Whitnall, "History of Zoning," *Annals of the American Academy of Political and Social Science,* 155, II, May 1931, p. 9; Carey McWilliams, *Southern California,* pp. 84–95.

16. Ray Nimmo, "Accomplishing," p. 9.

17. In the matter of Yick Wo, 68 Cal 300 (cited in W.L. Pollard, "Outline," p. 18).

18. The Industrial District Ordinance of 1908 (17135 N.S.) was somewhat modified on December 30, 1909. See Los Angeles City Ordinance 19,500 N.S.

19. Frank Backus Williams, *The Law of City Planning and Zoning* (New York: MacMillan, 1922), p. 267; Huber Earl Smutz, "Zoning in Los Angeles," *Annual Report,* Los Angeles Board of City Planning Commissioners, 1930, p. 58; Los Angeles Realty Board, Minutes of the Governing Committee, February 15, 1917, p. 2; March 1, 1917, p. 2.

20. J. M. Guinn, "How the Area of Los Angeles City was Enlarged," *Historical Society of Southern California Annual,* IX, III, 1914, pp. 173–80; Richard Bigger and James D. Kitchen, *How the Cities Grew* (Los Angeles: The Haynes Foundation, 1952), pp. 155–93; Robert Fogelson, *Fragmented,* pp. 224–27.

21. Ray Nimmo, "Accomplishing," p. 8.

22. W. L. Pollard, "Outline"; John Roberts, "Cases"; Rollin McNitt, *Law;* Jefferson Hardin, "Present Status"; Frank Williams, *Law.*

23. Lawrence Veiller, a leading city planner and a member of the two New York zoning commissions, described the Los Angeles zoning law and court cases in a 1914 speech to the National Conference on City Planning, stating that since

the Los Angeles law "is the only one which has been tested in operation through any considerable period of time and is also one which has been tested in the highest state courts, it assumes especial importance for the rest of the country." Lawrence Veiller, "Protecting Residential Districts," *Proceedings of the Sixth National Conference on City Planning* (Boston: Harvard University Press, 1914), p. 97; Charles Cheney, in reporting to his fellow Californians on the 1917 National Conference on City Planning, stated, "The great importance of zoning or districting of cities was emphasized at practically every session of the Conference. It was evident that the experts present without question regarded it as the first fundamental step. California's progress came in for a great deal of favorable comment, particularly as the decisions of the U.S. Supreme Court upholding the Los Angeles Zone Ordinance seemed to be the basis for districting in New York and most of the other cities in the country." *Pacific Municipalities,* 31, 7, July 1917, p. 306.

24. S. J. Makielski, Jr., *The Politics of Zoning: The New York Experience* (New York: Columbia University Press, 1966), p. 21; *Pacific Municipalities,* 29, 5, May 1915, pp. 201–2. (This is an excerpt from the 1913 *Report of the Heights of Buildings Commission,* New York City's first zoning commission.)

25. Albert Lee Stephens, "The Significance of the New Laws Relative to Zoning and Set-Back Lines," *Pacific Municipalities,* 32, 3, March 1918, pp. 129–36.

26. *Pacific Municipalities,* 27, 7, July 1913, p. 361; 28, 5, May 1914, p. 276; 28, 10, October 1914, p. 536; 29, 4, April 1915, p. 179; 31, 7, July 1917, p. 179; Civic Development Department, *City Planning and Zoning Accomplishments* (Washington, D.C.: Chamber of Commerce of the United States, 1927), table III.

27. Charles Henry Cheney, *Procedure for Zoning or Districting of Cities,* Bulletin Number 2 (San Francisco: California Conference on City Planning, September 1917).

28. *Oakland Tribune,* May 29, 1914, pp. 1 and 12. On Mayor Frank Mott's activities as a leader of Oakland and California realtors, see C. W. Taylor, "History," ch. 2, p. 5; *Real Estate,* II, 12, September 1913, p. 344.

29. Robert Fogelson, *Fragmented;* Frank Beach, "Transformation," pp. 152–53, 200; Margaret Gordon, *Employment,* pp. 172–73; Frank L. Kidner and Philip Neff, *An Economic Survey of the Los Angeles Area* (Los Angeles: The Haynes Foundation, 1945), pp. 7–9; Frank Kidner, *California,* p. 16; Mark Foster, "Decentralization," p. 174.

30. Frank Beach, "Transformation," pp. 211–14; Mark Foster, "Decentralization," pp. 40–41, 55.

31. Huber Smutz, "Zoning"; Huber Earl Smutz, "Zoning: Past-Present-Future," unpublished manuscript in possession of the author; Lawrence Veiller, "Protecting," pp. 102–4.

32. Robert Fogelson, *Fragmented,* pp. 70–84.

33. *Real Estate,* IV, 12, November 1915, p. 388; Remi Nadeau, *Los Angeles,* pp. 147–49; "war workers in Los Angeles were a negligible quantity with the exception of those employed in the shipyards at San Pedro and Long Beach during

the latter year of the war. It has been estimated that fully 20,000 laborers left Los Angeles between 1914 and 1918 for employment in manufacturing centers of the east and became engaged in war industries." Los Angeles Realty Board, response to U.S. Department of Labor questionnaire, January 30, 1919, p. 2. Also see note 5 in this chapter.

34. "The local Boards throughout the State having suffered on account of the depression in business activity," *Real Estate,* III, 11, October 1914, p. 329; "Many of the members were not disloyal to the State body, but, they were so busy trying to hold their private businesses together during trying times, that it left little leisure to attend meetings and aid in the things the Federation was striving for." C. W. Taylor, "History," ch. 5, p. 26, see also ch. 5, p. 25, ch. 7, p. 1; Los Angeles Realty Board, Minutes of the Governing Committee, September 29, 1915, p. 1; November 4, 1915, pp. 1–2; January 12, 1916, pp. 1–2; January 13, 1916, p. 4; May 22, 1917, pp. 1–2; June 9, 1917, p. 2.

35. Los Angeles Realty Board, Minutes of the Governing Committee, July 27, 1916, p. 1.

36. Letter from realtor-subdivider Patrick C. Campbell to Governing Committee, Los Angeles Realty Board, June 14, 1917; Los Angeles Realty Board, Minutes of the Governing Committee, July 12, 1917, p. 2; February 6, 1919, p. 2; Letter to the Governing Committee from the Committee on the Labor Department questionnaire, Los Angeles Realty Board, January 21, 1919; "There were a much greater number of forced liquidations of unimproved nonincome-producing properties in the war period—1917–18—than there were in previous corresponding periods. . . . War restrictions on construction during the war period—1917–18—materially operated to decrease the value of unimproved real estate in and about Los Angeles," Los Angeles Realty Board, response to U.S. Department of Labor questionnaire, January 30, 1919, p. 2; "The year has been a particularly trying one for the real estate fraternity. Never before has the Los Angeles Realty Board as an institution been put to so severe a test. With an embargo on building and practically no market for real estate, the individual Realtor has found it exceedingly difficult to command even a fair percentage of the usual volume of business, and, for this reason, has not been in a position to give the support to this organization which would be expected in normal times." Letter from the Governing Committee to the outgoing president, Los Angeles Realty Board, May 15, 1919, p. 2.

37. Los Angeles Realty Board, response to the U.S. Department of Labor questionnaire, January 30, 1919, p. 2; Los Angeles Realty Board, Minutes of the Governing Committee, March 25, 1920, p. 1.

38. Report of the Committee on the Housing Situation, Los Angeles Realty Board, May 12, 1920, p. 1.

39. Los Angeles Realty Board, response to the U.S. Department of Labor questionnaire, January 30, 1919, p. 2; Los Angeles Realty Board, Minutes of the Governing Committee, April 24, 1919, p. 3; August 7, 1919, p. 1; October 9, 1919, p. 1; October 16, 1919, p. 2; October 23, 1919, p. 2.

40. Los Angeles Realty Board, Minutes of the Governing Committee, Feb-

ruary 20, 1919, pp. 1–2; November 20, 1919, p. 1; December 4, 1919, p. 2; October 21, 1920, p. 1; October 22, 1920, p. 1; October 25, 1920, p. 1; October 28, 1920, p. 2; "On further motion duly made, seconded and carried it was the consensus of opinion of the Governing Committee that an appeal should be made to the newspapers to eliminate all reference to 'rent hog propaganda.' " Los Angeles Realty Board, Minutes of the Governing Committee, January 27, 1921, p. 2.

41. Mark Foster, "Decentralization," pp. 22–46, 172–94; Frank Beach, "Transformation," pp. 71–99, 204–42; Carey McWilliams, *Southern California*, pp. 135–37; Remi Nadeau, *Los Angeles*, p. 146; Los Angeles Realty Board, Minutes of the Governing Committee, March 20, 1919, p. 2.

42. Letter from Frank Ryan, Chairman of the Publicity Committee, to Governing Committee, Los Angeles Realty Board, March 25, 1920, pp. 1–2.

43. Los Angeles Realty Board, Minutes of the Governing Committee, May 29, 1919, p. 2; June 12, 1919, p. 2.

44. Los Angeles Realty Board, Minutes of the Governing Committee, May 27, 1920, p. 1.

45. Cuthbert Reeves, *The Valuation of Business Lots in Downtown Los Angeles* (Los Angeles: Bureau of Municipal Research, 1932), p. 15. As an example of the downtown representation among the Realty Board's leaders, William May Garland, 1917–18 NAREB president and founder and senior realtor of the Los Angeles Realty Board, was also president of the Central Business District Association of Los Angeles, *Real Estate*, III, 7, June 1914, p. 202.

46. Charles Cheney, *Procedure.*

47. *Los Angeles Times*, September 1, 1920, Part II, p. 5.

48. For an interesting discussion of the role of the oil industry in Los Angeles' development, see Fred W. Viehe, "Black Gold Suburbs: The Influence of the Extractive Industry on the Suburbanization of Los Angeles, 1880–1930," *Journal of Urban History*, 8, 1, November 1981.

49. *Los Angeles Times*, July 28, 1920, Part II, p. 1.

50. Ibid., May 28, 1920, Part II, p. 1.

51. William May Garland, for example, in addition to his role as a downtown realtor, also "subdivided the elite district in and around Westlake (now MacArthur) Park." Remi Nadeau, *Los Angeles*, p. 147; Los Angeles Realty Board, Minutes of the Governing Committee, November 21, 1918, p. 2.

52. Los Angeles Realty Board, Minutes of the Governing Committee, May 29, 1919, p. 2; see also May 22, 1919, p. 2; June 5, 1919, p. 1.

53. Ibid., June 12, 1919, pp. 1–2.

54. Ibid., March 20, 1919, p. 2; October 16, 1919, p. 1; November 6, 1919, p. 2.

55. Gordon Whitnall, "Tracing the Development of Planning in Los Angeles," *Annual Report*, Los Angeles Board of City Planning Commissioners, 1930, p. 40.

56. Ibid.; *Los Angeles Times*, April 13, 1920, Part II, p. 8. Of the 51 commissioners, seven were from the Chamber of Commerce and three were from the Realty Board. The chairman of the Commission and chairman of the Commission's nine-member Executive Committee was W. H. Pierce, chairman of the Chamber of

Commerce's City Planning Committee. On April 8, 1920, the Governing Committee of the Los Angeles Realty Board moved to request that W. H. Pierce appoint one of the three Realty Board members to the City Planning Commission's powerful Executive Committee. Two days later Chairman Pierce appointed Gilbert S. Wright, past president of the Realty Board and head of one of the largest realty firms in downtown Los Angeles, to this important position. In the same April 8 resolution, the Realty Board declared its intention to take control of zoning for the city: ". . . with the further understanding that an effort will be made by that particular representative of the Realty Board [Gilbert Wright], together with the assistance of the President [Realty Board President O. A. Vickrey], through Mr. Pierce to bring about a situation whereby the proposed plans for the zoning of the City of Los Angeles by the Executive Committee of Nine will be referred to the Los Angeles Realty Board as its particular duty, the work to be done and transmission of plans to the City Council to be made by the Los Angeles Realty Board," Governing Committee Minutes, April 8, 1920, p. 2. On Gilbert S. Wright, see letter from Gilbert Wright to Board of Governors, Los Angeles Realty Board, September 29, 1920. He was president of Wright-Callender-Andrews Co., which owned and was headquartered in a ten-story office building on Hill and Fourth Streets in downtown Los Angeles.

57. *Los Angeles Times,* April 6, 1920, Part II, p. 7; April 13, 1920, Part III, p.3; April 15, 1920, Part II, p. 1; May 16, 1920, Part II, p. 2; letter from the Publicity Committee Chairman, Frank Ryan, to the Governing Committee, Los Angeles Realty Board, March 25, 1920, pp. 1–2; Los Angeles Realty Board, Minutes of the Governing Committee, April 15, 1920, p. 1.

58. Los Angeles Realty Board, Minutes of the Governing Committee, May 27, 1920, p. 1.

59. *Los Angeles Times,* May 28, 1920, Part II, p. 1; June 6, 1920, Part II, pp. 1–2, 12; June 11, 1920, Part III, p. 3; Los Angeles Realty Board, Minutes of the Governing Committee, June 17, 1920, p. 1. The realtors who formed the opposition "Wilshire Improvement Association," while members in good standing of the Los Angeles Realty Board and the California Real Estate Association, were mostly brokers in the Wilshire area, whereas the members of the Governing Committee of the Realty Board were mostly the large downtown brokers and the large citywide high-income residential subdividers. See *California Real Estate Directory-Bulletin,* II, 1 (Sacramento: California State Printing Office, June 20, 1920); *Annals of Real Estate Practice* (Chicago: National Association of Real Estate Boards, 1929), division membership rosters, pp. 955–1041; files and correspondence of the Los Angeles Realty Board, 1903–1921; *California Real Estate,* various issues; *Los Angeles Realtor,* various issues; C. W. Taylor, "History."

60. Los Angeles Realty Board, Minutes of the Governing Committee, November 3, 1919, p. 2; February 5, 1920, p. 2; April 8, 1920, p. 1; June 17, 1920, p. 1; June 24, 1920, p. 1; July 8, 1920, pp. 1–2; July 14, 1920, p. 1; Letter from S. Ross Fenner, secretary, Los Angeles Realty Board, to Realty Board Zoning Committee, July 9, 1920.

61. *Los Angeles Times,* April 14, 1920, Part I, p. 6; July 15, 1920, Part II, p. 12. Cheney had been involved in the zoning of Berkeley, San Francisco, Alameda, Oakland, Palo Alto, Fresno, and Portland, Oregon. Charles Cheney, *Procedure; Pacific Municipalities,* 23, 5, May 1919, pp. 170–85; 23, 9, September 1919, pp. 343–44; *The Architect and Engineer of California,* 52, 3, June 1918 (special issue on Charles Cheney); Carl Abbot, *Portland: Planning, Politics, and Growth in a Twentieth-Century City* (Lincoln: University of Nebraska Press, 1983), pp. 71–92; Marc A. Weiss, "Urban Land Developers and the Origins of Zoning Laws: The Case of Berkeley," *Berkeley Planning Journal,* III, 1, 1986. The Los Angeles Realty Board had previously followed his activities through northern California realtors such as Duncan McDuffie, Fred Reed, and Charles Cheney's father, Warren Cheney. While the younger Cheney was working on the zoning of Portland, the Los Angeles Realty Board answered the Portland Mayor's query with the following telegram: "This Board is favorable to building zone regulations and believe them advisable. Committee active here on this question but no definite plan as yet advocated. We believe such regulations tend to stabilize values and help rents." Los Angeles Realty Board, Minutes of the Governing Committee, February 19, 1920, p. 1.

Charles Cheney, at a luncheon given in his honor by the Los Angeles Chamber of Commerce on April 13, 1920, "talked about the connection between home-building and homeownership on the one hand and zoning—the protection of the investor—on the other. . . . He advocated zoning to exclude apartment houses and flat buildings from home areas and also spoke of the sociologic advantages of the bungalow court over the apartment or flat houses." At a September 1 City Club luncheon, Cheney said, "In Los Angeles we see flats and apartments creeping into the Wilshire district. We see industries hesitating whether or not to come to Los Angeles for fear that after they are established here zoning ordinances will be passed ordering them to move. There are many other signs which point to serious damage and loss if city planning on a broad basis is not undertaken soon." *Los Angeles Times,* April 14, 1920, Part I, p. 6; September 2, 1920, Part I, p. 8. It was Cheney's special reputation, from the 1916 Berkeley zoning law, as a planner-advocate *both* of exclusive single-family residential zoning *and* of exclusive industrial zoning that made him so appealing both to the Los Angeles Realty Board, concerned primarily with the former, and the Chamber of Commerce and Merchants and Manufacturers Association, deeply interested in the latter. See *Los Angeles Times,* June 16, 1920, Part II, p. 3.

62. Los Angeles Realty Board, Minutes of the Governing Committee, July 19, 1920, p. 1. The Wilshire District meeting was held on Wednesday evening, July 21, at the Masonic Hall, 265 S. Western Avenue.

63. Los Angeles Realty Board, Minutes of the Governing Committee, July 22, 1920, p. 1; "Report of Property Owners Committee for the Wilshire Neighborhood," July 21, 1920. The report, written by Charles Cheney and Realty Board President O. A. Vickrey and Vice-President Frank Ryan, states: "This neighborhood is being seriously invaded by flats and apartments which we know threaten

to destroy all its present attractiveness and desirability as a home neighborhood. We therefore, most urgently and earnestly, recommend that immediate steps be taken by the City Planning Commission and the City Council to work out an ordinance limiting flats and apartments to certain definite blocks and protecting the home blocks from further invasions of this kind. We are in hearty accord with the protection of Wilshire Boulevard as one of the greatest show drives and thoroughfares in the city, and pledge ourselves to maintain it permanently as a residence street" (p. 2).

64. *Los Angeles Times,* July 29, 1920, Part II, p. 12.

65. Los Angeles Realty Board, Minutes of the Governing Committee, July 29, 1920, p. 1.

66. *Los Angeles Times,* August 27, 1920, Part II, p. 1.

67. Ibid., September 2, 1920, Part I, p. 8.

68. Ibid., September 1, 1920, Part II, p. 5.

69. Ibid., June 8, 1920, Part II, p. 3; June 16, 1920, Part II, p. 3; June 26, 1920, Part II, p. 8; July 1, 1920, Part II, p. 1; July 21, 1920, Part II, p. 3; July 9, 1920, Part II, p. 5; July 16, 1920, Part I, p. 14; July 23, 1920, Part I, p. 16; August 3, 1920, Part II, p. 5; September 24, 1920, Part II, p. 8; September 29, 1920, Part I, p. 5; October 8, 1920, Part II, p. 6; October 20, 1920, Part II, p. 2.

70. Ibid., September 9, 1920, Part II, p. 8; September 17, 1920, Part II, p. 5; September 24, 1920, Part II, p. 8.

71. Ibid., August 6, 1920, Part II, p. 8.

72. Los Angeles Realty Board, Minutes of the Governing Committee, September 9, 1920, p. 2; September 14, 1920, p. 1.

73. *Los Angeles Times,* October 31, 1920, Part I, p. 7. On the actual hearings, see August 7, 1921, Part IV, p. 12; August 16, 1921, Part II, p. 3; August 17, 1921, Part II, p. 1.

74. Los Angeles City Ordinance Number 45,666 N.S., passed unanimously by the City Council on October 18, 1921. See *Los Angeles Times,* September 30, 1921, Part II, p. 12; October 4, 1921, Part II, p. 7; October 7, 1921, Part II, p. 11; October 8, 1921, Part II, p. 7; October 13, 1921, Part II, p. 2; October 19, 1921, Part II, p. 2; October 20, 1921, Part II, p. 5; October 30, 1921, Part V, p. 4; November 6, 1921, Part V, p. 5; November 26, 1921, Part II, p. 1; December 23, 1921, Part II, p. 8.

75. George Soule, *Prosperity Decade: 1917–1929* (New York: Rinehart, 1947), ch. 5, especially pp. 102–3; *California Real Estate,* I, 9, August –September 1921, pp. 2, 8, 11; II, 3, December 1921, p. 2.

76. "During this period of depressed values in many lines of investments, the money put into homes and farms looms safe and secure. And if the real estate man who may feel that the flood tide of sales has passed him by, will but preach in his community the strength and satisfaction and solidarity of the family owning their own home he will reap the harvest of success in no stinted measure." *California Real Estate,* I, 8, June–July 1921, p. 27; I, 9, August–September 1921,

p. 13; II, 5, February 1922, p. 27; II, 6, March 1922, p. 24; III, 1, October 1922, p. 8; C. W. Taylor, "History," ch. 8, pp. 3, 9. The chairman of the California "Own Your Own Home and Build Now" campaign was Harry Culver of the Los Angeles Realty Board.

77. Los Angeles Realty Board, Minutes of the Governing Committee, June 2, 1921, pp. 2–3; *Los Angeles Times,* September 29, 1921, Part II, p. 9; see also note number 41 of this chapter.

78. Los Angeles City Ordinance Number 45,666 N.S.; *Los Angeles Times,* October 19, 1921, Part II, p. 2.

79. George H. Coffin, Jr., *Zoning and its Relation to Property Values* (Los Angeles: California Real Estate Association, 1936), p. 11.

80. H. A. Postlethwaite, "Supreme Court Decides Los Angeles Zoning Cases," *Pacific Municipalities,* 39, 3, March 1925, pp. 71–72, 85–87; Gordon Whitnall, Address to the Los Angeles Realty Board, April 10, 1925 (Whitnall Papers, Los Angeles City Planning Department Library). See also note number 22 in this chapter.

81. Huber Smutz, "Past-Present-Future," p. 10; Robert Fogelson, *Fragmented;* Mark Foster, "Decentralization." On the role of the FHA in changing local zoning, see chapter 6. Also see Fred W. Marlow, "Future Trends in Subdivision Development Methods and Pricing Subdivision Property," in Harrison R. Baker, ed., *Subdivision Principles and Practices* (Los Angeles: California Real Estate Association, 1936). The FHA director for southern California from 1934–38 was Fred Marlow, a member of the Los Angeles Realty Board and a leading subdivider and housing developer. His partner, Fritz Burns, was a founder in the 1940s of the Community Builders' Council of the Urban Land Institute. In the 1950s Fred Marlow was president of the Los Angeles Realty Board, director of the California Real Estate Association, and vice-president of the National Association of Home Builders.

82. *California Real Estate,* II, 4, January 1922, pp. 6–9; Los Angeles Realty Board, Minutes of the Governing Committee, February 10, 1916, pp. 2–3; August 24, 1916, pp. 1–2; October 12, 1916, p. 1; January 8, 1920, pp. 2–3; *Real Estate,* III, 6, May 1914, p. 144; *California Real Estate,* I, 8, June–July 1920, p. 20; II, 5, February 1922, p. 2.

83. *California Real Estate Directory-Bulletin,* II, 2 (Sacramento: California State Printing Office, October 15, 1920), pp. 130–280.

84. Mark Foster, "Decentralization," p. 180; Remi Nadeau, *Los Angeles,* p. 152; W. W. Robinson, "The Southern California Real Estate Boom of the Twenties," *Historical Society of Southern California Quarterly,* 24, 1, March 1942, pp.25–30.

85. William B. Munro, "A Danger Spot in the Zoning Movement," *Annals of the American Academy of Political and Social Science,* 155, II, May 1931, pp. 202–6.

86. Ibid., p. 203.

87. "The high point of Mr. Whitnall's talk was regarding zoning, where paid lobbyists were able to override the planning commission's recommendations and

by spot zoning absolutely ruin investments made by law-abiding citizens. This is a message that every one interested in his or her community should take well to heart, for much of the work of planning can be undone if politics are allowed to enter in." *Pacific Municipalities,* 44, 7, July 1930, p. 252; see also *Annual Report,* Los Angeles Board of City Planning Commissioners, 1928, p. 16; 1929, p. 5; 1930, pp. 7–11, 23–24, 58–64; Mark Foster, "Decentralization," pp. 237–42; Robert Fogelson, *Fragmented,* p. 257; Edward M. Bassett, "Spot Zoning," *City Planning,* 6, 3, July 1930, p. 229; Huber Smutz, "Past-Present-Future," pp. 9–10.

88. Ralph Hancock, *Fabulous Boulevard* (New York: Funk & Wagnalls, 1949), pp. 149–64; Remi Nadeau, *Los Angeles,* p. 150.

89. Robert Fogelson, *Fragmented,* pp. 261–62; Mark Foster, "Decentralization," pp. 248–51; Gordon Whitnall, "Zoning Attack" (Whitnall papers, Los Angeles City Planning Department Library).

90. *Report of the Property Owners Committee for the Wilshire Neighborhood,* July 21, 1920, O. A. Vickrey, Chairman, p. 2; the California Real Estate Association news bulletin called Vickrey "one of the best known real estate men in Southern California." He was appointed to the Los Angeles City Planning Commission in May 1921. See *California Real Estate,* I, 8, June–July 1921, p. 8.

91. *Los Angeles Times,* August 21, 1921, Part IV, p. 12. Some of the Wilshire protestors later changed their attitude: "Those realtors who a few years ago were somewhat skeptical about the rights of the city or county authorities to determine specifically the use to which land may be put and who were opposed to zoning on general principles are often now its strongest adherents. They realize that something must be done to stabilize values of property, and that, inasmuch as all value of property depends upon the use to which that property is put, zoning is a necessity." *Los Angeles Realtor,* VII, 7, April 1928, p. 24.

92. Bigger and Kitchen, *Cities Grew; California Real Estate,* II, 11, August 1922, p. 24; Gordon Whitnall, "Zoning," February 28, 1924 (Whitnall Papers, Los Angeles City Planning Department Library).

93. The full text reads: "The situation in this (Wilshire) district, in its present unregulated condition, has seriously interrupted business and has thrown the investing public, as well as the present property owners, into a very unhealthy frame of mind, with serious financial losses threatened. The spirit in which the Los Angeles Realty Board has entered upon this work of making such recommendations is, we believe, thoroughly understood, in that we are agreed that the greatest good to the greatest number might be recognized." *Los Angeles Times,* July 29, 1920, Part II, p. 12.

94. Gordon Whitnall, "Supply and Demand in Zoning," *Pacific Municipalities,* 41, 3, March 1927, pp. 107–9; Gordon Whitnall, "Supply and Demand in Business Zoning," *The Community Builder,* I, 3, February 1928, pp. 13–16; Huber Smutz, "Past-Present-Future," pp. 10–13; idem, "Zoning," pp. 61–62. "City planning is rapidly developing into an exact science." See *Annual Report,* Los Angeles Board of City Planning Commissioners, 1930, p. 7, and *Pacific Municipalities,* 45, 2, February 1931, p. 63.

95. *California Real Estate,* VIII, 8, May 1928, p. 12.

96. Gordon Whitnall, "Common Sense in Zoning," an address to the League of California Municipalities, August 1926 (Whitnall Papers, Los Angeles City Planning Department Library), p. 3.
97. Ibid., p. 10.
98. *Annual Report,* Los Angeles Board of City Planning Commissioners, 1930, p. 54.
99. Gordon Whitnall, "Subdivision Activity in 1924" (Whitnall Papers, Los Angeles City Planning Department Library). See also chapter 5, tables 5.1 and 5.2.
100. Huber Smutz, "Past-Present-Future," p. 11.
101. See successive semi-annual volumes of the *California Real Estate Directory-Bulletin* (Sacramento: California State Printing Office).
102. George H. Coffin, Jr., "To What Extent Should Business Areas Be Limited?," *California Real Estate,* VI, 9, June 1926, pp. 52–53; idem, *Pacific Municipalities,* 40, 7, July 1926, pp. 273–81; idem, "Appraising Property Zoned for Business," *Journal of the American Institute of Real Estate Appraisers,* III, 1, October 1934, pp. 29–33; idem, *Zoning and its Relation to Property Values;* Carl Bush, "Zoning," *Los Angeles Realtor,* VII, 8, May 1928, pp. 12–13, 42–43, 48–49; VII, 9, June 1928, pp. 24, 28–32; W. L. Pollard, "Determining the Amount, Character, and Location of Business Property a Subdivision Needs," *Annals of Real Estate Practice* (Chicago: National Association of Real Estate Boards, 1928), pp. 621–32; idem, "City Planning—Why the Realtor Should be Interested," *Los Angeles Realtor,* VII, 6, March 1928, pp. 24, 35–36; idem, "Economic Effects of Zoning a City," *Annals of Real Estate Practice* (Chicago: National Association of Real Estate Boards, 1929), pp. 501–12; idem, *What Blighted Districts Mean in our Communities* (Los Angeles: Chamber of Commerce, Civic Development and Real Estate Department, 1931); Peter Hanson, "Relation of Zoning to Appraisals," *National Real Estate Journal,* 32, April 13, 1931, pp. 49–50; George LeRoy Schmutz, "Economic Effects of Zoning," *Annals of the American Academy of Political and Social Science,* 155, II, May 1931, pp. 172–77; Harry H. Culver, "A Realtor's Viewpoint on Zoning, Present and Future," *Annals of the American Academy of Political and Social Science,* 155, II, May 1931, pp. 207–12.
103. George H. Coffin, Jr., "Zoned into Oblivion," *City Planning,* X, 4, October 1934, p. 189.
104. Gordon Whitnall, "Supply and Demand in Zoning," p. 109; see also Huber Earl Smutz, "Zoning Business Frontage," *City Planning,* V, 4, October 1929, pp. 269–71.
105. Los Angeles City Ordinance Number 66,750 N.S.
106. Huber Smutz, "Past-Present-Future," p. 18; idem, "The Value and Administration of a Zoning Plan," 1951 (Whitnall Papers, Los Angeles City Planning Department Library), p. 11.
107. See note number 102 in this chapter; also Mark Foster, "Decentralization."
108. Edward Bassett, "Spot Zoning."
109. Quoted in Mark Foster, "Decentralization," p. 239.
110. Huber Smutz, "Past-Present-Future," p. 18; on the realtor's role in stand-

ardizing zoning administration throughout Los Angeles County, see *Pacific Municipalities,* 44, 7, July 1930, p. 266.

111. Ibid., pp. 8–10; also see letter from Gordon Whitnall to the Commonwealth Club of California, September 2, 1924, p. 1 (Carl J. Rhodin Papers, Bancroft Library, University of California, Berkeley).

112. City of Los Angeles, *Charter,* Article VIII, Sections 94–99; Mel Scott, "Fletcher Bowron of Los Angeles: An Achievement of the People," 1940, unpublished manuscript in the possession of the author; Fred W. Viehe, "The Recall of Mayor Frank L. Shaw: A Revision," *California History,* 59, 4, Winter 1980–81. For a perspective on zoning in Los Angeles during and after the 1940s, see Administrative Services Division, *City Planning in Los Angeles: A History* (Los Angeles: Department of City Planning, March 1964); Robert W. Glendinning, "Zoning," in George W. Robbins and L. Deming Tilton, eds., *Los Angeles: Preface to a Master Plan* (Los Angeles: Pacific Southwest Academy, 1941); Judith Norvell Jamison, *Coordinated Public Planning in the Los Angeles Region* (Bureau of Governmental Research, University of California at Los Angeles, June 1948); Martin J. Schiesl, "City Planning and the Federal Government in World War II: The Los Angeles Experience," *California History,* 59, 2, Summer 1980; Fred E. Case and James Gillies, "Some Aspects of Land Planning: The San Fernando Valley Case," *The Appraisal Journal,* 23, 1, January 1955; Fred E. Case, *Los Angeles Real Estate: A Study of Investment Experience* (Real Estate Research Program, University of California at Los Angeles, 1960).

5. The California Real Estate Association and Subdivision Regulations

1. California Statutes, 1893, p. 96; W. Sumner Holbrook, Jr., "Subdivision Control Methods," *Los Angeles Realtor,* VII, 1, October 1927, p. 22; Charles D. Clark, "Subdivision Plotting and Map Filing," in Harrison R. Baker, ed., *Subdivision Principles and Practices* (Los Angeles: California Real Estate Association, 1936), p. 36.

For general background on California state politics in the years covered by this chapter, see Carey McWilliams, *California: The Great Exception* (New York: Current Books, 1949); Walton Bean, *California: An Interpretive History* (New York: McGraw-Hill, 1973); Winston W. Crouch and Dean E. McHenry, *California Government* (Berkeley: University of California Press, 1945); Dewey Anderson, *California State Government* (Stanford: Stanford University Press, 1942); Spencer C. Olin, Jr., *California's Prodigal Sons: Hiram Johnson and the Progressives, 1911–1917* (Berkeley: University of California Press, 1968); Mansel G. Blackford, *The Politics of Business in California, 1890–1920* (Columbus: Ohio State University Press, 1977);

Gerald D. Nash, *State Government and Economic Development: A History of Administrative Policies in California, 1849–1933* (Berkeley: Institute of Governmental Studies, University of California, 1964); Dean E. McHenry, "The Third House: A Study of Organized Groups Before the California Legislature" (M.A. thesis, Department of Political Science, Stanford University, 1933).

On the California economy, see W. W. Robinson, *Land in California* (Berkeley: University of California Press, 1948); Margaret S. Gordon, *Employment Expansion and Population Growth, The California Experience, 1900–1950* (Berkeley: University of California Press, 1954); Frank L. Kidner, *California Business Cycles* (Berkeley: University of California Press, 1946); Robert Glass Cleland and Osgood Hardy, *March of Industry* (Los Angeles: Powell, 1929); Gerald D. Nash, "Stages of California's Economic Growth, 1870–1970: An Interpretation," *California Historical Quarterly*, 51, 4, Winter 1972.

2. C. W. Taylor, "History of the California Real Estate Association" (unpublished manuscript, dated 1955, in the library of the California Association of Realtors), ch. 2, page 8. See also *California Realty Bulletin*, 1, 1, May 1908, p. 4. The California Land Title Association was formed in 1907 to represent the title companies, who also supported the Map Act. The California State Realty Federation was formed in 1905 at the initiative of the Los Angeles Realty Board. The original purpose of the 80-member organization was to lobby for state licensing of brokers and salesmen. The group, which had grown to more than 400 members by 1907, also took positions on other issues, including support of the 1907 Map Act, a bill to force owners of vacant lots to keep them clean (this was a very important issue with the Los Angeles Realty Board, because vacant lots were ubiquitous in that city since the subdivision boom and crash of 1887–90), and bills to repeal the state mortgage tax and strengthen landlords' ability to evict tenants.

The CSRF reached its peak membership in 1912, but in the next few years the real estate crisis caused membership to dwindle back down to 70 members, and the Federation nearly dissolved. In 1917 it was renamed the California Real Estate Association (CREA), and with the help of the new 1917 license law (which was declared unconstitutional in 1918, but a new permanent one passed in 1919) and the real estate boom starting in 1922, CREA reached a membership of 5,000 by 1927. During the 1920s CREA published a monthly newsletter which eventually became a thick magazine. This official organ was published under three different names, but for the sake of simplicity, I have called it *California Real Estate* throughout. This was its longest-running name, and the volume numbers are consecutive from 1920 on. Today CREA is called CAR, the California Association of Realtors.

For some further background on the California real estate industry in the 1920s, see George A. Schneider, *California Real Estate Principles and Practices* (New York: Prentice-Hall, 1927); Ivan A. Thorson, *Essentials of California Real Estate* (Los Angeles: Realty Research Bureau, 1929). On CSRF/CREA and the license law, in addition to C. W. Taylor, see *California Real Estate,* III, 9, June 1923, p. 16, and IV, 1, October 1923, p. 42.

3. California Statutes, 1907, pp. 90–92; Sumner Holbrook, "Subdivision Control," p. 22; Charles Clark, "Subdivision Plotting," p. 36.

4. California Statutes, 1913, p. 568; Sumner Holbrook, ibid., p. 22; Charles Clark, ibid., p. 36.

5. Charles Henry Cheney, *What City Planning Commissions Can Do,* Bulletin Number 1 (San Francisco: California Conference on City Planning, June 1915); *Transactions of the Commonwealth Club of California,* IX, 14, January 1915, pp. 746–48; *Pacific Municipalities,* 28, 10, October 1914, pp. 503, 511, 513–15; 29, 4, March 1915, p. 115; 29, 7, July 1915, pp. 320–21.

6. California Statutes, 1915, ch. 756, pp. 1512–14; California Statutes, 1921, p. 1002; Sumner Holbrook, "Subdivision Control," p. 22; California Statutes, 1923, ch. 163, pp. 378–80.

7. See Los Angeles Realty Board, Minutes of the Governing Committee, July 8, 1915, p. 1. On Duncan McDuffie, see Marc A. Weiss, "Urban Land Developers and the Origins of Zoning Laws: The Case of Berkeley," *Berkeley Planning Journal,* III, 1, 1986. See also Werner Hegemann, *Report on a City Plan for the Municipalities of Oakland and Berkeley* (The City Club and Civic Art Commission of Berkeley, and the Chamber of Commerce and Commercial Club of Oakland, 1915), pp. 120–23. On NAREB-NCCP cooperation and "The Best Methods of Land Subdivision," see chapter 3.

8. Margaret Gordon, *Employment,* pp. 112–20; Lewis A. Maverick, "Cycles in Real Estate Activity," *Journal of Land and Public Utility Economics,* 8, 2, May 1932, pp. 191–99; idem, "Cycles in Real Estate Activity: Los Angeles," *Journal of Land and Public Utility Economics,* 9, 1, February 1933, pp. 52–56; idem, "Real Estate Activity in California," *Journal of Land and Public Utility Economics,* 10, 3, August 1934, pp. 291–95; Remi Nadeau, *Los Angeles* (New York: Longmans, Green, 1960), pp. 147–49; Wilfred George Donley, "An Analysis of Building and Loan Associations in California, 1920–1935" (Ph.D. diss., Department of Economics, University of California, Berkeley, 1937); John Beatty Dykstra, "History of the Physical Development of Oakland, 1850–1930" (M.C.P. thesis, Department of City and Regional Planning, University of California, Berkeley, 1967); Robert Luther Williams, "Eighty Years of Subdivision Design: An Historical Evaluation of Land Planning Techniques in San Mateo County, California" (M.C. P. thesis, Department of City and Regional Planning, University of California, Berkeley, 1952); Elizabeth Kates Burns, "The Process of Suburban Residential Development: The San Francisco Peninsula, 1860–1970" (Ph.D. diss., Department of Geography, University of California, Berkeley, 1974).

9. Bryant Hall, *The History of City Planning in California* (Los Angeles: California Conference on City Planning and Los Angeles Chamber of Commerce, 1929), p. 5; Charles Cheney, *City Planning,* p. 18; *Pacific Municipalities,* 30, 8, August 1918, pp. 287–92; 32, 3, March 1918, pp. 138–41; *The Architect and Engineer of California,* 52, 3, June 1918.

10. Bryant Hall, *History*, p. 5; Civic Development Department, *City Planning and Zoning Accomplishments* (Washington, D.C.: Chamber of Commerce of the United States, 1928), Table III.

11. See chapter 4.

12. Civic Development Department, *Accomplishments*, Table IV.

13. "It is difficult to explain how a new City Planning Commission consisting, partly at any rate, of individuals who had been instrumental in devising the state legislation regulating the process of land subdivision should have overlooked the duty imposed on the Commission. It is a fact, however, that many weeks passed following the appointment of the Commission before attention was given that most important duty. The dozens of new subdivision plats that were recorded during that period were happily saved any possible future embarrassment by the simple expedient of a blanket resolution of approval and by that act several skeletons were hung in the closet of the new department." Gordon Whitnall, "Tracing the Development of Planning in Los Angeles," *Annual Report* (Los Angeles Board of City Planning Commissioners, 1930), p. 42; idem, "Regional Planning and Commercial Development," *Transactions of the Commonwealth Club of California*, XVIII, 6, November 1923, p. 263; *Proceedings of the Sixteenth National Conference on City Planning* (Baltimore: Norman, Remington, 1924), pp. 105–28, 150–65; *Planning Problems of Town, City and Region* (Philadelphia: Wm. F. Fell, 1926), pp. 40–48.

14. Stuart O'Melveny, "What Title Insurance Means to Los Angeles," *Los Angeles Realtor*, VIII, 6, March 1929, pp. 14–15, 25–26.

15. *California Real Estate*, IV, 8, May 1924, p. 12; James Charles Stephens, "The Development of County Planning in California" (M.A. thesis, Department of Political Science, University of California, Berkeley, 1938), pp. 24–26; for a colorful description of boom sales practices, see "An Old Promoter Forty Years in the Field of Real Estate," *Sunshine and Grief in Southern California* (Detroit: St. Clair, 1931). For the concern of the Los Angeles Realty Board with the *control* of "excursion tickets" and other subdivision sales practices, see Los Angeles Realty Board, Minutes of the Governing Committee, April 5, 1921, p. 3; May 5, 1921, p. 1; May 19, 1921, p. 1; May 26, 1921, p. 1, and "Memoranda of Agreement of Subdividers, Establishing a Standard of Ethics for Operations, which Agreement has been reached upon Request of Ray L. Riley, Real Estate Commissioner of the State of California," pp. 1–2; June 9, 1921, p. 2; June 14, 1921, p. 1.

16. *Los Angeles Realtor*, VIII, 10, July 1929, p. 32.

17. James Stephens, "County Planning"; Bryant Hall, *History*, p. 8; *Proceedings of the First Regional Planning Conference of Los Angeles County*, January 21, 1922; Hugh Pomeroy, "Two Years of Regional Planning in Los Angeles County," *City Planning*, 1, 1, April 1925, pp. 47–49; idem, "Personal and Community Benefits from Subdivision Control," *Pacific Municipalities*, 39, 12, December 1925, pp. 441–42, 459–71; idem, "How Regional Planning is Beneficial to Cities," *Pacific Municipalities*, 40, 11, November 1926, pp. 432–36, 451–63; *Pacific Municipalities*, 37, 11, November 1923, pp. 428–29; *City Planning*, 7, 1, February 1931, pp. 42–48;

City Planning, 9, 1, February 1933, pp. 15–17. There also was a somewhat complicated and ineffective Monterey Peninsula Regional Planning Commission carved out of several different counties in 1927, but this was replaced by LACRPC-style county planning commissions after 1929.

18. *California Real Estate*, IV, 8, May 1924, p. 13; W. W. Robinson, "The Southern California Real Estate Boom of the Twenties," *Historical Society of Southern California Quarterly*, 24, 1, March 1942, pp. 25–30; Remi Nadeau, *Los Angeles*, pp. 149–57; Mark Stewart Foster, "The Decentralization of Los Angeles During the 1920s" (Ph.D. diss., Department of History, University of Southern California, 1971), pp. 172–90; also see note 8 in this chapter.

19. *California Real Estate*, IV, 8, May 1924, p. 17.

20. Ibid., IV, 3, December 1923, p. 44.

21. Ibid., IV, 9, June 1924, p. 94; V, 3, December 1924, pp. 13–14; Fred T. Wood, "Selling Subdivisions," *Annals of Real Estate Practice*, III, Home Building and Subdividing (Chicago: National Association of Real Estate Boards, 1925), pp. 48–49.

22. *California Real Estate*, IV, 7, April 1924, p. 27; IV, 8, May 1924, p. 14; C.C.C. Tatum, "Syndicate Financing and Subdivision Work," *Annals of Real Estate Practice*, III, Home Building and Subdividing (Chicago: National Association of Real Estate Boards, 1926), p. 101.

23. *California Real Estate*, IV, 3, December 1923, p. 17.

24. Ibid., IV, 1, October 1923, p. 74.

25. Ibid., III, 4, January 1923, p. 54.

26. Ibid., III, 5, February 1923, p. 39. For the 1887 boom and bust, see Glenn S. Dumke, *The Boom of the Eighties in Southern California* (San Marino: The Huntington Library, 1944).

27. *California Real Estate*, IV, 4, January 1924, p. 6.

28. Ibid., IV, 8, May 1924, p. 12. Edwin Keiser was a realtor and true friend of CREA. As commissioner he openly promoted CREA and actively encouraged licensed brokers and salesmen to join local realty boards. The CREA annual convention proceedings were reprinted in the official state *California Real Estate Directory-Bulletin*, published by Commissioner Keiser's Real Estate Department. When Keiser was first appointed by the governor, the editor of *California Real Estate* said, "For a number of years he was in the real estate business and is one of California's best known Realtors." His appointment was strongly supported by CREA. See *California Real Estate*, I, 9, August–September 1921, p. 3; C. W. Taylor, "History," Chapter 7, p. 9.

29. *California Real Estate*, IV, 9, June 1924, pp. 33, 43.

30. Ibid., V, 3, December 1924, p. 26.

31. Ibid., V, 4, January 1925, p. 13 and front cover.

32. Ibid., V, 6, March 1925, p. 7.

33. Ibid., V, 8, May 1925, front cover.

34. Ibid., p. 9.

35. Ibid., V, 7, April 1925, p. 7; V, 8, May 1925, p. 45; *Pacific Municipalities*, 39, 2, February 1925, p. 69; 39, 6, June 1925, p. 207.

36. Hugh R. Pomeroy, "Subdivision in Relation to Community Building," *Annals of Real Estate Practice*, III, Home Building and Subdividing (Chicago: National Association of Real Estate Boards, 1925), pp. 269–70. See also Hugh R. Pomeroy, "The Realtor in Regional Planning," *California Real Estate Directory-Bulletin*, V, Supplement, December 1924 (Sacramento: California State Printing Office, 1924), pp. 72–75.

37. *California Real Estate*, VI, 4, January 1926, p. 8.

38. Ibid., VI, 9, June 1926, pp. 39 and 54.

39. Ibid., VII, 2, November 1926, p. 7; VII, 3, December 1926, pp. 44 and 58; VII, 4, January 1927, pp. 66–67; VIII, 9, June 1928, p. 156; *Pacific Municipalities*, 41, 12, December 1927, pp. 533–39; Fred E. Reed, "Realtors and City Planning Progress," *City Planning*, 4, 3, July 1928, pp. 208–13.

40. *California Real Estate*, VI, 7, April 1926, p. 5; VI, 10, July 1926, p. 5.

41. Ibid., VI, 9, June 1926, pp. 44–62; *Pacific Municipalities*, 40, 6, June 1926, p. 215.

42. *California Real Estate*, VI, 9, June 1926, p. 16.

43. Ibid., p. 69.

44. Ibid., p. 39.

45. Ibid., p. 56.

46. *Real Estate*, III, 9, August 1914, p. 276; *California Real Estate*, VI, 12, September 1926, p. 29; Guy Rush, "Elements to Consider in Financing a Subdivision," *Annals of Real Estate Practice*, V, Real Estate Finance (Chicago: National Association of Real Estate Boards, 1927), pp. 185–97.

47. *California Real Estate*, VII, 2, November 1926, p. 26.

48. Ibid., VII, 5, February 1927, pp. 5–6.

49. Ibid., VII, 3, December 1926, p. 7; VI, 3, December 1925, p. 7; VII, 5, February 1927, pp. 5–6.

50. Ibid., VII, 1, October 1926, p. 16; VII, 2, November 1926, p. 5; VII, 3, December 1926, pp. 7, 9, and 34; *Pacific Municipalities*, 41, 9, September 1927, p. 315. C. C. Young was vice-president of Mason-McDuffie, one of the largest brokerage and development firms in northern California. See Marc Weiss, "Urban Land."

51. *California Real Estate*, VII, 3, December 1926, p. 10.

52. Ibid., VII, 5, February 1927, p. 6; VII, 6, March 1927, pp. 5, 11, 35; *Pacific Municipalities*, 41, 1, January 1927, pp. 3–4; 41, 2, February 1927, p. 53. Senator Arthur Breed was president of A. H. Breed and Sons, one of Oakland's oldest and largest realty firms. The CREA general counsel was Herbert Breed, the senator's brother. See *California Real Estate*, VII, 9, July 1927, p. 21; and VI, 12, September 1926, p. 17.

53. *California Real Estate*, VII, 7, April 1927, p. 6.

54. Ibid.

55. Ibid., VII, 6, March 1927, p. 7; VII, 7, April 1927, pp. 12–35; *Pacific Municipalities*, 41, 2, February 1927, pp. 61–65; 41, 12, December 1927, pp. 533–39.

56. *California Real Estate*, VII, 7, April 1927, p. 31.

57. Ibid.,VII, 4, January 1927, p. 27. Also see chapter 3.

58. Fred Reed, "Realtors"; *California Real Estate*, VII, 6, March 1927, p. 7.

59. *California Real Estate*, VII, 7, April 1927, p. 7; James Stephens, "County Planning," pp. 32–37. On the "Hoover" model, see Helen C. Monchow, "The California Planning Act of 1927," *Journal of Land and Public Utility Economics*, 4, 2, May 1928, pp. 209–12.

60. *California Real Estate*, VII, 7, April, 1927, p. 7.

61. Ibid., p. 26.

62. Ibid., p. 35; VII, 4, January 1927, p. 59.

63. Ibid., p. 35; VII, 8, May 1927, p. 8.

64. Ibid., pp. 10 and 38; VII, 9, June 1927, p. 10.

65. *Pacific Municipalities*, 41, 7, July 1927, pp. 234 and 247.

66. *California Real Estate*, VII, 9, June 1927, p. 10.

67. Ibid.

68. Ibid., VII, 10, July 1927, p. 18.

69. Ibid., VII, 11, August 1927, p. 39.

70. Ibid., VII, 10, July 1927, p. 29.

71. Ibid., VIII, 6, March 1928, p. 42; *Pacific Municipalities*, 41, 10, October 1927, p. 360. S.B. 585 became California Statutes 1927, Chapter 874, pp. 1899–1913.

72. *California Real Estate*, VII, 10, July 1927, p. 25.

73. Ibid.; see also Charles H. Cheney, *The California Planning Act of 1927*, Bulletin Number 5 (Palos Verdes Estates: California Conference on City Planning, August 1927); Charles Henry Cheney, "The California City Planning Act of 1927," *The Community Builder*, 1, 1, December 1927, pp. 41–44, and 1, 2, January 1928, pp. 37–41. Cheney sent a telegram to former U.S. Senator James D. Phelan in San Francisco on May 29, 1927, with the following message:

> Please wire Governor C. C. Young Sacramento urging signature senate bill five eighty five standard city planning act recommended by Herbert Hoover and National Real Estate Association which while only optional not mandatory authorizes cities to establish master plans requires hearings stabilizes city planning procedure on street plans and regional planning and better protects real estate particularly the small man. Opposition from few subdividers may influence governor to veto this important legislation unless proponents promptly wire him.

After Governor Young signed S.B. 585, Cheney wrote to the members of the California Conference on City Planning:

> I do not know whether you were one of those who wired the Governor at the last moment as requested but he evidently heard from so many different places that he felt obliged to sign the act despite the opposition of some selfish subdividers in Southern California.
>
> I have promised the Governor that we will all stand together to see that the act is properly interpreted and that if amendments are found necessary we will join with the State Real Estate Association and others in preparing them well in advance of the next session.

The letter and the telegram are in the James D. Phelan Papers, Bancroft Library, University of California, Berkeley.

74. *California Real Estate*, VIII, 4, January 1928, pp. 18 and 21.

75. Ibid., p. 19. Guy Rush continued to be one of the main advocates for subdivision control among California's community builders. See Guy M. Rush and W. Sumner Holbrook, Jr., "Subdivision Control Methods: A Nation-Wide Survey," *National Real Estate Journal*, 29, July 23, 1928, pp. 42–45.

76. *California Real Estate*, VIII, 4, January 1928, p. 19; VII, 12, September 1927, p. 35; VIII, 2, November 1927, p. 25.

77. Ibid., VIII, 5, February 1928, p. 23; VIII, 2, November 1927, p. 15; VIII, 7, April 1928, p. 23.

78. Hal G. Hotchkiss, "The Annual City Planning Conference of the California Real Estate Association," *The Community Builder*, I, 3, February 1928, pp. 17–18; "California City Planning Conference," *The Community Builder*, I, 5, April 1928, pp. 43–44; *Los Angeles Realtor*, VII, 7, April 1928, p. 24; *California Real Estate*, VIII, 8, May 1928, p. 11. Pages 9–69 of this issue provide a great deal of evidence of the intense political backlash within CREA over the issue of subdivision regulation.

79. *California Real Estate*, VIII, 8, May 1928, p. 41.

80. Ibid., p. 17.

81. Ibid., pp. 9, 62.

82. Ibid., VIII, 12, September 1928, p. 27.

83. Ibid., VIII, 9, June 1928, p. 158; VIII, 8, May 1928, p. 62; Kenneth Gardner, "Subdivision Control," *Pacific Municipalities*, 42, 1, January 1928, pp. 15–20 and 35.

84. *California Real Estate*, VI, 10, July 1926, p. 29.

85. Ibid., VIII, 4, January 1928, p. 24; Gordon Whitnall, "The Place of the Subdivision in Community Expansion," *The Community Builder*, 1, 1, December 1927, pp. 15–20.

86. *California Real Estate*, VIII, 9, June 1928, p. 158.

87. Charles D. Clark, "Penalties of Excess Subdividing," *City Planning*, 10, 2, April 1934, pp. 51–61. On the special assessment crisis, see W. L. Pollard, "The Assessment Problem in California," *Annals of Real Estate Practice* (Chicago: National Association of Real Estate Boards, 1930), pp. 379–94; and *California Real Estate*, X, 12, September 1930, p. 29.

88. *California Real Estate*, VIII, 8, May 1928, p. 25: "Newspaper comments from leading papers north and south, especially the papers that carry vast amounts of subdivision advertising, are in support of cleaning up the land business . . . it is the indiscriminate foisting on the market of unbalanced and unnecessary subdivisions that tends to convince the public that more certain protection by law is needed."

89. Ibid., VII, 2, November 1926, pp. 26–27; VII, 4, January 1927, pp. 22 and 25; VII, 9, June 1927, pp. 19 and 57; VII, 11, August 1927, pp. 28 and 39; VII, 12, September 1927, pp. 19, 23, and 37; VIII, 6, March 1928, p. 30; VIII, 8, May 1928, p. 52; IX, 3, December 1928, p. 29; IX, 5, February 1929, p. 18.

90. Ibid., VI, 9, June 1926, p. 67; IX, 7, April 1929, p. 47; *Rancho Santa Fe,*

California, Protective Restrictions, Charles H. Cheney, consultant in City Planning, April 1928. In the mid-1920s, Hugh Pomeroy wrote a letter to developer Walter Leimert praising the deed restrictions in his large Los Angeles subdivision:

Dear Mr. Leimert:

Accept my congratulations upon the establishment of protective restrictions for Leimert Park and the formation of a Community Association.

I have had the privilege of visiting several communities throughout the United States which have used this general type of restrictions. They are outstanding examples of the best means of developing a high standard of community life. The use of such restrictions in Leimert Park is a real contribution to the welfare of Los Angeles, adding, as it does, the element of protected excellence which is so needed in our residential developments.

You are providing for those who will make their homes in Leimert Park the assurance of the practical application of a high ideal in community building and home life.

Respectfully,
Hugh R. Pomeroy, Secretary
Los Angeles County Regional Planning Commission

See *Leimert Park Community Association,* Walter H. Leimert Co., Los Angeles, 1927, p. 3. Unfortunately both Rancho Santa Fe and Leimert Park were restricted to "caucasians only."

91. Ibid., IX, 4, January 1929, p. 9; IX, 8, May 1929, p. 12.
92. Ibid., VIII, 8, May 1928, p. 41; VIII, 9, June 1928, p. 70.
93. Ibid., IX, 11, August 1929, p. 46.
94. Ibid., VIII, 11, August 1928, p. 27.
95. Ibid., IX, 2, November 1928, p. 84.
96. Ibid., p. 12.
97. Ibid., IX, 4, January 1929, p. 55.
98. Ibid.
99. Ibid., p. 9.
100. Ibid., p. 43.
101. Ibid.
102. Ibid., IX, 5, February 1929, pp. 12 and 16.
103. Ibid., IX, 6, March 1929, p. 12.
104. Ibid., IX, 5, February 1929, p. 25.
105. Ibid., IX, 6, March 1929, p. 12.
106. *Los Angeles Realtor,* VIII, 7, April 1929, p. 14; VIII, 10, July 1929, pp. 7 and 32; *California Real Estate,* IX, 7, April 1929, p. 45; IX, 8, May 1929, pp. 13–14; *Pacific Municipalities,* 43, 4, April 1929, p. 175.
107. *California Real Estate,* IX, 7, April 1929, p. 45.
108. Ibid.; IX, 8, May 1929, pp. 10, 13–14; IX, 9, June 1929, p. 371; *Pacific Municipalities,* 43, 3, March 1929, p. 123.
109. *California Real Estate,* IX, 7, April 1929, p. 45; *Los Angeles Realtor,* VIII, 8, May 1929, pp. 8 and 35.
110. James Stephens, "County Planning"; *Western City,* VI, 2, February 1930,

pp. 13–18, 48–49; California County Planning Commissioner's Association, *A Manual of County Planning* (California State Chamber of Commerce, March 1934); *The Regional Planning Commission, County of Los Angeles* (Los Angeles: Hall of Records, 1929); San Mateo County Planning Commission, *The Subdivision of Land, San Mateo County,* 1932; L. Deming Tilton, "The Districting Plan of Orange County, California," *Journal of Land and Public Utility Economics,* 12, 3, August 1936; *City Planning,* 5, 4, October 1929, p. 261; 6, 1, January 1930, p. 45; *California Real Estate,* X, 1, October 1929, pp. 46–47.

111. Fred B. Wood, *Comparative Analysis of "The Planning Act" of 1927 with Senate Bill Number 615—1929 Legislation,* Bulletin Number 10 (Los Angeles: California Conference on City Planning, 1929); James Stephens, "County Planning," pp. 55–60.

112. *California Real Estate,* IX, 10, July 1929, pp. 15–16. S.B. 614 became The Map Act, California Statutes, 1929, ch. 837, pp. 62–68; S.B. 615 became The Planning Act, California Statutes, 1929, ch. 838, pp. 1806–21.

113. *California Real Estate,* X, 1, October 1929, p. 40; XI, 1, October 1930, p. 36.

114. Ibid., X, 7, April 1930, p. 14.

115. *Pacific Municipalities,* 44, 3, March 1930, p. 78.

116. *California Real Estate,* XI, 6, March 1931, p. 15; XI, 3, December 1930, p. 29.

117. Ibid., X, 4, January 1930, p. 29; X, 8, May 1930, p. 38; X, 11, August 1930, p. 29; Wilfred Donley, "Building and Loan" *Proceedings of the 22nd Annual Convention of the California Building-Loan League,* 1927, p. 31. See also note number 88 in this chapter.

118. *California Real Estate,* XI, 11, August 1931, p. 38.

119. Ibid., XII, 2, November 1931, p. 42.

120. L. Deming Tilton, "The Direction of Land Subdivision—A County Responsibility," *Planning Problems of Town, City, and Region* (Philadelphia: Wm. F. Fell, 1930), pp. 31–32.

121. *California Real Estate,* XII, 6, March 1932, p. 14.

122. Ibid., XIII, 1, October 1932, p. 33.

123. Ibid., XIII, 3, December 1932, p. 31.

124. Ibid., XII, 2, November 1931, pp. 34–35.

125. Ibid., XIII, 1, October 1932, p. 33.

126. Ibid.

127. The only mention was an announcement of the upcoming conference, June 16–18 in Hollywood. See ibid., XIII, 6, March 1932, p. 14.

128. *Western City,* IX, 3, March 1933, p. 20.

129. *California Real Estate,* XIV, 8, May 1933, p. 5.

130. Ibid., XIV, 4, January 1933, p. 14.

131. Ibid., XIV, 5, February 1933, p. 17.

132. Ibid., XIV, 7, April 1933, p. 11.

133. Ibid., XIV, 9, June–July 1933, pp. 60–61.

134. *Western City,* IX, 7, July 1933, p. 23.
135. *California Real Estate,* XIV, 11, August 1933, p. 12.
136. Ibid., XIV, 5, February 1933, pp. 17 and 21.
137. Ibid., XIV, 11, August 1933, pp. 6 and 12.
138. *Western City,* IX, 7, July 1933, p. 23.
139. Keiser later served as a CREA director, as president of the Pomona Realty Board and as president of the Associated Realty Boards of Los Angeles County. Gabbert later served as president of the Riverside Realty Board and as an active CREA member. Perhaps in their roles as realtor "insiders," Keiser and Gabbert helped persuade other CREA leaders to adopt their previous "outsider" position in favor of state Real Estate Department regulation of urban subdivision sales. See *California Real Estate,* XII, 1, October 1931, p. 36; XIV, 4, January 1933, p. 21; XIV, 11, August 1933, p. 11.
140. *California Statutes,* 1937, ch. 665 and 670.
141. *California Statutes,* 1935, ch. 112. For admiring commentary, see Helen C. Monchow, "New Departures in Subdivision Control," "Subdivision Legislation in 1937," and "California's Subdivision Control Sustained," in *Journal of Land and Public Utility Economics,* 12, 4, November 1936, pp. 417–19; 14, 1, February 1938, pp. 83–84; 15, 1, February 1939, pp. 97–98.
142. FHA basically required deed restrictions in new subdivisions in order to qualify for mortgage insurance. On FHA, see chapter 6. One example of the shift in *design and engineering* as well as power over *coordination* and *control* brought about by FHA is the fact that Charles D. Clark, chief subdivision engineer for the Los Angeles County Regional Planning Commission, was appointed to head FHA's new Land Planning Division field office for the western states, headquartered in Los Angeles. See Charles D. Clark, "Penalties of Excess Subdividing"; idem, "Subdivision Plotting"; and idem, "Federal Housing Administration Standards for Land Subdivision," *The Planners' Journal,* 4, 5, July–August 1938. On FHA in California, see also Fred W. Marlow, "Future Trends in Subdivision Development Methods and Pricing Subdivision Property," in Harrison Baker, *Subdivision Principles;* and Fred W. Marlow, *Memoirs and Perceptions,* self-published, Los Angeles, 1981.
143. For an excellent overview of the four-part subdivision planning and control system (city and county land-use regulations, state licensing and investigation, federal financing assistance, and private deed restrictions and subdivision design), see Harrison Baker, *Subdivision Principles.* On later developments, see D. D. Watson, *Subdivision Control in California,* Report to the California State Senate Finance Committee, Sacramento, March 11, 1953; Paul F. Wendt, James A. Bailey, and Marybeth Branaman, *Special Report to the Advisory Committee to the California State Senate Interim Committee on Subdivision Development and Planning* (Berkeley: Real Estate Research Program, University of California, September 1954). The Advisory Committee was chaired by Harrison R. Baker. Senator Arthur H. Breed, Jr., who succeeded his father in the Senate and in the real estate brokerage and subdivision development business, was chairman of the Senate

Interim Committee. D. D. Watson, the California Real Estate Commissioner in 1953, had been president of CREA in 1930.

6. COMMUNITY BUILDERS AND THE FEDERAL HOUSING ADMINISTRATION

1. See chapters 3 through 5. On the status of local planning, see Robert A. Walker, *The Planning Function in Urban Government* (Chicago: University of Chicago Press, 1950); U.S. National Resources Committee, *Status of City and County Planning in the United States*, Circular 10, May 15, 1937, Washington, D.C.; U.S. National Emergency Council, *Comprehensive Housing Legislation Chart*, March 1, 1937, Washington, D.C.

2. John M. Gries and James Ford, eds., *Planning for Residential Districts* (Washington, D.C.: National Capital Press, 1932). The two key points are best represented as follows:

(1)"The ideal arrangement is one in which the original developer controls an area sufficiently large to comprise a complete neighborhood unit, namely, an area of from one-quarter square mile to one square mile, planned as a self contained unit, and bounded on all sides by natural or artifical barriers of major traffic streets. If the original developer controls a large amount of land, even though it may not be a complete community unit, and there is retention of the natural features, streets of good basic design, proper provision for open spaces, and adequate provision for all needed utility services, the prospective home owner will find much greater satisfaction than in the average 'subdivision'" (pp. 74–75, Report of the Committee on Subdivision Layout).

(2) "Planning by neighborhood units is such a large undertaking that it is not possible to complete a unit within a short time. It is, however, essential to establish the plan at the very beginning and to adhere to it; otherwise, the same chaos will continue to arise that we face in our cities today. Private initiative does not have the means, nor the power, to preserve and to create values at the large scale which in the long run will be in the public interest. This is the province of the city plan, as has been elsewhere stated" (p. 122, Report of the Committee on Subdivision Layout).

On the evolution of the "neighborhood unit" idea, see James Dahir, *The Neighborhood Unit Plan* (New York: Russell Sage Foundation, 1947).

3. For a list of the committee members, see ibid., pp. vii–viii; Louis Eppich was NAREB president in 1923, Harry Culver in 1929, Harry Kissell in 1931, Lawrence Stevenson in 1932, William Miller in 1933; on Harland Bartholomew and NAREB, see *Annals of Real Estate Practice* (Chicago: National Association of Real Estate Boards, 1930), p. 480; of the other planners, Jacob Crane, Henry Hubbard, John Nolen, and Robert Whitten were all private consultants, and Henry Wright was the codesigner of Radburn, the model of a neighborhood unit for middle-income homeowners—see Henry Wright, "How Long Blocks Cut Down Street Costs, and Other Economies of Modern Planning," and Alex-

ander M. Bing, "Community Planning for the Motor Age," in *Annals of Real Estate Practice* (Chicago: National Association of Real Estate Boards, 1929).

4. See Report of the Committee on Subdivision Layout, in Gries and Ford, *Planning*, pp. 46–124; the basic ideas and recommendations are contained within pp. 46–84.

5. Ibid., p. 49.

6. Ibid., p. 64.

7. *First Annual Report of the Federal Housing Administration* (Washington, D.C.: U.S. Government Printing Office, 1935), p. 14. The 1934 National Housing Act listed its purposes as simply "To encourage improvement in housing standards and conditions, to provide a system of mutual mortgage insurance, and for other purposes." 73rd U.S. Congress, Public Law Number 479, p. 1. The best account of the origins of FHA is in William Lindus Cody Wheaton, "The Evolution of Federal Housing Programs" (Ph.D. diss., Department of Political Science, University of Chicago, 1953). For other accounts, see Mark I. Gelfand, *A Nation of Cities: The Federal Government and Urban America, 1933–1965* (New York: Oxford University Press, 1975); Miles L. Colean, *A Backward Glance: The Growth of Government Housing Policy in the United States, 1934–1975* (Washington, D.C.: Mortgage Bankers Association of America, 1975); Nathaniel S. Keith, *Politics and the Housing Crisis Since 1930* (New York: Universe Books, 1973); Marriner S. Eccles, *Beckoning Frontiers: Public and Personal Recollections* (New York: Alfred A. Knopf, 1951); Federal Housing Administration, *The FHA Story in Summary, 1934–1959* (Washington, D.C.: U.S. Government Printing Office, 1959); Gertrude S. Fish, "Housing Policy During the Great Depression," in Gertrude Sipperly Fish, ed., *The Story of Housing* (New York: MacMillan, 1979); and Kenneth T. Jackson, *Crabgrass Frontier: The Suburbanization of the United States* (New York: Oxford University Press, 1985).

8. Section 203(c) of the 1934 National Housing Act said "but no mortgage shall be accepted for insurance under this section (mutual mortgage insurance) unless the Administrator finds that the project with respect to which the mortgage is executed is economically sound." 73rd Congress, p. 4.

9. In the first meeting of the FHA Administrator's Housing Advisory Council, Deputy FHA Administrator J. Howard Ardrey acknowledged Hugh Potter's role in the passage of the National Housing Act. Federal Housing Administration, *Confidential Report of Housing Advisory Council Meeting*, December 17–18, 1934, Washington, D.C. Hugh Potter later utilized FHA mortgage insurance to construct the River Oaks Gardens "large-scale housing project" adjacent to his River Oaks development. See Federal Housing Administration, *Fifth Annual Report* (Washington, D.C.: U.S. Government Printing Office, 1939), pp. 22, 127. On NAREB enthusiasm for FHA, in addition to William Wheaton, "Evolution," and the other sources in note 7, see also Federal Housing Administration, *Proceedings of the Realtors' Housing Conference, Arranged by the National Association of Real Estate Boards* (Washington, D.C.: U.S. Government Printing Office, 1938); House Select Committee on Lobbying Activities, 81st Congress, 2nd session,

Housing Lobby (Washington, D.C.: U.S. Government Printing Office, 1950); *California Real Estate*, XV, 7, May 1935, p. 30; and for a somewhat later view of the close relationship between FHA and the real estate industry trade associations, see Richard O. Davies, *Housing Reform Under the Truman Administration* (Columbia: University of Missouri Press, 1966).

10. On Ayers J. DuBois, see *California Real Estate*, XV, 1, November 1934, p. 24; XIV, 9, June–July 1933, p. 8; FHA, *Confidential Report of Housing Advisory Council*, Real Estate Committee, Washington, D.C., March 6, 1935, p. 1. On Fred Marlow, see Fred W. Marlow, *Memoirs and Perceptions*, self-published (Los Angeles, 1981); idem, "Future Trends in Subdivision Development and Pricing Subdivision Property," in Harrison R. Baker, ed., *Subdivision Principles and Practices* (Los Angeles: California Real Estate Association, 1936); on FHA praise for the Los Angeles office, see FHA, *Confidential Report of Housing Advisory Council Meeting*, Washington, D.C., January 21, 1935, p. 3, and January 22, 1935, pp. 177–78, and FHA, *Fourth Annual Report* (Washington, D.C.: U.S. Government Printing Office, 1938), p. 111. Ernest Fisher was NAREB Director of Education and Research in the 1920s; see Ernest M. Fisher, *Principles of Real Estate Practice* (New York: MacMillan, 1923). Frederick Babcock, a famous real estate appraiser, also published a book in the NAREB-YMCA-Richard T. Ely Land Economics Series: Frederick M. Babcock, *The Appraisal of Real Estate* (New York: MacMillan, 1924). On the private sector backgrounds of other early FHA officials, see *The FHA Story in Summary*.

11. Federal Housing Administration, *Underwriting Manual* (Washington, D.C.: U.S. Government Printing Office, 1938); FHA, *Confidential Report*, December 17–18, 1934, pp. 25–29, 32–38; FHA, *Second Annual Report* (Washington, D.C.: U.S. Government Printing Office, 1936), pp. 25–26. 1938 was the first published edition of the *Underwriting Manual*. Beginning in 1934, FHA printed typescript copies for their staff. See also Kenneth T. Jackson, "Race, Ethnicity, and Real Estate Appraisal: The Home Owners Loan Corporation and the Federal Housing Administration," *Journal of Urban History*, 6, 4, August 1980.

12. Federal Housing Administration, *Operative Builders*, Circular Number 4, December 15, 1934 (Washington, D.C.: U.S. Government Printing Office, 1934), p. 4. For a later revision, see FHA, *Procedures for Operative Builders*, Circular Number 4, May 1, 1938 (Washington, D.C.: U.S. Government Printing Office, 1938).

13. Ibid., p. 4.

14. Ibid., pp. 5–7; Kenneth Jackson, *Crabgrass Frontier*, p. 238.

15. William Wheaton, "Evolution," pp. 165–66.

16. This goal was recognized from the very start of FHA's operations. For example, the *First Annual Report* states: "Once the plan comes into wide-spread operation, the following results may reasonably be anticipated: . . . (d) Improvement in subdivision layouts—subdivisions that are regarded as specially good by the Federal Housing Administration will receive more favorable loan rating." FHA, *First Annual Report* (Washington, D.C.: U.S. Government Printing Office,

1935), p. 18. See also the actual standards: FHA, *Subdivision Development*, Circular Number 5, January 10, 1935 (Washington, D.C.: U.S. Government Printing Office, 1935).

17. Seward H. Mott, "Land Use Requirements and Subdivision Planning Under Section 203," in FHA, *Proceedings of the Realtors' Housing Conference*, pp. 27–30; FHA, *Fifth Annual Report* (Washington, D.C.: U.S. Government Printing Office, 1939), pp. 38–40; *Sixth Annual Report* (Washington, D.C.: U.S. Government Printing Office, 1940), pp. 16–17; *Seventh Annual Report* (Washington, D.C.: U.S. Government Printing Office, 1941), pp. 22–23; Charles D. Clark, "Federal Housing Administration Standards for Land Subdivision," *The Planners' Journal*, 4, 5, September–October, 1938; Fred Marlow, "Future Trends"; Miles Colean, *Backward Glance.*

18. FHA, *Subdivision Development;* see also a revised version, Federal Housing Administration, *Subdivision Standards*, September 1, 1939 (Washington, D.C.: U.S. Government Printing Office, 1939); FHA, *Planning Neighborhoods for Small Houses*, Technical Bulletin Number 5, July 1, 1936 (Washington, D.C.: U.S. Government Printing Office, 1936); see also the revised version, dated July 1, 1938; FHA, *Planning Profitable Neighborhoods*, Technical Bulletin Number 7 (Washington, D.C.: U.S. Government Printing Office, 1938); FHA, *Successful Subdivisions*, Land Planning Bulletin Number 1 (Washington, D.C.: U.S. Government Printing Office, 1940).

For Miles Colean's views, see his classic book *American Housing: Problems and Prospects* (New York: Twentieth Century Fund, 1944), and his oral history memoirs, *A Backward Glance.* Seward Mott left FHA in 1944 to become executive director of the Urban Land Institute. He coedited *The Community Builders Handbook* (Washington, D.C.: Urban Land Institute, 1947). Mott, who was a member of the Board of Governors of the American Institute of Planners (1946–49), presented his views to AIP in 1939 on the FHA Land Planning Division's role under his supervision in promoting new residential subdivision development in "suburban districts"; see Seward H. Mott, "Planning Considerations in the Location of Housing Projects: The Case for Fringe Locations," *The Planners' Journal*, 5, 2, March–April 1939. An example of FHA's influence concerning the planning of residential subdivisions is the book review by the editor of *The Planners' Journal*, Frederick J. Adams, on FHA's 1938 Bulletin, *Planning Profitable Neighborhoods:* "The Federal Housing Administration is to be complimented for the manner in which they have presented the essentials of good neighborhood planning, under a title which is designed to appeal to the private real estate developer. The bulletin indicates by means of a series of illustrations showing typical good and bad plans for specific sites how proper planning not only improves the amenities of the neighborhood but also results in a more secure investment for the operator." See *The Planners' Journal*, 4, 6, November–December 1938, p. 153.

19. FHA, *Subdivision Development*, p. 3.

20. Ibid., p. 5.

21. FHA, *Fifth Annual Report*, p. 39. Frederick Babcock was director of FHA's Underwriting Division throughout the 1930s. See FHA, *Confidential Report of Housing Advisory Council*, December 17–18, 1934, pp. 25–29; FHA, *Underwriting Manual*; Frederick Babcock, *Appraisal*; idem, "Underwriting Eligibility Requirements Under Section 203," in FHA, *Realtors' Housing Conference*, pp. 30–33. Ernest Fisher was director of FHA's Economics and Statistics Division throughout the 1930s. He recruited other economists, including Homer Hoyt, Richard Ratcliff, and Arthur Weimer, to engage in research on a variety of urban growth and real estate market and valuation issues. See FHA, *Confidential Report*, 1934, pp. 34–38; FHA, *Second Annual Report*, pp. 40–42; *Third Annual Report* (Washington, D.C.: U.S. Government Printing Office, 1937), pp. 17–19; *Fourth Annual Report*, pp. 25–27; *Fifth Annual Report*, pp. 40–43; *Sixth Annual Report*, pp. 14–15. Two key documents are FHA, *Analysis of Housing in Peoria* (Washington, D.C.: U.S. Government Printing Office, 1935), prepared by Ernest M. Fisher, Richard U. Ratcliff and J. Bion Philipson; and FHA, *The Structure and Growth of Residential Neighborhoods in American Cities* (Washington, D.C.: U.S. Government Printing Office, 1939), prepared by Homer Hoyt. For fuller background, consult the textbook written by Ernest M. Fisher for the American Institute of Banking, *Home Mortgage Lending* (New York: American Bankers Association, 1938); Arthur M. Weimer and Homer Hoyt, *Principles of Urban Real Estate* (New York: Ronald Press, 1939); Richard U. Ratcliff, *Urban Land Economics* (New York: McGraw-Hill, 1949); Chester Rapkin, Louis Winnick, and David M. Blank, *Housing Market Analysis*, U.S. Housing and Home Finance Agency (Washington, D.C.: U.S. Government Printing Office, 1953).

22. FHA, *Subdivision Development*, p. 7.

23. *Oakland City Planning Commission Activities and Accomplishments*, March 1, 1935, Annual Report to the City Council, Oakland, California p. 3. On Oakland politics, see Fred E. Reed, "Realtors and City Planning Progress," *City Planning*, 4, 3, July 1928, pp. 211–12. On the Los Angeles Realty Board, see chapter 4.

24. FHA, *Realtors' Housing Conference, p. 28.*

25. FHA, *Planning Neighborhoods for Small Houses*, 1936, pp. 31–32. See also Charles H. Cheney, "Architectural Control," *The Planners' Journal*, 6, 2, March–April 1936.

26. FHA, *Planning Neighborhoods for Small Houses* (revised), 1938, p. 31; Charles Clark, "FHA Standards," p. 112; Charles Abrams, *Forbidden Neighbors* (New York: Harper, 1955), pp. 229–37.

27. FHA, *Realtors' Housing Conference*, p. 29.

28. FHA, *Sixth Annual Report*, pp. 2–19.

29. Ibid., p. 17.

30. FHA, *Seventh Annual Report*, p. 23.

31. Paul Opperman, "The Tri-Cities Planning Project: A Pilot Case in Cooperative Planning," *The Planners' Journal*, 8, 3, July–September 1942; see also the Land Planning Division's important book: FHA, *A Handbook on Urban Redevel-*

opment for Cities in the United States (Washington, D.C.: U.S. Government Printing Office, 1941); Earle S. Draper, who was director of Land Planning and Housing for the Tennessee Valley Authority (TVA) in the 1930s, was president of the American Institute of Planners in 1942.

32. An example of FHA's leading role in promoting local planning is the creation by the American City Planning Institute (ACPI) in 1937 of a "Committee to Confer with the Federal Housing Administration." This ACPI Committee, chaired by Walter Blucher and consisting of Jacob Crane, John Nolen, Jr., and Ladislas Segoe, represented the first major cooperative effort between ACPI and real estate developers since the NAREB-ACPI *Joint Statement on Subdivision Control* in 1927, the "Hoover" Committee on Subdivision Layout in 1931, and the Department of Commerce Advisory Committee's *Model Subdivision Regulations* in 1932 (see chapter 3). It is interesting that FHA, though a federal agency with no "private" representation, nevertheless acted through its Land Planning Director, Seward Mott, as spokesman for the interests of community builders from NAREB. See "FHA to Advise Municipalities on Planning and Zoning," *The Planners' Journal*, 3, 5, September–October 1937, p. 130. On the importance of Section 701 of the 1954 Housing Act, see Carl Feiss, "The Foundations of Federal Planning Assistance: A Personal Account of the 701 Program," *Journal of the American Planning Association*, 51, 2, Spring 1985. On the NRPB, see National Resources Planning Board, *National Resources Development Report for 1943* (Washington, D.C.: U.S. Government Printing Office, 1943); NRPB, *Action for Cities: A Guide for Community Planning* (Chicago: Public Administration Service, 1945); Phillip Funigiello, *The Challenge to Urban Liberalism* (Knoxville: University of Tennessee Press, 1978); Marion Clawson, *New Deal Planning* (Baltimore: Johns Hopkins University Press, 1982). On the continuing influence of FHA's Land Planning Division on general housing and planning policies, see U.S. Housing and Home Finance Agency, *Suggested Land Subdivision Regulations* (Washington, D.C.: U.S. Government Printing Office, February 1952).

33. FHA, *Subdivision Development*, p. 4.

34. For examples of "Suggested Revised Plans" with the disclaimer, see FHA, *Planning Profitable Neighborhoods* and *Successful Subdivisions*. Also, on the final two pages of each Bulletin FHA presents the basic service information for developers who may want their proposed subdivisions to be analyzed by an FHA land planning consultant. On the market for "competent subdivision designers," see Charles H. Diggs, "Subdivision Design," *The Planners' Journal*, 5, 2, March–April 1939.

35. FHA, *Confidential Report of Housing Advisory Council*, January 21, 1935, Washington, D.C., p. 12.

36. FHA, *Fourth Annual Report*, p. 22.

37. FHA, *Fifth Annual Report*, p. viii.

38. R. J. Saulnier, Harold G. Halcrow, and Neil H. Jacoby, *Federal Lending and Loan Insurance* (Princeton: Princeton University Press, 1958), table 66, p. 340. On FHA and the need for new state banking legislation, see FHA, *First Annual*

Report, p. 19; *Second Annual Report*, pp. 27, 35–36, 51; FHA, *Confidential Report of Housing Advisory Council*, December 17–18, 1934, pp. 14, 29–32.

39. William Wheaton, "Evolution" p. 338.

40. Ibid.; FHA, *Sixth Annual Report*, p. 19. See also FHA, *FHA Homes in Metropolitan Districts* (Washington, D.C.: U.S. Government Printing Office, 1942).

41. FHA, *Seventh Annual Report*, pp. 56, 59, 62.

42. Ibid., p. 22.

43. Ibid., p. 23.

44. FHA, *Sixth Annual Report*, p. 17.

45. Bureau of Labor Statistics, "Builders of 1-Family Houses in 72 Cities," U.S. Department of Labor, *Monthly Labor Review*, 51, 3, September 1940, p. 735.

46. Ibid., pp. 732–39.

47. Kenneth Jackson, *Crabgrass Frontier*, ch. 13; Barry N. Checkoway, "Suburbanization and Community: The Postwar Development and Planning of Lower Bucks County, Pennsylvania" (Ph.D. diss., Department of History, University of Pennsylvania, 1977); Alfred S. Levitt, "A Community Builder Looks at Community Planning," *Journal of the American Institute of Planners*, 17, 2, Spring 1951; Herbert J. Gans, *The Levittowners: Ways of Life and Politics in a New Suburban Community* (New York: Alfred A. Knopf, 1967). On FHA and the post-1940 transformation of residential subdivision development, see Joseph Laronge, "The Subdivider of Today and Tomorrow," *Journal of Land and Public Utility Economics*, 18, 3, August 1942; Sherman J. Maisel, *Housebuilding in Transition* (Berkeley: University of California Press, 1953); Miles Colean, *American Housing;* Leo Grebler, *Production of New Housing* (New York: Social Science Research Council, 1950); Charles Abrams, *The Future of Housing* (New York: Harper, 1946); idem, "The Residential Construction Industry," in Walter Adams, ed., *The Structure of American Industry* (New York: MacMillan, 1950); Community Builders' Council, *The Community Builders Handbook* (Washington, D.C.: Urban Land Institute, 1947); Stanley L. McMichael, *Real Estate Subdivisions* (New York: Prentice-Hall, 1949); *Home Builders Manual for Land Development* (Washington, D.C.: National Association of Home Builders, 1950); James Gillies and Frank Mittelbach, *Management in the Light Construction Industry* (Real Estate Research Program, University of California at Los Angeles, 1962); Charles M. Haar, *Federal Credit Aid and Private Housing* (New York: McGraw-Hill, 1960); Saulnier, Halcrow and Jacoby, *Federal;* William Wheaton, "Evolution"; Richard Ratcliff, *Urban;* Mark Gelfand, *Nation;* Gertrude Fish, ed., *Story;* Glen H. Beyer, *Housing and Society* (New York: MacMillan, 1965); Edward P. Eichler and Marshall Kaplan, *The Community Builders* (Berkeley: University of California Press, 1967); President's Committee on Urban Housing, *A Decent Home* (Washington, D.C.: U.S. Government Printing Office, 1968); National Commission on Urban Problems, *Building the American City* (New York: Praeger, 1969); Marion Clawson, *Suburban Land Conversion in the United States: An Economic and Governmental Process* (Baltimore: Johns Hopkins University Press, 1971); Leo Grebler, *Large Scale Housing and Real Estate Firms* (New York: Praeger, 1973); Martin Mayer, *The Builders*

(New York: Norton, 1978); Barry Checkoway, "Large Builders, Federal Housing Programs, and Postwar Suburbanization," *International Journal of Urban and Regional Research,* 4, 1, March 1980; Gwendolyn Wright, *Building the Dream: A Social History of Housing in America* (New York: Pantheon, 1981); Ned Eichler, *The Merchant Builders* (Cambridge: MIT Press, 1982); Kenneth Jackson, *Crabgrass Frontier.*

48. On J. C. Nichols, see chapters 2 and 3. On ULI, see *Community Builders Handbook;* Garnett Laidlaw Eskew, *Of Land and Men: The Birth and Growth of an Idea* (Washington, D.C.: Urban Land Institute, 1959). On NAHB and NAREB, see Pearl Janet Davies, *Real Estate In American History* (Washington, D.C.: Public Affairs Press, 1958); on NAHB, see Michael Sumichrast and Sara A. Frankel, *Profile of the Builder and His Industry* (Washington, D.C.: National Association of Home Builders, 1970); Joseph B. Mason, *History of Housing in the U.S., 1930–1980* (Houston: Gulf, 1982).

49. See *The Planners' Journal* and the *Journal of the American Institute of Planners* for the 1940s and 1950s.

50. S. Herbert Hare, "Federal Housing Administration Standards for Land Subdivision," *The Planners' Journal,* 5, 1, January–March 1939, pp. 18–19.

51. Charles Abrams, *Future,* p. 238.

CONCLUSION:
MODERNIZING THE REAL ESTATE INDUSTRY

1. Allen Manvel, *Local Land and Building Regulations,* Research Report Number 6, National Commission on Urban Problems (Washington, D.C.: U.S. Government Printing Office, 1968). See also chapters 2, 3, and 6.

2. See chapter 3.

3. The phrase comes from the famous preamble to the Housing Act of 1949. See Public Law 171, 81st U.S. Congress, Section 2, "Declaration of National Housing Policy."

4. Federal Housing Administration, *Confidential Report of the Planning Committee Meeting,* Housing Advisory Council, January 18, 1935, Washington, D.C., pp. 40–41.

5. Sherman J. Maisel, *Housebuilding in Transition* (Berkeley: University of California Press, 1953), pp. 22–23.

6. Alfred D. Chandler, Jr., *The Visible Hand: The Managerial Revolution in American Business* (Cambridge: Harvard University Press, 1977), p. 490.

7. At the 1931 President's Conference on Home Building and Home Ownership, the legislative recommendations of the Committee on Subdivision Layout called for the creation of planning commissions to prepare master plans and "provide for administrative control over subdivision development." See ch. 7, "Legislation and Administration," in John M. Gries and James Ford, eds., *Housing Objectives and Programs* (Washington, D.C.: National Capital Press, 1932), p. 106.

8. For interesting analyses in business-government history, though not on urban development or real estate, see Louis Galambos, "The Emerging Organizational Synthesis in Modern American History," *Business History Review*, 44, Autumn 1970; idem, "Technology, Political Economy, and Professionalization: Central Themes of the Organizational Synthesis," *Business History Review*, 57, Winter 1983; and Thomas K. McCraw, *Prophets of Regulation* (Cambridge: Harvard University Press, 1984).

INDEX

Adams, Thomas, 68
Allen, Harry B., 120, 123-125
All-Year Club (Los Angeles), 95
American City Planning Institute (ACPI),
15, 57-59, 62, 73, 75-76, 77-78, 122,
141; Committee on Subdivision Con-
trol, 73, 77
American Community Builders (Park For-
est, Ill.), 147
American Institute of Planners, 57, 157
American Title Association, 37
Apartment House Association (Calif.), 89
Atterbury, Grosvenor, 69

Babcock, Frederick, 146, 149
Baker, Harrison, 123, 126, 130-32, 135,
138
Ball, Charles, 67
Baltimore, Md., 290
Barbour, Henry, 115
Bartholomew, Harland, 143
Bartlett, Dana, 82; *The Better City,* 82
Bassett, Edward, 61, 67, 76
Beaumont, Jack, 124, 129-30, 132, 134
Bettman, Alfred, 67
Bing, Alexander, 70
Bouton, Edward H., 50, 57-59, 69
Breed, Arthur, 121

California, xiii, 6-10, 12-14, 17-18, 22,
25, 27-28, 55-58, 70, 79, 83-84, 85-86,
105-6, 109-11, 114-17, 118-20, 122,
125-27, 132-35, 136, 138-40, 155; Alameda, 86; Atascadero, 57; Berkeley, 12,
58, 86, 91; Beverly Hills, 7, 47, 101;
Burlingame, 86; Colegrove, 85; Culver
City, 47, 111, 118; Fresno, 131; Hollywood, 95-96; Long Beach, 13; Modesto, 84; Oakland, 86, 111, 118, 121-
22, 138, 150; Palo Alto, 86; Pasadena,
13, 86, 123, 126, 138; Pebble Beach,
123-24, 130; Piedmont, 86; Planning
Act of 1915, 9-10, 110-11, 114; of
1927, 14, 122, 125, 130-31, 134; of
1929, 14, 131, 133-36, 139; of 1933,
135; of 1937, 139; Real Estate License
Bill of 1913, 18, 25; of 1917, 12-13,
18, 25, 120; Redondo Beach, 86; Sacramento, 86, 131-32, 134-35; San Bernardino, 9; San Diego, 111, 126; San Jose,
115, 138; San Mateo, 86; Santa Barbara, 14, 114, 134; State Department of
Real Estate, 27, 108, 116, 118-20, 135,
137-40; Subdivision Map Act of, 1893,
109; of 1907, 109, 123, 129, 130; of
1913, 9-10, 110; of 1915, 110-11,
114; of 1921 and 1923, 110; of 1925,
126; of 1927, 125-26, 129, 131; of
1929, 131, 132-36, 138; of 1933, 135,
138-39; of 1937, 139; Turlock, 86;
Zoning Enabling Act of 1917, 91
California Bankers Association, 115
California Conference on City Planning,
14, 58, 110, 118-19, 121, 126, 131;
Resolutions Committee, 119, 122
California Land Title Association, 37, 132,
135, 137
California Real Estate, 37, 138
California Real Estate Association
(CREA), 6, 8, 14, 16, 18, 26-27, 37,
45, 47, 55-56, 63, 83, 107-40, 146;
California Conference, 14; California
State Realty Federation, 17-18, 86,
109; City Plan and Zoning Committee,